Winning the H Factor

Also available from Continuum

Winning the H Factor

The Secrets of Happy Schools

Alistair Smith with Sir John
Jones and Joanna Kurlbaum

network
continuum

Continuum International Publishing Group
The Tower Building
11 York Road
London
SE1 7NX

80 Maiden Lane, Suite 704
New York
NY 10038

www.continuumbooks.com

British Library Cataloguing–in–Publication Data
A catalogue record for this book is available from the British Library

ISBN: 9781855395701 (paperback)

Library of Congress Cataloging–in–Publication Data
A catalog record for this book is available from the Library of Congress

Typeset by Fakenham Photosetting Ltd, Fakenham, Norfolk
Printed and bound in Great Britain by Bell & Bain Ltd, Glasgow

'Our remedies oft in ourselves do lie.'
Shakespeare, *All's Well that Ends Well*

Some Clues to Winning the H Factor

'Happiness is more like wrestling than dancing.'
Marcus Aurelius, *Meditations*

'Happiness is a butterfly, which, when pursued, is always beyond our grasp, but which, if you will sit down quietly, may alight upon you.'
Nathaniel Hawthorne

Contents

Acknowledgements

Alistair Smith

Happiness is more than the absence of misery – so a big thanks to anyone who ever at any time cheered me up! Principal cheerleaders include Ani, the team at Alite, James who hasn't had a mention before but has been my friend for 50 years, and my various mates in football who clear my head every Saturday. Many thanks also to those who chipped in and kindly bought me the 'Death Clock' to load on the computer and remind me of my mortality. Finally, to Gerry who gave constructive and practical feedback along the way.

Sir John Jones

To Alistair whose idea and inspiration made the book happen. To Joanna whose skill and dedication made it real. To Jenny, Alex, Ben and Lizzie who replenish my contentment cup each day. And to all those staff and children who filled my 34 years as a teacher with such joy.

Joanna Kurlbaum

My heartfelt thanks go to the many pupils, teachers and school leaders who have taken the time to share with me what they do on a daily basis to make their schools and classrooms happy places. Also to Jan for her flexibility, to Heather for her faith in me in the first place and to my ever positive husband, Phillip, for keeping me on track.

Preface

'Lately in a wreck of a Californian ship, one of the passengers fastened a belt about him with two hundred pounds of gold in it, with which he was found afterwards at the bottom.

Now, as he was sinking – had he the gold? Or had the gold him?'

John Ruskin, 'Unto This Last', 1862

A miner returns home triumphant having been a rare winner in the California Gold Rush. We can imagine the man's excitement at the prospect of returning wealthy from the Klondike. His life is transformed. His status as a man of means has been secured. He may have indulged himself a little on board ship, wary of being too relaxed with his travelling companions but keen nevertheless to assert himself as someone to be admired. But then … the ship grounds, it begins to break up and there are calls to abandon. What could have gone through his mind as he jumped into the deep, wrapped in the very wealth that was to suck him down to his death? Had he committed so much to the idea of the gold transforming his life that he was unable to let go of his dream?

John Ruskin's description of the man attempting to journey home with his newfound gold captures some of the happiness dilemma. The man is alone with his wealth. Every muscle and sinew in his body is wracked and telling him to hold on to what he has got; all sense has been abandoned; no vision of a future without the gold is possible. Eyes bulging, down into the dark he goes – no chance of reprieve – plummeting into the abyss. The image is a vivid one. A desperate pursuit of wealth becomes his undoing.

Go anywhere in the world and ask people what they want most and you get the same reply – long and happy lives. We know that the popular conceptions of what makes us happy (wealth, fame, material possessions, beauty, enviable status) are not supported by the evidence of our everyday lives, by the existing research nor by the wisdom of the years. And yet many – including many young people – are transfixed like the drowning miner with securing gold around their waists.

It seems that the more we strive for it, the more elusive happiness becomes. Nathaniel Hawthorn, the great American writer, likened the pursuit of happiness to catching a butterfly; extra effort goes unrewarded, but if you sit quietly for a while happiness will come to you. Are we prepared to sit quietly and wait for happiness? Maybe we would do so if we could be persuaded it would work. If we can't sit quietly and wait are there other alternatives?

'Happiness is a butterfly, which, when pursued, is always beyond our grasp, but which, if you will sit down quietly, may alight upon you.' (Nathaniel Hawthorne, 1851)

We know enough about happiness to itemise its benefits. This book spends time doing just that. We explain how happiness correlates to increased life expectancy, better quality of life, greater job satisfaction, improved personal relationships, more extended social networks and improved immunity to illness. Presumably we all want those benefits, but are we able to throw away our gold and sit quietly for a while? This book hopes to persuade you to do so and to show you how.

Our key proposition is that individuals, groups and communities can be happier. To be so requires our equivalent of Hawthorne's sitting quietly – that is, studied self-scrutiny. Our book contains a model to allow this self-scrutiny to take place. You will then follow this self-scrutiny with some strenuous exercise! Our model will also provide you with some strenuous happiness activities – that is, suggestions, ideas and activities to increase levels of happiness. Happiness is a bit like running the 100 metres – we can't all run it under 10 seconds, but our percentage performance improvement can be massive – with training!

We will help you build, broaden and balance three areas – head, heart and health – at individual, classroom and whole school levels. When you do so, you will win the Happiness Factor!

Alistair Smith
November 2008

Our summary

Happiness, for us, is more about fulfilling potential and flourishing (eudaimonia) than about acquiring material goods or pleasant experiences (hedonism).

*

In a world of dramatic change there is an increasing need for young people to develop the 'soft skills' associated with happiness.

*

Despite 50 years of improving affluence we in the UK are no happier. However, we can do something about it.

*

There is a growing body of quality research across different disciplines on what constitutes happiness.

*

The 'science' of happiness suggests that unhelpful patterns of thinking can be reversed and more positive patterns taught in their place. Such remediation takes time and practice.

*

Building, balancing and broadening the components of the H Factor is our recommended strategy at individual, group and community levels.

*

Our findings point towards the importance of providing access to supportive social networks and developing those networks. Schools have a key role to play in this.

*

Schools should constantly revisit their core purpose and can use the H Factor to help with this.

How to use this book

The organization and structure of the book

This book is organized for simple navigation. This means that people with all sorts of reading preferences will be able to quickly and easily find the information they need.

Chapters

Each chapter looks at one aspect of our happiness model. If you are especially interested in the theory of happiness and want to know more about the origins of our model, start with the chapter 'Defining the H Factor'. If you are interested in what our model says to you personally, then start with 'Happier Individuals'. If you are a classroom teacher and want to know how to make your classroom a happier place then you could start by reading 'Happier Classrooms'. If you are a school leader, read 'Happier Schools'. 'Happier Ever After' indicates some further reading. Of course, there is nothing to stop you from starting at the beginning and reading through to the end! Do what suits you best.

Top and tail

Each chapter is preceded by a series of questions. We answer these questions in the body text. To skim read the book, focus on these questions.

Summaries

We provide boxed summaries of the essential background research upon which we base our model.

Case studies

Case studies of some of the schools we have worked with are provided to illustrate key points.

Introduction: Why bother finding the H Factor?

In this section we focus on the following topics:

> **The significance of social networks**
>
> **Affluence and its relationship to happiness**
>
> **The dangers of demonizing youth**
>
> **Reversing the trend in psychology**
>
> **The bottom line**

And answer the following questions:

> *In what ways does the welfare of others affect my happiness?*
>
> *Are our society's children to be feared or revered?*
>
> *Is my cup half empty or half full?*
>
> *How much happiness is enough?*
>
> *What are the benefits of a happier workplace?*

- Society does matter
- Wealthy but miserable
- Toxic attitudes
- Minus five to zero
- The benefits of happiness

Society does matter

When driving past his local pub recently, Alistair was reminded of one of former Prime Minister, Margaret Thatcher's, announcements: 'We are a grandmother.' Outside the pub, which is the hub of the local community, the landlord had placed a sign announcing, 'We are of twins.' He and his wife had become grandparents.

Another of Mrs Thatcher's comments also came to mind. In October 1987, a month during which a storm caused chaos across the south of England killing 23 people and fifty billion pounds was wiped off shares in the London Stock Market after panic on Wall Street, the then Prime Minister gave an interview to Women's Own magazine in which she said,

> And, you know, there is no such thing as society. There are individual men and women, and there are families. And no government can do anything except through people, and people must look to themselves first.[1] (Thatcher 1987)

Sadly, here in the UK, we have been taking her advice too seriously for too long. Now we are picking up some of the bill.

We worry about Alistair's pub. And not just because we like a drink! The celebrated English ideal of the 'local' has gradually been eroded and, towards the end of 2008, five pubs in the UK were closing down a day. The closure of bingo halls up and down the country has been labelled by researchers as:

> The disappearance of a unique social support network ... Bingo closures also appear to be both a manifestation and catalyst for a wider breakdown of local communities that could have a negative impact upon society.[2] (Hicks 2007)

In his book, *Bowling Alone*, Robert Putnam laments the demise of organized social activities (such as bowling and softball leagues) in the USA. He points to the importance of such informal networks, which sit outside family and employment groups and provide an outlet for people. Terrifyingly, he puts a good argument together to show that the consequence of not socializing in such groups can lead to an increase in the risk of a person dying over the next year: 'Of all the domains in which I have traced the consequences of social capital, in none is the importance of social connectedness so well established as in the case of health and well being.'[3] (Putnam, 2000)

In 1985, the UK government created a wandering underclass at a stroke by limiting benefit claims in centres of population such as London, Birmingham, Manchester and Glasgow to eight weeks, in other inland locations to four weeks and in seaside towns to two weeks. 45,000 benefit claimants – mostly young people – were told that they must move on and out of their area for at least six months. So, rather than encouraging them to stay in a supportive community that may have been able to help them find work, they were pushed onwards to claim benefit elsewhere.

We disagree with Mrs Thatcher. Society *does* matter. Being connected is important. Having a sense of belonging is vital for well–being and mental health.

In his 2008 book, *Outliers*, Malcolm Gladwell explains why it was that a community of Italian-American citizens who believed in society and who were able

to stay together lived longer lives than any other comparable group in the whole of the USA. The group lived in a town called Roseto, Pennsylvania. The researchers looking for an explanation as to why these people lived longer were confused because their diet was no better than that of other communities, they smoked and drank as much and they exercised no more and no less than other people.

> What Wolf began to realise was that the secret of Roseto wasn't diet or exercise or genes or location. It had to be Roseto itself. As Bruhn and Wolf walked around the town, they figured out why. They looked at how the Rosetans visited one another, stopping to chat in Italian on the street, say, or cooking for one another in their backyards. They learned about the extended family clans that underlay the town's social structure. They saw how many homes had three generations living under one roof, and how much respect grandparents commanded. They went to mass at Our Lady of Mount Carmel and saw the unifying and calming effect of the church. They counted twenty-two separate civic organizations in a town of just under two thousand people. They picked up on the particular egalitarian ethos of the community, which discouraged the wealthy from flaunting their success and helped the unsuccessful obscure their failures.[4] (Gladwell 2008).

The secret of longer life, it transpired, had something to do with being connected, with enjoying a sense of belonging and with being part of a supportive community. The Rosetan social infrastructure, which left no-one alone, played a part in helping them towards better health and longer and more fulfilled lives. The researchers also noted their belief that as these people became more Americanized the 'Roseta effect' would wear off. In 1992, they returned to the town and found this to be true. According to the American Journal of Public Health, the Rosetans now suffer from as many heart attacks as people in any other community!

> ... people's mood states are not just a matter of heredity, but depend on our social relationships and fulfillment in life.[5] (Steptoe 2008)

For years it has been known that people in poorer countries tend to recover from mental illness more quickly because of reliable kinship networks. In January 2009, the *British Medical Journal* contained a study[6] that related better health to the quality and extent of social networks. The study was a follow-up to an earlier piece and showed how behaviours such as happiness spread over time from one person to another. This occurs through people's 'immediate and more distant social contacts'. The study, entitled 'The Dynamic Spread of Happiness in a Large Social Network', showed that happiness is a collective phenomenon. That is, happiness clusters in groups of people. And these groups can extend as far as three degrees of separation – to the friends of our friends' friends! The study also showed that happiness can be spread through social networks and that the characteristics of the network will independently predict which individuals will be happier in the future. The key conclusion was that, 'people's happiness depends on the happiness of others with whom they are connected'.

According to the above study, a friend who is happy and who lives within a mile (about 1.6 km) of you increases the probability that you will be happy by 25 per cent. Similar effects were seen in co-resident spouses (if your partner is happy, you are 8 per cent more likely to be happy), siblings who live within a mile of each other (14 per cent) and next-door neighbours (34 per cent).

The study analysed results from the Framlington Heart Study that had traced 4,739 individuals between 1983 and 2003. The researchers knew that emotional states can be transferred directly from one individual to another by mimicry (sometimes called 'emotional contagion'). This could take place in a number of ways including the copying of emotional behaviour, mimicking and replicating facial expressions, and replicating mood. The research found that the participants of the study who were surrounded by many happy people and those who were central in their network were the most likely to become happy in the future.

Longitudinal statistical models suggest that clusters of happiness come about from the actual *spread* of happiness and not just from a tendency for people to associate with others who are of a similar mindset to themselves. Effects were not, however, seen between co-workers. The effect decayed with time and with geographical separation.

So, our own personal happiness depends on the happiness of others with whom we are connected.

Society matters!

Is there something our schools can learn from this model of happiness networking? Perhaps we in schools can reproduce this beneficial networking effect?

Research summary
You will be happier in the future if:
- you are surrounded by happy people
- you are central to your social network
- your co-habiting spouse is happy
- your neighbours are happy
- siblings and friends who live nearby are happy.

Wealthy but miserable

As a nation, we sit somewhere between Plato and Prozac. Are we happy or are we not? It is decidedly difficult to get a true picture. Are our answers philosophical or chemical? Has the box labelled 'material wealth' which arrived in a much heralded moment proven to be empty – or maybe the toys inside turned out to be less satisfying than playing with the box itself?

A recent study by the UK Office for National Statistics reported that we are no happier now than we were 30 years ago. In fact, our reported levels of contentment have remained static at around 86 per cent since 1971.[7] This is despite having households full of labour and time-saving devices – washing machines, tumble dryers and dishwashers – and gadgets for our entertainment – televisions, DVD players, computers and computer games. They are all tantalisingly affordable: the cost of a computer has decreased by 100 per cent in the past ten years. 50 per cent of UK children aged 5–10 years now own a mobile phone.[8]

We are travelling more. UK residents made a record 45.3 million trips abroad in 2006, which is an increase of 153 per cent since 1986.[9]

We are also becoming generally healthier. In 1995, the total expenditure on health as a percentage of gross domestic product was 6.9 per cent. In 2006, this had increased to 8.5 per cent. The total number of doctors in England increased by 44 per cent in the decade to 2001 and surgery hours have recently been extended to improve access to our GPs. Between 1992 and 2006, there were no child deaths from measles in the UK, compared to 857 total deaths from measles in 1940, 98 in 1959 and 42 in 1970.[10]

We are living for longer thanks to constantly improving medical resources and healthier nutrition and lifestyles. Since just 1996, our average life expectancy at birth has increased by three years. However, your life expectancy may depend on where in the country you live. For example, adults living in the Shettleston area of Glasgow – where Alistair's mother was born and brought up – have a shorter life expectancy, estimated at 11 years less on average, than their peers living in Bournemouth!

The over-55s are growing in number and the over-75s in particular are forecast to represent more than a tenth of the population by 2030. The proportion of under-16s is in decline in Britain today. Children account for less than a fifth of the overall population, representing a significant shift since 1961 when they made up 25 per cent of the total.

Yet, despite all of these advantages to living in the twenty-first century, the World Health Organization has predicted that, by 2020, depression will be second only to heart disease as the world's leading disability. Economist and government advisor, Richard Layard, has said that mental illness costs the UK economy (in terms of lost output) about 2 per cent of its GDP.[11] He states that the cost to the Exchequer is about £10 billion, which is spent on incapacity benefits, and some £8 billion spent on mental health services. According to Layard, mental health issues are a bigger social problem than unemployment and poverty – although, of course, there is an obvious link between poor health (both physical and mental) and poverty.

So why is it that here in the UK we report ourselves as no happier, despite all of the advancements outlined above? The standard arguments that are often given for our lack of reported happiness despite our improved economic well-being are outlined below.

Basic needs

Firstly, economists argue that once our average income reaches a certain level our satisfaction with life levels out. So, money is important to us as far as meeting our basic needs is concerned but, once we have food to eat, clothes on our back and a roof over our heads, a higher income will not increase our happiness.

Expectations

Secondly, as our wealth increases so do our expectations. We get used to having a certain standard of living and we expect to, at the very least, maintain it and, if we can, improve it. And here's the rub; however much our disposable income increases, there is likely to always be something more that we want, something that we feel would make our lives better, easier or more fun. Our thirst for the latest gadget becomes unquenchable. This is a partial explanation of the fact that, in 2006, nearly half of people in Britain had some form of unsecured debt. In fact, in 2007, newspapers reported that the total debts of people in the UK (including credit cards, loans and mortgages) was greater than the entire value of the country's economy.[12] The root cause of much of our unhappiness is unbridled desire.

Outside agency

Apparently, we individuals alone are not to blame for this hedonistic desire for more. Outside forces are at work on us. We are constantly encouraged to want, and to confuse our wants with our needs. From every angle we are bombarded by messages that shout at us that if we buy this latest gadget or that fast car it will improve our lives for the better. And, of course, however hard we work and however many 'things' we collect, there is always going to be someone, somewhere with more than us. It makes us vulnerable. Our naïveté is exposed. The German car manufacturer, BMW, was bombarded last year by consumers who were keen to purchase their latest model with the centrally positioned steering wheel allowing instant left- or right-hand drive. The model launched on 1 April of course!

Fractured time

The social cost to our desire for more is a further explanation given for us feeling no happier. As a result of the fact that we are working longer, harder and faster we are seeing less of our families and friends. Often we work in irregular shift patterns, travelling alone to and from work in our secure steel motorized box, communicating with our children at the end of tiring days when we are not always at our best. Time becomes a commodity to be conquered and controlled rather than indulged and enjoyed. In such small parcels our capacity to build trusting relationships and to function meaningfully with others is limited. It takes Google just 0.28 seconds to find 8,320,000 dating agencies. Some claim that 80 per cent of marriages in the USA in 2008 were of couples who first met online! If you ask the fractured time generation about why they may not yet have found a suitable partner, you may be told that they haven't had the time! If we could ask the birds and the bees the same question, we doubt they would come up with the same answer – there's nothing natural about being in a rush!

Our argument in this book will be that the rush towards hedonism should be replaced with a slow walk around eudaimonism. In other words, there is more joy in playing with the box than in the toys that were in the box. Hedonism is about the accumulation of personally satisfying moments, experiences and objects. Eudaimonism is about the fulfilment of one's potential, about achieving something, however small, of true worth and about finding space to reflect on such achievements. Our model suggests that there is an antidote to being wealthy but miserable and that it lies in building, broadening and balancing the key elements of happiness – the H Factors. And, if we should be concerned about the happiness of adults, what about the happiness of the children of our nation?

Toxic attitudes

Authors, academics, politicians and commentators have joined the queue to declare that childhood is 'under threat' (UNICEF 2005), 'toxic' (Palmer 2006) or 'disappearing' (Postman 1994).[14] One day the call is that young people are not allowed enough freedom to develop and to discover things for themselves and the following day the shout goes out that they are hanging around on street corners with nothing organized to do.

This surge of moral panic over childhood has left us with the fear that the lives of young people today are falling apart due to broken homes, poor diet, working mothers, lack of open spaces, a disastrous curriculum and an avaricious media intent on driving sales into the kindergarten: 'We live in a violent and suspicious world. None of us feel safe any more, whether we are in our own homes or out on the street.'[15] (Gibson 2007).

But when you get closer to home, the evidence begins to change. Do you feel unsafe in your own home or on the streets where you live? Consider the children you know. Are your own children unhappy? What about the children of your friends? And those you teach? Is there really a great difference between the happiness of children today and that of children 40 years ago?

When giving presentations to large groups around this country and in the USA we often ask delegates to raise their hands if they believe that the quality of childhood today is poorer than in the past. We usually get a very large affirmative response. Yet, when we subsequently ask all of those who are parents to keep their hands up if they believe that their own child's childhood is poorer than it would have been in the past all the hands go down. For some reason, it seems that this disastrous childhood is happening everywhere else, but not to our own children.

While it is true that the nature of childhood is changing and that the pressures exerted by those changes may bring a heavy price, it is too easy to assume the worst. There is an alternative, less gloomy picture.

> A certain myth of decline surrounds the concept of family life as many people believe that parents do not provide the same quality of upbringing that they did in the past. Indeed, 80% of the population believe that parents used to spend more time with their children than they do now. However, when we examine the facts, a

somewhat different picture emerges. Time spent on childcare has actually increased over time, jumping from an average 34 minutes per day in 2000 to 45 minutes per day in 2005.

Although more mothers now work (and work at much higher career levels) than in previous generations, time-saving technologies, the outsourcing of household chores and greater gender equality within household responsibilities have freed time for both mothers and fathers.

Parents seem keen to preserve the routine of family time together. Although one might assume that the tradition of the evening meal together en famille is fading and being replaced by unstructured meal-time patterns and greater fluidity, it remains very much in place. Many families still ensure that they sit down together regularly to spend time as a unit and catch each other's news; indeed, the average family eats just under four evening meals together a week according to the latest findings from the British Household Panel Survey (2008).[16] (Rand 2008)

According to the Future Foundation, in 2009 children feel satisfied with family life on the whole. Parents are spending more time with them and family relationships are more open than they were in the past. In the last two years, children's nutrition in particular has become more strictly regulated by parents as a result of the governmental drive to achieve healthier eating.

Yet we wonder how many people know about the Future Foundation's report, in comparison to those who know about the UNICEF report of 2007[17] in which children of the UK were found to be languishing at the bottom of the industrialized world's league table of well-being? Rather than looking at anything positive, our nation's sense of doom and gloom prefers to feed a hysteria over our children's futures. This, in turn, is becoming a self-fulfilling philosophy. The more we panic over the future of our young people and the more we tell them that they are unhappy and depressed, the more they will become so.

Recently, we took part in an activity during which a room full of people aged 30+ were asked to discuss the most memorable play activity from their childhood. When asked by the presenter for a show of hands as to how many of these activities involved a pre-manufactured toy only one or two hands were raised. The point being made was that, should you ask today's children the same questions when they are in their 30s, many more hands would be in the air. Is that bad? Is that scary? Or is it just different? Maybe children don't get outside as much as they did in previous years, maybe they don't get to explore the world on their own, but let's not romanticize the 'golden days' of childhood as something that they may not always have been. Had the press been as aggressive 30 years ago as it is now, maybe the focus would have been on children being kicked out of the house and ignored by mothers who prioritized having a clean home over spending time with their children. How much time did the mothers of 30 years ago actually spend listening to and engaging with their children and how much time was spent polishing parquet flooring, scolding them for getting their clothes dirty and kicking them out of the house to 'explore their world'?

Of course, back in the good old days, children didn't have to worry about how many friends they had on Facebook, how well they would do in their exams, global warming, family break-ups or having the latest Wii console. They may have, however, worried about how many friends they had in their class, passing their 12 plus, dying from Aids or in a nuclear war, family arguments and having the latest BMX bike.

The lives of children today are different – not necessarily worse. Ask yourself this. Are the statistics and the scary headlines you read backed up by what you see on a daily basis? Listen to the evidence of your daily life. What do you see in the households of your friends and family, in the classrooms where you teach and on the streets where you live?

So, is childhood today different? Let's break it down.

Futures

Looking into the future, many young people believe that happiness will come from being rich or famous. And if asked how they will achieve this fame and fortune, it is not unusual for them to genuinely believe that they will win a television talent show, a game show or the National Lottery. In February 2006, a Learning and Skills Council survey of 777 16–19 year olds in England reported that one in ten young people would drop out of school or college if they had a chance of TV fame. Sixteen percent of the children surveyed believed that they would actually realize this ambition.

The LSC research showed that many of the young people had no idea that the odds of being selected to appear on a reality TV show such as Big Brother are slim and that the odds of actually maintaining fame after the show is over are negligible. Almost one in ten of the children surveyed said that they thought that being a celebrity was a great way to earn money without skills or qualifications, and more than half of the teenagers who stated a desire to become famous gave money and success as the principal reasons for this. Yet previous research in the UK has shown that staying on at school after taking your GCSE exams can increase your lifetime earnings by as much as £185,000.

> If making money is the reason a young person wants to become famous, by staying on in education or training they can significantly increase their future earning power through gaining these essential qualifications.[18] (Bullen 2006)

Play and exploration

The locations for play *are* changing. Gardens are getting smaller. There may well be a media-fed fear of letting children out of sight to play on their own and a tendency to trust in the electronic babysitter. Perhaps some children today get outside less and spend more time watching television and playing computer games but, where children in the past may have played in the streets and woods locally, they may now instead be taken to dance classes, swimming lessons, brownies and cubs. In addition, many councils and libraries make activities available for young people during school holidays – many of these are free of charge and targeted at areas of deprivation. There is an awareness that young people need something stimulating to do and, very often, this is provided.

Of course, the evidence of our everyday lives tells us that, yes, there are some young people who hang around on street corners, perhaps with nothing better to do. But they, and their parents, are caught between a rock and a hard place. If they stay in the assumption is that they are rotting their minds with violent video games, but if they go out they are accused of have nothing better to do than hang about, ignored by their irresponsible working parents.

Ask yourself this – are those young people on the street corner waiting to cause trouble or are they just chatting with friends? Are the noisy boys at the back of the supermarket breaking the wall, or are they simply kicking a ball against it?

And for those young people who do have nothing to do but cause trouble, we come back to the fact that society matters. Let's begin to build a society in which, rather than ostracize young people, we begin to engage them.

Outside agencies at work

Another fear that is often expressed is that, instead of exploring their world on their own, children are all too often told or shown who they should be, how they should behave and what they should want. To an extent, this has always been true – is it not an age-old syndrome that adults feel that they know better than their children because of their life experience? Has there not always been a tendency to feel that if something is good it must be bad for you? It is not new for children to be told how to think, how to behave and what to want. The prevalent fear today comes from the fact that it is not parents who are doing the telling. Instead, marketing and technology mean that there are influences possibly beyond the control of adults.

All the more reason to help children become free-thinking individuals who understand how marketing and technology work and who can distinguish between their wants and their needs.

Access to friendship groups

In the past, children may have played with their siblings, their neighbours' children and one or two other friends. The field has widened considerably today. It is not unusual for young people to have 'friends' who they have never met – friends in countries far away, with different cultures and beliefs. There is, of course, a possibility that these people are not what we would consider a good influence; they may not even be who they say they are. So let's provide our children with the tools that they need to stay safe and with the strength of character and self-confidence to behave according to their own values and beliefs. The same things as those that were needed for children 30 years ago to stand up to peer-pressure and to avoid 'stranger danger'. If we do this we can start to celebrate the fact that our children have access to a world of opportunity – they can discuss differences and similarities and have their minds opened to different cultures and traditions at the press of a button.

Diet

Our diet today has changed and, yes, there are worrying signs. But, again, we would like to warn against promoting the feeling that life is falling apart and that there is nothing we can do to save the souls and waistlines of our young people. Apparently, one in three children in the UK is obese or overweight,[19] and in America warnings have been so stark as to compare the potential effects of obesity to those of the Black Plague![20]

If, however, 'for all children aged between two and fifteen, the figure for those either overweight or obese has risen from 24 per cent to 33 per cent'[21] (Kirby 2006), how is it that children are also being forced by pictures in magazines to be a size zero?

We do not deny that there is a problem with food and nutrition and that people are getting larger. But one in three children? Where are they? That means that in every classroom across the country there are ten overweight or obese children. Are we building bigger classroom chairs to accommodate the 400 or so obese children in the large secondary schools?

> 'I, perhaps rather scarily, find myself agreeing with Janet Street Porter, who claims that "obesity is a growth industry".'[22] (Joanna Reid).

It has been suggested that the Dr Foster Research into obesity[23] was funded by a pharmaceutical company that produces an anti-obesity drug. This may or may not be the case, but it does point up the need to ask questions.

In Australia, scientists have found that the 'obesity epidemic' among children has halted. Yet people are still clinging to it. Here's what one scientist, Professor Olds, has to say about it:

> It's a sensational story for the media, academics have built careers in dealing with and treating childhood obesity and, frankly, the success of their grants depends on a sense that it's a national crisis that's continuing.[24] (Olds 2009)

And, looking on the positive side, parents are now armed with information, school nutrition has improved somewhat and the government is addressing the issue.

Pester power

Pester power has moved from chocolate at the checkout to the worldwide web. Large businesses may be grooming young people to become the most consumerist society we have ever seen and technology means that they can bombard children from all angles. Adverts are not just aimed at making them want something now, but at turning them into customers for life. While this is an undesirable state of affairs, it does not stop parents from doing the same now as they did at the checkouts years ago and using that little word, 'no'. Alternatively, it hasn't been unheard of for children to be asked to do additional chores around the house to earn money to buy something that they want.

Young people can easily be targeted by companies that want to sell them something and to programme them to want and to feel that they *need* the next latest thing in order to make them happy. According to research conducted by the Girl Guides with the Mental Health Foundation, 43 per cent of girls feel either angry or sad about the pressure to own cool gadgets or particular clothes and a quarter of girls feel worried or bad about themselves when under this pressure. You could look at this another way – more than half of the girls questioned didn't feel pressurised despite the best attempts of the marketers and three in four girls were resilient enough to cope with this pressure and not let it bother them.

People talk in shocked tones of the fact that 83 per cent of young people influence their parents' technological decisions such as broadband providers.[25] The levels of horror increase when they hear that children as young as eight are often given a say which family car is purchased![26] But let's consider the exact wording of these phrases: 'have an influence on' and 'given a say in' do not exactly amount to 'dictate to parents which technological items they must buy' or 'get their parents' credit cards out and buy the family car for them'. Perhaps what parents are actually doing is talking to their children and allowing them to express an opinion and a preference. Perhaps parents recognize that their children know more about technology than they themselves do. These survey results could be a sign of the fact that families are, in actual fact, communicating!

Join the clubs

One of the extraordinary conclusions in Robert Putnam's 2000 book, *Bowling Alone*, is that active membership of a club or society can extend your life expectancy. In the UK we are club enthusiasts. If you take one letter of the alphabet at random – let's say 'b' – and scratch the surface to find the clubs, you get the following: badminton, bingo, boats, bowls, business, bird watching, bereavement, board games, Beavers and Brownies. Where Joanna lives in Cheltenham there is an 18 month waiting list for the Brownies! We can envisage a situation where parents will be secretly renting houses to be near a Brownie pack of their choosing; estate agents will advertise homes near the Brownies and uniforms will trade on eBay for vast sums!

Schools offer a myriad of clubs and activities for children today. Even before the extended schools programme, children were being offered a huge variety of extra-curricular activities. Joanna recalls having to wait until secondary school before being offered the odd hockey match or drama production, and these were all put on hold during the teaching strikes of the 1980s. (Not that she is bitter, of course!) In contrast, her daughter's infant school offers at least one club every night of the week. The small body of staff works exceedingly hard to provide activities that will catch the interest of all children.

Technology

Technological advances have perhaps brought about the greatest changes to childhood. Many of these would have been unimaginable just 20 years ago. The downside is that young people are open to influences other than those of family, friends and teachers. On the upside, however, technology allows young people to find advice and support when they need it from a variety of sources that weren't available just 15 years ago.

There is more than one way to look at things. Most 11 year olds own a mobile phone! Should we stand back in shock at this news or consider the fact that a mobile phone can be used as a useful tool for keeping in touch with our children? Four year olds can use the computer better than many adults and can download CBeebies all on their own! We could find this disastrous for any number of reasons, or we could consider it a sign of the fact that they are remarkably able to adapt to our rapidly changing times.

In a 2007 Populus survey, parents voted overwhelmingly that technology can and does help their children to learn, bring subjects to life, engage children in subjects they find difficult and give them flexibility to learn at home and school. As the Good Childhood Enquiry points out, access to the internet and technology makes them 'ever more free to communicate, learn and play on their own terms.'[27]

Sexualization of girls

Premature sexualization and a pressure to grow up too fast are two of the key things that make girls aged between 10 and 15 unhappy.[28] The way girls are sexualized has been found to be leading to higher rates of depression, eating disorders and to poor academic performance.[29] And it is not just girls who are affected. According to America's National Institute of Mental Health, one in four preadolescent cases of anorexia occurs in boys, and binge-eating disorder affects roughly the same number of females and males.

In a quest to see if things have really changed greatly over past generations, Joanna browsed some old copies of the magazine *Jackie*. Titles of features in the 1970s magazines included, 'How sexy are you?' and 'Dresses for men – how to wear a dress to impress your man'. Features on attracting the opposite sex are not a new phenomenon.

> The letters sent in to the advice column of one of Britain's most widely-read youth magazines – *Just Seventeen* – reveal a disturbing level of distress, fear and ignorance among British teenagers. Many of the problems raised are health-related.'[30] (McFadyean 1986).

And there we have it – another shocking statement. Young people are distressed, ignorant and fearful! But this one was written in 1986! So, we ask, are things really that bad today, or is it simply a fact that growing up can be difficult and that the letters in magazines represent a tiny minority of young people?

> Below is a summary of the problem pages of three teen magazines:

The topics included the following:

> 1970s

- I'm in love with my stepfather and I'm having an affair with him.
- My boyfriend wants me to prove my love for him by having sex.

- I haven't started my periods yet.
- The older boys in school want 'one night stands' with me and my mates, but won't 'go steady'.

1984

- How can I get the pill without telling my mum?
- I liked it when I 'made out' with another girl. What's wrong with me?
- I can't tell my parents about my black boyfriend.
- I'm pregnant and the baby's father has gone off with someone else.

2009

- I hate my mum smoking.
- Did the cervical cancer jab make my periods start?
- My boyfriend hates condoms.
- Should I go out with my best friend?

Subject of problems	*Just 17* 1970s	*Just 17* 1984	*Sugar* 2009
Career/university	5 (26%)	2 (17%)	0
Sex/sexuality	1 (5%)	2 (17%)	0
Pregnancy/contraception	2 (11%)	2 (17%)	1 (10%)
Bullying	0	1 (8%)	0
Boyfriend problems	6 (32%)	3 (25%)	4 (40%)
Teacher problems	0	1 (8%)	0
Family problems	0	0	2 (20%)
Periods	1 (5%)	1 (8%)	2 (20%)
Looks	3 (16%)	0	1 (10%)
Exams	1 (5%)	0	0
Total	19	12	10

Although far from a scientific study, this would indicate that the key problems for young people have not changed greatly over the decades.

Body image

Many accusations are thrown at magazines today for making young people insecure in their own bodies. Pictures of beautiful people, size zero models and A-list celebrities, and fad diets abound. The fact that these pictures and trends are out there is not something we can deny. But they are not necessarily new. Joanna's old copies of the *Jackie* (1970s) magazine are full of pictures (illustrations rather than photographs) of skinny girls in bikinis. So the pressure to be thin has long been there. Barbie dolls have been around for about 60 years now, and they have always been a source of complaint about body image. In 1965, the Slumber Party Barbie was sold with a book entitled *How to Lose Weight* which advised, 'Don't eat'. In 1997, Barbie was redesigned to have a wider waist, although today if copied to scale as a life-sized woman she would be an anatomically improbable 36-18-28!

Despite media reports that teenagers are filling the waiting rooms of cosmetic surgeons (some with, some without parental support), a 2005 survey indicated that it is actually older people who are increasingly requesting cosmetic procedures.

> In a qualitative survey, members of the BAAPS (British Associations of Aesthetic Plastic Surgeons) were asked about age trends they noticed in their private practices. Most reported that there has been no discernible jump in requests from teenagers but have, in fact, seen more of an increase in older people seeking cosmetic treatments.[31] (BAAPS 2005)

Not that it is a desirable state of affairs, but Joanna notes that there are not many women of a similar age to her who do not worry about their weight. She suspects her mother would say the same! It could be that Barbie and magazines for teenagers had an influence on them all those years ago, and that this, combined with the even more aggressive trends of today, could be having an even bigger effect on young people. However, another thing that Joanna has noticed is that mothers do not hesitate to discuss their concerns in front of their children. Surely, children are as (or more) likely to learn about body image from their closest role models as they are from pictures in magazines.

Demonization of boys

An Ipsos MORI study in 2004[32] looked at 603 newspaper articles on or about young people. The study found that, of these, only 14 presented young people in a positive light.

> When news coverage about productive, non-violent youth is the exception rather than the rule, violence fills the void, and audiences with little or no other contact with young people are particularly vulnerable to the perception that youth are violent and 'out of control'.[33] (Dorfman 2001)

Figures show that more than half the stories about teenage boys in national newspapers in 2008 were about crime. Research[34] showed that the best chance a teenage boy has of sympathetic coverage would be if they died. Of 8,629 items in national and regional newspapers, the words most commonly used were yobs (591), thugs (254), sick (119) and feral (96). Fewer than one in ten articles about young people actually interviewed, quoted or shared their perspective. Boys are now being influenced by their negative media portrayal to such a degree that they are becoming frightened of other boys. The survey of nearly 1,000 teenage boys cited 51 per cent who said that they are always or often wary of teenage boys they don't know.

Take, for example, reports on the 2008 youth survey.[35] 'One third of children admit to carrying a gun or knife'[36] (Russell 2009) shouts the *Independent*, accompanying the story with a picture of a hooded, faceless 'youth' grasping a flick knife in a hand covered in gold rings. What they fail to point out is that the figures include penknives and that the most common use suggested for carrying these 'weapons' was 'for hobbies, activities and sports'.[37] The *Telegraph* chooses to show a picture of two hooded young people pointing fingers at a policeman with the headline, 'One crime committed every two minutes by British youths'[38] (Telegaph.co.uk 2009). The newspaper does not see fit to state that a huge 68 per cent of young people have not committed any crimes at all, nor that the crimes they talk of include not paying when travelling on the bus, train or tube. Try asking a group of adults if they have committed a crime in the past 12 months – including driving above the speed limit – and perhaps the headlines would read something like, 'One crime committed every three seconds in the UK'?

Self-perception

Self-perception studies have shown that children in the UK and the USA report themselves as among the least happy in the world.[39] Let us take some time to consider what is driving these views. Children in both the USA and the UK are told that they are unhappy, that they cannot be trusted, are feral and do not live up to adults' expectations of them. 'Youth' has almost become a dirty word. Aware that they are supposedly greedy, narcissistic and abandoned, is it any wonder that they too may believe that the whole world is going to pot?

The effect that the media can have on our perceptions is perhaps nowhere clearer than in Bridgend, Wales. After a series of suicides, the national press picked up on the 'fact' that they could have been due to an internet suicide pact. The reports that followed led the assistant police constable to state that the common factor among further suicides was the press itself:

> We are speaking to young people in Bridgend and what we are getting from them is that the media is starting to contribute to their thoughts in terms of how they feel, pressures they are under and Bridgend becoming stigmatised through the media.[40]
> (Morris 2008)

All things considered, is life for young people today so bad? Whilst our aim is not to belittle the fact that growing up can be hard and that young people can and do have problems, we would like to refocus the collective mind of adults in the UK. We are not trying to deny the fact that there are, indeed, young people who are unhappy or who do cause trouble and flout the rules. We are not saying that there is no problem at all. Of course growing up can be difficult. Of course our world is changing. And of course young people have to cope with these changes (although, most of them seem remarkably resilient and able to do so; sometimes it is older people who find it more difficult!). It is simply that we would like to get things a little more into perspective.

Sue Bailey, who heads the faculty of child and adolescent psychiatry at the College of Psychiatrists, London, disputes statistics that suggest that one in ten children has a clinically diagnosed mental health disorder.[41] She maintains that there is little or no evidence to support this. Others such as David Healy, a consultant psychiatrist, believe the figure to be nearer one in 100. They say the high figures can be explained by two factors; first, pressure from the drugs industry to prescribe and, second, the ever-widening definition of the term 'depression'.

The Chief Executive of the Mental Health Foundation has this to say, 'Modern life puts our young people under terrible pressure while we offer them precious little support to help them cope, with profound consequences for their mental health and future chances in life.'[42] (McCulloch 2008) Is this not a little unfair? Who is this 'we' who offer them precious little support? Us as parents, grand-parents, aunts and uncles, or us as teachers, school leaders and professionals? Rather than accept comments like this, should we not be crying out from the rooftops that many of us are doing more than ever to support the young people we know?

Please take the time to ask yourself the following; is the problem as huge and far reaching as we are being led to believe by people who have it in their own interests for us to believe it? Or are the vast majority of young people responsible, thoughtful and happy individuals? Do the young people you know actually have many things in their lives to be joyful about and are they not robust enough to overcome the pressures that they may be under and to become responsible adults?

You want to see obese people? You'll see them. If you want to see groups of unruly youngsters with nothing to do, you'll spot them on every corner. But could it be that you are noticing them because you are constantly being told that they are there? Do you believe that everyone nowadays is rude? We'll bet that the next time you go to the supermarket you'll spot someone rude. We would like to challenge you. Spend the rest of today – even better, the rest of the week – looking for healthy people, great children who are happy, well dressed and socializing well with their peers, and polite, smiling people at the supermarket. We'll bet you'll see more of those than usual!

In a single lesson with a secondary school class of 14 year olds in Scotland, Alistair took the topic 'Getting to know us' and asked the class to work in groups to list some of the positive things they had done over the last week. These things were to have nothing to do with school and had to be things that no-one else in the class already knew about. Among the many things that – eventually – came back were:

- went shopping for a neighbour
- returned an old man's dog that had been lost
- ran the line at a football match
- gave directions to strangers
- washed the dishes(!)
- cared for mum (who happened to be an invalid as a consequence of a dependency)
- cleaned up a cupboard at the Boys' Brigade

- baby sat for a younger sister
- sang in the church choir for a charity 'do'.

Growing up can be difficult but most children come through it just fine! We cannot help them by removing problems from them, and we certainly won't help them by demonizing them. But we can help them develop the resilience they need to cope with problems both as children and as adults and we can give them the support they need to make their own way in the world. Part of the way we can do that is to look more closely at what helps individuals, groups, organizations and communities be more positive and ultimately happier.

> Children are not only our future, they are our present and we need to start taking their voices very seriously … We must listen carefully to what young people have to say and give them every opportunity to speak. We must reach out to them and encourage them to participate in the decision-making processes that affect their lives.[43] (Bellamy 2001)

We come back to our point that society matters – communities matter. And schools should be at the very centre of their communities. One of the things that the Mental Health Foundation highlights as having a significant contribution to young people's mental health is, 'going to a school that looks after the well-being of all its pupils'[44] (Mental Health Foundation 2008).

> Other factors that are also stated as important are:

- feeling loved, trusted, understood, valued and safe
- being interested in life and having opportunities to enjoy themselves
- being hopeful and optimistic
- being able to learn and having opportunities to succeed
- accepting who they are and recognizing what they are good at
- having a sense of belonging in their family, school and community
- feeling they have some control over their own life
- having the strength to cope when something is wrong (resilience) and the ability to solve problems.

These are all things that schools can, and should, provide. *Winning the H Factor* will give you the start you need to do so.

Minus five to zero

The 2008 film, *Happy Go Lucky*, is described by its director Mike Leigh as an 'anti-miserablist' film. It contains a central character, Poppy, who is irrepressibly happy. Poppy is a primary school teacher. The story follows her as she experiences various challenges to the durability of her optimism. Her relationship with a driving instructor – a loner, who dislikes his customers and is given to wild flights of fancy about Egyptian gods – provides her biggest test. Scott, the driving instructor, is an angry man who overcomes his emotional reticence to develop an attraction for Poppy that is not shared. In the end, Scott proves too much even for Poppy. The film's final scene has Poppy being asked to consider the possibility that she is over-optimistic.

Although *Happy Go Lucky* would not make Alistair's list of top ten feel-good films, with Poppy's enthusiasm beginning to grate shortly after the first scene, it did highlight the huge distance between pessimism and optimism. Until recently, research into people's well-being went only so far as to look at people who weren't coping and to try to discover why and to take out the negatives. If you look at the scale below, psychiatrists were concentrating on people like Scott, the driving instructor, who function from minus five to zero.

–5	0	+5
unhappy	getting by	flourishing
struggling	coping	doing well

Thankfully, more recently scientists and psychologists have begun to look at the science of happiness – to look at the Poppy's of this world and find out more about what these people do to flourish, stay positive and function at +5.

Language and self-perception

Generally, it is so ingrained onto our human psyche to avoid showing off that we tend to talk about ourselves as at the lower to middle part of the scale above. Consider your own standard response when someone asks how you are. If it is along the lines of; 'Fair to middling', 'Can't complain' or 'Oh, surviving', perhaps it is time to give yourself a good talking to! Think about your language. What might the impact be of saying 'I'm great', or 'Fantastic, thanks!' or 'I'm feeling really good today!'?

Our language is so closely tied in to our self-perception that we don't even notice its power. Think about the last time someone complemented you on something – it could be some work you have done, your haircut, your clothes or a sporting result. What was your response? Did you accept the complement graciously, or did you put yourself down – 'It was nothing/Hmm, not sure about the colour though/What, this old thing?/Oh, you know, it was a lucky break'?

If you are told not to think of an orange kangaroo, probably the first thing that pops into your mind will be exactly that; an orange kangaroo. In the same vein, if you talk about your well-being in terms of 'dodging along' or 'getting by', then that is exactly what you are likely to do. Simply surviving and getting by is not enough. Rather than hovering around the middle of the scale, we want you to move up towards the +5; to be a little more like Poppy. If you focus on the positive you will get more of the positive. When you are happy you will build better relationships with those around you, including your family, friends, your colleagues and your pupils. Of course bad things will happen, but the H Factor will help you build a buffer around yourself that will help protect you from the not so pleasant things that life throws at you.

> We need to help people to recognize the things that make them feel good and truly satisfied with their lives, so that they spend more time doing these things.[45] (Steptoe 2008)

Could it be that, as a nation here in the UK, we are terribly prone to look at the grey side of life? Do we tend to put ourselves down before anyone else gets a chance to step in and do it for us? This seems to be particularly notable in the realms of sport – think of how we treat the likes of Tim Henman. Rather than celebrating Henman for at one stage being ranked the fourth best tennis player in the world, we berate him for never winning Wimbledon. And, when Murray fought his way into the semi-finals of a major tournament, the emphasis was put upon his opponent's brilliance and great drop shots and his own 'head-shaking, shoulder-dropping, bottom-lip-sagging bewilderment'.[46] (Harman 2009) In fact, one journalist went so far as to headline the fact that Murray 'could not stop himself from crashing stomach first into the net, and he was left folded over the top of the white tape like a wet towel draped over a radiator'.[47] (Hodgkinson 2009) And this was a match he actually won!

Listen to yourself and your friends and colleagues for a while and see. In just one week, Joanna came across at least half a dozen examples of negative talk that completely prevented people from enjoying the moment. Perhaps unsurprisingly, two of these were to do with the weather! That week the weather was unseasonably beautiful – blue skies, plenty of sun and very warm for the spring. Yet, when she commented on the beautiful weather to a lady she met when waiting for a bus, rather than rejoicing in it, the lady said, 'Oh, yes, but you wait until next week. It's going to snow, you know. I mean, can you believe it? Snow in March.

Terrible really.' Shortly afterwards she heard someone else complaining that they didn't know whether to put their jumper on or take it off, and, 'Oh dear, this sun; one minute you need your sunglasses and the next you are in the shade!'

How much happiness is enough?

Being happy doesn't mean that everything is perfect. It means that you've decided to look beyond the imperfections. (Unknown)

Surely Alistair was not alone in his dislike of Poppy's blind optimism. The possibility of being overly optimistic is an intriguing one. Is it truly realistic to expect everyone to be functioning at +5 at all times? Probably not. Being naïvely happy could be dangerous in many life situations. It is both normal and healthy to feel sadness and other negative emotions.

In the book *Uglies* by Scott Westerfield everybody in the futuristic society willingly agrees to an operation at the age of 16 to make them supermodel beautiful. As a consequence, their government claims, they are all happy and lacking any bad feelings such as jealousy. What the government fails to tell its people is that, during the operation to make them pretty, a part of their brain is also removed so that they lose the ability to think freely. The people may be happy, but at what cost? The converse is also true. Just because someone is flourishing it does not mean that that their life is lacking in unhappiness. Happiness is not the opposite of unhappiness. However, having the H Factor gives us the ability to cope with negative events and to move on. It is about building strengths and bringing everyone up to the point where they are flourishing.

Equally, it is not desirable to have all members of staff and all pupils in schools blindly optimistic and happy at all times. This is very likely to lead to stagnation and lack of motivation for change and improvement. We are not looking to hide weaknesses, but to support people through them. And we should certainly not be removing challenge or aiming to remove any kind of problem from the lives of our young people.

In an interview on Radio 4's Today programme, Carol Craig (Chief Executive of the Centre for Confidence and Well-being in Glasgow) warned against making children narcissistic by allowing them to think that everything is all about them. She referred to the fact that parents complain to schools if their children receive a knock to their confidence by, say, not getting the lead role in a play or failing a spelling test. 'Schools should be resisting ... they shouldn't be accepting this role. It is not one they will be able to fulfil.'[48] (Craig 2009).

The H Factor is not about preventing children from having bad experiences. Nor is it about making them feel that their feelings are the most important things in the world. In fact, it is quite the opposite. It is about helping them build resilience so that they can cope with bad experiences and about teaching them other key skills such as building and maintaining friendships, being flexible and working within a team, so that they are aware of the needs and feelings of others.

We make children resilient by constantly pushing them to the edge of their comfort zones in an environment where it is safe to take risks and to make mistakes. And we believe that schools can, absolutely, do just that.

There are those who will argue that, by calling for schools to consider the happiness of all of those within them, we are going soft. Yet, you only need to go into the self-help section of any book shop – often you need to call on air-sea rescue to get you out – to know that there is a need for the 'soft' skills nowadays. Alternatively, try Googling 'self-help'. In less than 14 seconds Google will offer about 75,000,000 hits. If you type in 'self-help groups' you'll get around 527,000, and more than 15,000,000 for 'life coach'.

The going rate for a life coach in London is somewhere around £100 per hour. The minimum wage is £5.73 per hour for people aged over 22. Private GCSE tuition is £20 to £30 per hour. What does that tell you about the value we place on the H Factor?

Of course, the same people who think we are going soft will also shout defiantly that 'it's a tough world out there and we should be preparing children to cope with it'. We would argue that giving children the H Factor will not only prepare them to cope with that 'tough world' but also to flourish in it and, maybe, to make it just a little less tough for those who share it with them.

Nowadays, the so called 'soft skills' are as much or more in demand by employers than academic results.[49] Naturally a good, solid academic base is important, but that alone is not enough. Employers are also looking for people who are trustworthy, cooperative and positive. These soft skills include being able to persist at a task, to apply oneself and to concentrate. It has been found that poor children who have high levels of application and concentration are 14 per cent more likely to be well-off by the age of 30, than the average poor child.[50]

Today's focus on teaching content can prevent us from considering the so-called soft skills such as how to form and maintain positive relationships, how to manage emotions, to communicate and to be optimistic, but these are becoming increasingly important.

> It has become almost an annual ritual to focus on the literacy and numeracy of school leavers – but our research shows employers want more focus on communication, interpersonal skills and developing a work ethic ... findings suggest that the education system might help close the 'employability gap'.[51] (Clarke 2006)

The benefits of happiness

Staff

Work is important to us – we are there for a large part of our day and for a large chunk of our lives! But it is not just a case of bringing in the pounds. Most of us would say that our work is a part of our identity and that it gives structure to our days and weeks. In fact, in a meta-analysis of 225 studies on the topic of well-being,[52] it was found that the one factor that appears to influence our happiness most is ... work. This study also found that people whose work is varied and allows them to be autonomous are by far the happiest.

Research Summary

Some of the findings of Lyubomirski et al.'s meta–analysis are below.

- People who are happy at work are more creative and productive.
- Happy people perform better.
- Jobs that offer autonomy and variety make workers happier.
- Supervisors are happier than subordinates.
- People who are highly rated by customers are happier than those who are poorly rated.
- People who talk positively when at work are more likely to get positive reviews from their managers three and a half years later.
- Happiness leads to successful outcomes, rather than simply being a result of them.
- The happier someone is, the more likely they are to be offered a job, to keep it and to get a new job if they ever lose it.
- People who report that they are happy at the age of 18 become more financially independent and do better at work by the time they are 26.

When your members of staff are happy, they will be more creative, which will make it easier for them to solve problems. They will also be more productive and more likely to go the extra mile for you. Happy people are more likely to turn up to work every day and less likely to be ill. They will also stay in post and not look to move to another job, offering your school and its students greater stability.

> When people feel happy, they tend to feel confident, optimistic, and energetic and others find them likable and sociable. Happy people are thus able to benefit from these perceptions. (Lyubomirsky 2005)

Students

The emotional well-being of children should be as important to us as their physical health, and schools in the UK are now expected to have well-being at the top of their agendas. A child who is supported emotionally is much more likely to learn effectively in school and to develop the social skills necessary to become an engaged, well-rounded adult. The sociability of a child in school has an impact on future earnings, with each friend representing a 2 per cent increase in income at the age of 35![53] Does it make you wish that you'd been nicer to more people during your own school days?

In 2008, 25 per cent of children who said that they didn't intend to go into further education stated that this was because they 'do not enjoy learning'.[54] When Nottingham City Council decided to measure well-being in the locality, young people completed detailed questionnaires. Not only did both their satisfaction with life and their curiosity in life both fall as they got older, but also their satisfaction with their school experience plummeted between primary and secondary school, never to recover.[55]

Interestingly, if you look at the results of the study below, you will see that there is a correlation between finding school interesting and the amount children appear to learn. It isn't rocket science – the more interesting lessons are, the better the learning outcome.

	Primary	Secondary
Found school interesting	65%	12%
Learned a lot in class	71%	18%

One of the things that the study also stressed was that there is a connection between children's well-being and their curiosity about life (curiosity was defined as a need to strive for more and to learn more). If we can grab children's attention, harness their natural curiosity for life and feed it with fantastic lessons that concentrate on the learning, not just on getting through content, then we will also increase their levels of well-being.

Every teacher and every teaching establishment, however good they are, should constantly endeavour to improve standards. Some standards are easily measurable – standards of attendance, results in public tests and examinations, standards of behaviour and appearance to name but a few. You may be aware that these measurable standards in your school could be better. Results aren't what they could be and, perhaps, behaviour could be better too. If so, ask yourself the following three questions:

'Are staff and students happy?'
'If they were happier, would standards improve?'
'What could be done to change this?'

It may be that the children in your school get good academic outcomes. Perhaps your department, year group or your personal results shine out within your establishment. Everything is, shall we say, ticking along quite nicely. If it isn't broken, why fix it? Take a look at the figures below and you decide.

In the UK, a child starting school in September 2009 will be expected to remain in education until at least 2021. During this time, they will spend at least 14,000 hours in an educational establishment.

Now, if the aforementioned child goes on to become a teacher, the number of hours (including A-levels, and 40 years working in a school, but excluding degree and teaching qualification) increases to nearly 74,000 (and that's a conservative estimate). And, of course, we want you to win the H Factor for every member of your school community.

The H Factor is neither a bolt-on initiative, nor a series of happiness lessons. Instead, it is something that we hope will become part of the culture of your school. It should be infused into the very foundations and be spread among every member of the establishment, be they pupil, governor, teaching or support staff. As such, it will not compete with the curriculum, but will become part of every single subject, lesson and meeting.

Winning the H Factor in your school will help you to unlock the potential of staff and pupils. Not only will it make your establishment a more pleasant place in which to learn, teach and work, but it will make teaching and learning more effective and more enjoyable. It will also provide pupils with another invaluable life skill that will be just as useful to them as they progress through life as any examination results.

> We need to give young learners far more than skills for employment alone, even if such skills are key to the country's economy.[56] (Pring 2008)

Now, if you still need to be convinced that the H Factor is worth winning, below is a summary of some research projects into how happiness can positively affect lives.

Sisters are doing it for themselves

> If you are happy you are likely in the future to have less in the way of physical illness than those who are unhappy.[57] (Cox 2006)

In the 1930s, the members of an order of nuns known as the American School Sisters of Notre Dame were asked to write their autobiographies for their Mother Superior. At that time, the average age of the nuns was 22. Some 70 years later, a group of researchers[58] divided these autobiographies into four groups based on the number of positive and negative words and phrases used. Group 1 contained the autobiographies of those nuns who showed the least positivity, and who wrote comments such as:

> I was born on September 26, 1909, the eldest of seven children, five girls and two boys ... My candidate year was spent in the Motherhouse, teaching Chemistry and Second Year Latin at Notre Dame Institute. With God's grace, I intend to do my best for our Order, for the spread of religion and for my personal sanctification.

In contrast, Group 4 was highly positive. Below is a section from one of the Group 4 autobiographies:

> God started my life off well by bestowing upon me a grace of inestimable value ... The past year which I have spent as a candidate studying at Notre Dame College has been a very happy one. Now I look forward with eager joy to receiving the Holy Habit of Our Lady and to a life of union with Love Divine.

The researchers found that there was a very distinct relationship between positivity and longevity; that's to say, the higher the number of positive words and emotions expressed, the longer the life expectation. In fact, the average life expectancy of those nuns in Group 1 was 86.6 years and that of the nuns in Group 4 was 93.5 years! So, among a collection of people with very similar lifestyles, support, access to medical care and socioeconomic status, those with a positive attitude added an average of 6.9 years to their lives.

The link between depression and poor health has long been known. Someone who is depressed is more likely to become ill due to a drop in the effectiveness of their immune system. But what of the potential positive effects of happiness on an individual's health? While there is little evidence that being happy can help people overcome an illness, there is plenty to show that a happy outlook on life can actually prevent you from becoming ill.

In 2003, a team of researchers[59] asked a group of 334 healthy 18–54 year olds questions about their emotional state (for example, were they happy, pleased, relaxed, anxious, hostile or depressed?) and then gave them nasal drops containing a cold virus. They found that the volunteers who described more positive emotions were less likely to catch the cold than those who had been more negative.

Furthermore, in his analysis of 30 worldwide studies on health and happiness[60] Ruut Veenhoven found that happiness can actually add up to ten years to your life. This led him to conclude that the effects of happiness on longevity in healthy populations are 'comparable to that of smoking or not'. While the reasons as to how this can be are still under discussion, there is evidence that being happy reduces the levels of harmful hormones in your body. This is backed up by a study that showed happier people to have lower levels of fibrinogen,[61] which is a clotting factor known to increase the risk of heart disease.

> The effect of happiness on longevity in healthy populations is remarkably strong. The size of the effect is comparable to that of smoking or not.[62] (Veenhoven 2008)

Further research[63] by the same team tested 3,000 healthy British adults for the levels of cortisol (a stress hormone that is linked to high blood pressure, abdominal obesity and dampened immune function) in their bodies at various stages of the day. As they were tested, the volunteers were asked to describe their mood. It was found that people who were in a more positive mood when tested had lower levels of cortisol than those who were feeling more negative. The conclusion here is that being happy can have a positive physical effect on your health in the same way as being stressed has a negative effect;

> '... people who are happy and unstressed are likely to have less potentially dangerous stress chemicals in their bodies'[64] (Weisberg 2005).

In addition, happy people are more likely to make good life choices than those with a more negative outlook. They build better social networks,[65] are more self-confident and are likely to smoke and drink in moderation.[66] They are also more likely to watch their weight,[67] to exercise more and to live generally healthier lives. Babies born to mothers who lived close to the World Trade Centre during the month after its collapse when they were pregnant were smaller than those born to mothers who lived further away at the time.[68] Early positive bonding is crucial to lifelong well-being.

A study in 1986 found that happy people are more likely to see the bright side of things, pray, directly struggle with problems and seek help from others.[69]

In contrast, unhappy people are more likely to engage in fantasy, blame others and themselves and avoid working on problems. Happiness has also been linked to people who have high self-esteem and who are extraverted.[70] With all of the above leading to further happiness, they are, if you like, caught in an ever increasing circle of well-being.

Olivia Giles was 37 years of age when she caught meningococcal septicaemia. She was a young, energetic lawyer who had come through a broken marriage and had just begun to develop a new relationship with a man called Robin. One afternoon at work she began to feel ill. She was taken to hospital where she slipped into a coma in which she remained for four weeks. When she came out of the coma she discovered that in order to save her life her hands and feet had been amputated. She had to start learning everything over again.

It would have been easy for Olivia to become morose and embittered. Instead, she describes the elation of the day when she first walked on prosthetics: 'I managed a couple of steps and it was euphoric, I felt like I was floating. I had to lie down and just lay there weeping. I realised I was going to be ok.'[71] (Giles 2007) It would also have been easy for Olivia to retreat into self-pity but for her she had embarked upon a new life.

> My life is so much better now than before the illness. I make a deliberate effort to seek out opportunities, and not put off things. My experience hasn't changed my personality … but now I can put things into perspective. I have fewer regrets about the five years since my illness than about the time before it.[72] (Giles 2007)

Olivia is an extraordinary woman who, by the way, is still with Robin, but this sort of response to profound trauma is not unusual. Paraplegics and quadriplegics have, after their life change, been found to soon return to previous levels of happiness.[73]

And finally, it *is* possible to learn to become happier. In a six-year study Headley and Wearing found that 31 per cent of their participants improved their positive affectivity by more than one standard deviation.

Research summary*

- People who report themselves as happy at 18 will earn higher incomes in their 30s than their less happy peers.
- Those who report themselves as the *most* happy at 18, however, will do worse. Could it be that being too happy can dampen ambition?
- Happier people are more likely to enter mutually supportive long-term relationships and to have more friends.
- The least happy group of people are those living in the West who are trapped in unhappy marriages.
- Partners who are similar in personality, ability, physical attractiveness, attitudes, interests, values and politics are more likely to experience marital satisfaction, remain married and to avoid conflict and infidelity.
- In individualistic cultures co-habiting couples are happier than married couples.
- In collectivist cultures co-habiting couples are unhappier than married couples or single people.

* Author notes Happiness and Its Causes Conference, London October 2007.

1

What the research tells us about happiness

In this chapter we focus on the following topics:

Common mistakes about happiness

Researching happiness

An outline of what constitutes happiness

The views of four contemporary thinkers

A summary of our own research

And answer the following questions:

Can fame, wealth, beauty or possessions make me happy?

How do we know what we know about happiness?

To what extent is happiness inherited from our parents?

Do academics ever agree about happiness?

Can you summarize happiness in five words?

- What happiness isn't!
- Measuring happiness
- What happiness is
- Contemporary thinkers on happiness
- What does our research say?

What happiness isn't!

A rich man lay dying. He lay in his bed, wrapped in sumptuous silk sheets, in a beautiful house with a large swimming pool and a garage full of expensive cars. All around him his wealth was evident in every belonging and in the sheer quantity of famous doctors who were attending him.

The doctors agreed that this was a hopeless case, but there was one slim possibility. If the shirt of a happy man could be found and placed beneath the rich man's head then, perhaps, there would be a chance that he could survive.

Messengers, soldiers, police and even released prisoners were sent to the four corners of the kingdom to find a happy man. But everywhere they looked they found only misery and despondency. In the cities and in the villages, in the mountains and in the valleys it was the same story; the people had nothing to share but trouble and woes.

Eventually, when all hope seemed to be gone, some of the searchers met a shepherd who had been spending the summer in a high and remote valley. He often laughed as he worked, cheerfully singing his way through each day and smiling to himself as he watched his sheep graze. When asked he said, 'Am I happy? I can't imagine anyone who could be happier than I am.'

'Then please give us your shirt', said the searchers, 'for we need it to save the life of a rich man'.

'I wish I could help, but I don't possess a shirt', replied the shepherd. 'Never have.'

When this news was given to the rich man he dismissed everybody from his bedroom and considered the information deeply for seven days. At the end of his contemplation he had made a decision. He sent out the order that all of his expensive clothes, jewellery, cars, paintings and the contents of his vast treasure chests should be distributed among the people.

From that day on the health of the rich man began to improve.

Money

Money doesn't buy happiness and, in our heart of hearts, most of us know that happiness is not defined by how wealthy we are. Much research has shown that, once our basic needs for food and housing have been met, having more money does not make us happier. For example, a 1985 study found that Americans who earned more than $10 million per year only reported slightly higher levels of happiness than average Americans.[74]

> Money never made a man happy yet, nor will it ... The more a man has, the more
> he wants. Instead of filling a vacuum, it makes one. (Benjamin Franklin)
>
> http://quotationsbook.com/quote/40990/ date accessed 13.10.09.

But if you're still hankering after that lottery win, we suggest you save your hard-earned cash. Lottery winners do experience an initial surge in their levels of happiness. (That's not really surprising – look in a jacket pocket and find a ten pound note that you had forgotten about and you'll feel pretty pleased.) But this rush doesn't last long. Within five years, the winners' levels of happiness have usually returned to the levels they were at before their big win.

In the same American study,[75] lottery winners appeared to gain less pleasure from everyday activities such as reading, talking to friends and having breakfast than non-winners. In many cases, of course, lottery winners seem to have a particularly hard time; you don't have to search far to find stories of lottery winners committing suicide, abusing drugs or alcohol, losing their wealth or being ostracized by their communities.

Comparisons

> I do not try to dance better than anyone else. I only try to dance better than myself.
> (M. Baryshnikov)

Why do these lottery winners find their new lives don't live up to their expectations? Often because they have given up their jobs and moved house, thus losing contact to friends and colleagues. Their social support network is gone. They then find themselves with a whole new peer group and, parked next to someone else's 50 ft yacht, their 30 ft yacht looks quite small actually. We are creatures of comparison and, wherever we are, there will always be someone waving at us from further along the road.

The much publicized 2007 UNICEF report on child well-being found no relationship between GDP per capita and levels of child well-being, with the Czech Republic ranking significantly higher than wealthier countries such as France, the UK and the USA. So, once everyone in a society has had their basic needs met, they should all be happy, right? Wrong. If a society has a great divide between rich and poor, the well-being of the poor declines. Comparing ourselves to others who are better off than us leads to unhappiness. As Karl Marx pointed out:

> A house may be large or small; as long as the neighbouring houses are likewise small, it satisfies all social requirement for a residence. But let there arise next to the little house a palace, and the little house shrinks to a hut … the occupant of the relatively little house will always find himself more uncomfortable, more dissatisfied, more cramped within his four walls.[76]

> http://thinkexist.com/quotation/i-do-not-try-to-dance-better-than-anyone-else-i/361529.html date accessed 13.10.09

A Chinese study found that members of households that are poor in relation to other households in their village are more likely to migrate elsewhere than those with the highest incomes in that village. In other words, people see moving as an effective means of improving their *relative* position economically.[77]

Inequalities

At the beginning of this century in the USA, 33 per cent of wealth was owned by 1 per cent of the population. In the UK this decade over a fifth of the country's wealth has been owned by only 1 per cent of the population. In contrast, half the population shares between 5 and 10 per cent of the country's wealth![78] Perhaps that is contributing to the fact that these countries are mouldering at the bottom of well-being tables? html://thinkexist.com/quotation/i-do-not-try-to-dance-better-than-anyone-else-i/361529.html

In Richard Wilkinson and Kate Pickett's Book, *The Spirit Level: Why More Equal Societies Almost Always Do Better,*[79] the authors chart the level of health and social problems against the level of income inequality in 20 of the world's wealthiest nations. This is a quality piece of work with more than 50 years of research behind it. The authors report that in countries where there is a big gap between the incomes of the rich and the poor the number of cases of mental illness, drug and alcohol abuse, obesity and teenage pregnancy are higher, as are the murder rates. Life expectancy in these countries is shorter and children's educational performance and literary scores are worse. The authors point out that it is not only the poor who suffer. Rates of mental illness are likely to be as much as five times higher in the population *as a whole* in the most unequal countries.

The authors describe experiments with monkeys in which the power of status and position within the troop was studied (the animals were housed in groups). Social hierarchies were observed carefully and then, somewhat bizarrely, the monkeys were taught to administer powerful sedatives to themselves by pressing a lever. Dominant monkeys abstained; they didn't need the drugs. Subordinate monkeys, however, took a lot of drugs in order to alleviate the pain of low social status.

Try this test
Imagine that you can to choose between:
A. An income of £50,000 per year. Everyone else will get half that amount.
B. An income of £100,000 per year. Everyone else will get more than double the amount.

Just like the monkeys, human beings are remarkably attuned to relative position and status. As a famous decade-old study[80] has revealed, people prefer to live in a world in which they receive an annual salary of $50K (when others are pulling in $25K) than an annual salary of $100K (when others are making $200K). The Harvard graduates who took the test above were happy to be poorer, so long as they got ahead of everyone else. The real significance of wage rises is that people care as much about the wages of others as they do about their own. Intense wage rivalry tends to remain within our own reference group – work colleagues, friends or family. In UK schools, the introduction of a performance-related pay structure will have had its most difficult passage when comparisons within reference groups provoked feelings of 'injustice'. Levels of discontent could be correlated to the number of opportunities for comparisons fostered by the system.

Along similar lines, some researchers in the UK have claimed that we will readily give up our own cash to destroy other people's earnings. Students have been shown to prefer to be given negative feedback for a task if other students receive even worse feedback, than to receive positive feedback when the feedback others are given is even better than their own![81] To some, such findings reflect a dark side of human nature, but to us they reveal an all-too-human truth. We care more about social comparison, about status, about rank and about so-called positional goods than about the absolute value of our bank accounts or reputations.

Andrew Clark has shown that being laid off hurts less if you reside in a community with a high unemployment rate, being overweight stings less if you live in a country full of the super-sized and even being married to an unhealthy or plump spouse makes it easier to cope with your own health or weight problem. Shockingly, if you are unemployed you will, on average, be happier if your spouse is also unemployed than if he or she is working!

In research cited in *The Spirit Level: Why More Equal Societies Almost Always Do Better* mentioned above, a new social enclave was created by placing high-status monkeys from different groups together. Over time within the new group some monkeys began to dominate, while others became subordinate. The latter group accumulated abdominal fat and developed a rapid build up of atherosclerosis in their arteries. We all do better when we pay heed to the H Factor!

And as if that wasn't bad enough, another study[82] found that, as they get older, the brains of people with a low sense of self-worth are likely to shrink more than the brains of people with high levels of self-esteem. People with low self-esteem are more likely to suffer from memory loss as they get older than their more confident counterparts. In this study, the brain scans of 92 senior citizens were studied over 15 years and it transpired that the brains of those with low self-worth were up to a fifth smaller than those who felt good about themselves.

However the lead researcher, Dr Lupien, believes that teaching those with a negative mind set to change the way they think could reverse their mental decline. He said,

> This atrophy of the brain that we thought was irreversible is reversible – some data on animals and some data on humans shows that if you enrich the environment, if you change some factors, this brain structure can come back to normal levels. (Lupien 2005)

According to Dr Felicia Huppert of Cambridge University, it is possible to reverse this pattern by getting things in balance:

> There are interventions which talk about focusing on positive things in everyday life and savouring good moments even at times when life is difficult. Little tiny things may give you pleasure so there are skills involved in how to derive pleasure from the ordinary things in life.[83] (Huppert 2003)

Possessions

> Most people are under the impression that if they only had more of something, that would fulfill them and it's usually not the case and you don't know that until you reach that goal.[84] (Brody 2007)

Say we are feeling a bit down (maybe because we haven't won the lottery!) should we engage in a bit of retail therapy? Will that bring us happiness? Maybe a brief moment of satisfaction (akin to finding the tenner in our wallet), but not long-term contentment, no. The term 'retail therapy' is a dangerous one. All that collecting possessions does is help us part with our money (or credit!), but the pleasure is fleeting. Soon we are ready for our next fix and are looking out for something else to buy. And this something will probably need to be bigger and better than the last to give us the same rush. Quite simply, our brain becomes conditioned to the pleasure of a new purchase and the response to it wears off. The explanation comes back to the fact that we are creatures of comparison. As we adapt, our expectations about what will make us happy rise. We compare ourselves to where we want to be, to what we want to have, and to other people. This is known as the hedonic treadmill. Then, as we achieve our goals, we find someone else we can compare ourselves to and, along with them, a new source of unhappiness! As Van Boven puts it: '… people receive more enduring pleasure and satisfaction from investing in life experiences than material possessions'[85] (Van Boven 2003).

Beauty

So, if winning the lottery and/or having lots of stuff won't make us happy, how about losing that bit of weight, having some plastic surgery or just being that bit more physically attractive? We're afraid not. The Greek philosopher, Sappho, claimed, 'What is beautiful is good'. However, today's scientists have come to a more sophisticated understanding of how, when and why our physical appearance can make a difference to us.

The number of cosmetic surgical procedures undergone in the UK has been increasing year on year for the last decade. Despite the credit crunch, people are still requesting cosmetic procedures – although it appears that they are currently going for the less expensive non-surgical procedures such as Botox. Male breast reduction figures rose from 22 to 323 between 2003 and 2008.[86] We do seem to associate looking good with feeling better.

However, women who face the possibility of losing a breast to cancer have been shown to have incredible strength. In a study by UCLA professor, Shelley Taylor, these women described the illness as a wake-up call. They found that it made them take stock of their lives and reorder their priorities, with many of them reinstating their families above work and chores. Shelley calls this phenomenon 'tend and befriend' and suggests that it is the female response to stress – as opposed to the male tendency to respond with fight or flight. In the animal kingdom, males need the fight or flight reaction to stress as it is most appropriate in the situations they find themselves in – either as potential prey, or trying to get a mate. Females, however, are more likely to turn towards their family and support system.

Despite Hollywood's attempts at persuading us otherwise, being beautiful does not make us more self-assured, nor does it bring happiness. (On the other hand, beating ourselves up about not looking good enough sure can make us unhappy.) It may be, however, that coming somewhere in the middle of the beauty scale could have advantages socially. In one study,[87] students were labelled by other students as 'rejected', 'accepted' or 'unknown'. The rejected students tended to be the most attractive, the accepted students were the next most attractive and the unknown students were unattractive. And, while it could be argued that people who are physically attractive are more likely to be treated positively by others and will thus have increased levels of self-esteem that may lead them to ultimately feel more happy, research has shown otherwise.

In a study entitled 'Physical Attractiveness and Subjective Well-being',[88] scientists found that there is no relationship between physical good looks and high levels of self-esteem. They did this by asking people to rate how they felt about themselves and by taking photographs of these people (firstly with, then without make-up). They showed these photographs to an independent panel, which rated them for attractiveness. When the panel looked at the completely unadorned pictures, there was absolutely no correlation between the people they found attractive and those who felt good about themselves. The more self-assured people, however, did seem to make more of an effort to make themselves look attractive with make-up and jewellery. This is an interesting change in culture since the eighteenth century, when British law allowed men to annul their marriage if they found out that their wives had deceived them with make-up or wigs!

Actress, Drew Barrymore, argues that we should turn the idea that beauty brings you happiness on its head: 'I just think happiness is what makes you pretty. Period. Happy people are beautiful. They become like a mirror, and they reflect that happiness.' Seeing as Drew Barrymore hasn't exactly been slapped in the face with the ugly stick, the response, 'That's easy for you to say', does spring to mind. However, if you think about her words, she is right. Think back to the last time you saw someone who was truly happy (a child playing with his friends, a mother holding her newborn baby or a newlywed, for example) and it is true – the chances are that they looked more beautiful at that time than at any other. Being beautiful does not make us happy – feeling good about ourselves does.

Research summary

- We tend to attribute the success of attractive people of the opposite sex to ability, whilst we attribute the success of non-attractive opposite-sex people to luck.[89]
- We tend to attribute the success of attractive people of the same sex to luck.[90]
- Females who judge other women to be beautiful also judge them to be vain, materialistic and egotistic.[91]
- Women expect other attractive women to engage in extra-marital affairs and to have little parental competence.[92]
- Being of medium attractiveness could make you more successful socially.[93]
- People with high levels of self-esteem may make more of an effort to appear physically attractive.
- Justice is not blind! Attractive law-breakers are less likely to get caught and less likely to be reported to the authorities. Ugly defendants are more likely to be found guilty of a crime than attractive defendants.[94]

Fame

> My career brought me success, fame and fortune when I was still in my teens. And I found those things did not bring me happiness, which means I had to begin a search for meaning and happiness.[95] (Farrow 2008)

Money and possessions won't work, then. Nor will beauty. What about landing that job on TV, in films or in the recording studio? Will fame make us happy?

In short, the answer is no. In recent years there has been a huge increase in the number of television programmes in which normal people can sing, juggle, dance or act their way to fame and fortune. This has led many people today to believe that, not only is fame something incredibly desirable, but that it is also easy to achieve. Forget the hard work, talent and training that most people put into it. And evidence that fame does not buy happiness is readily available; you only have to look at the likes of Kurt Cobaine, Kate Moss and Britney Spears to name just a few. According to Professor Jib Fowles, famous people are almost four times more likely to commit suicide than the average person. And it's not really surprising considering the way famous people are treated by the paparazzi. Having pictures of a partner's affair displayed to the world in a not-so-glossy magazine would not do wonders for anyone's well-being, nor would most of us be overjoyed at being snapped when running out to the rubbish bin in our pyjamas first thing on a Sunday morning.

That said, winning an Oscar may not be a bad idea! It may be hard to tell whether the smiles and speeches at the ceremony are genuine, but it does seem that the award does Oscar winners good in the longer term. Actors and directors who win an Oscar have been found to live almost four years longer than the nominees who don't win.[96]

Measuring happiness

Happiness is a mystery, like religion, and should never be rationalized.[97] (Chesterton 1910)

By aiming to develop a model to measure happiness, we did not set ourselves an easy task. Measuring happiness is difficult! It can be done using a combination of research methods. For example, by keeping diaries and comparing the subjective interpretation of everyday experiences with those of others. Or using inventories – Ed Diener developed a simple five-question survey known as the 'satisfaction with life scale'. There are other more complex scales – Martin Seligman has a choice of 19 on his website,[98] some of which (such as the 'meaning in life question-naire') sound improbable, others (such as the 'optimism test') seem more familiar. Another method is called 'day reconstruction', during which participants log a day and then rate their experiences on a given scale. Mihalyi Csikszentmihalyi has even pioneered a method, called 'experience sampling', during which participants have hand-held computers onto which he periodically places a prompt question such as, 'How are you feeling?'

Subjects are often tested before and after an intervention to measure any changes in their levels of happiness or well-being. Twin studies are also often used in research, in this case for measuring the extent to which our happiness may be predetermined. David Lykken gathered data on 4,000 sets of twins[99], coming to the conclusion in a 1996 University of Minnesota paper that about 50 per cent of our happiness is set by genetic programming. Other more obvious research methods are peer nomination – these are exceptionally positive people whom we know; peer observation – this is how they behave, what they say and do; and peer profiling using inventories such as those described above.

Rationalizing happiness may be difficult and describing happiness may begin to diminish it, but we consoled ourselves with the fact that we were going where others had already trodden! As part of our research on the H Factor we looked at different conceptual models and the following three emerged as important.

Hedonism

Hedonism is a bit like being the 4 year old who pees his pants. It has an instant effect on everyone. We all see it – but it's only the little boy who actually gets any enjoyment out of it. And hedonism, just like pee, begins to turn cold and smelly after a bit! Even the little 4 year old feels guilty after a while!

The main principle of hedonism is that all pleasure is good and that, to be happy, we should fill our lives with as much pleasure and as little pain as possible. There are several problems with this theory. First, it can be difficult to define what pleasure is – we all have a different take on what brings us pleasure. Some of us may derive pleasure from an event or an experience, others from a possession, others from a state of being.

Second, some pleasures may lead to pain in the longer term – for example overdoing your alcohol intake may be pleasurable at the time, but can lead to all sorts of pain the following morning! Furthermore, pain can sometimes bring about good things, especially if it causes a change for the better – for example, if we burn ourselves on a hot pot, the pain is warning us to take our hands off. Third, as we have previously mentioned, pleasure is reduced when we get things too readily and we simply raise the baseline. The more we have, the more we want. And, finally, philosopher Robert Nozick's imaginary machine put the theory of hedonism firmly in its place and gave woody Allen an idea for his 1973 film, *Sleeper*.

In his famous experiment, Nozick offered people the theoretical opportunity to be plugged into a machine that would bring them every pleasure they wished for, be it having a novel published or making a friend, while all the time they would be floating in a tank with electrodes on their heads. Most people declined to take up the opportunity, showing that there are things that matter more to us than sheer pleasure. People were not prepared to miss out on the experience itself of actually struggling to write the book or meeting the friend along with the ups and downs of the experience. Similarly, in *Sleeper*, Woody Allen's character, Miles Monroe, experiences the *Orgasmatron* and decides that it is not for him!

Desire-satisfaction theory

The desire-satisfaction theory states that, if all of our desires are met (regardless of whether they bring us pleasure or not), then our well-being will increase.

There are two major arguments against this theory. First, we may desire something without knowing that it will have a negative effect on our lives – take for example those children in the Learning and Skills Council survey who said that their desire was to become a famous singer. Let us grant them this desire. It is only when they win the *X-Factor* and their desire is satisfied that they become fully informed of the more negative aspects of stardom!

Second, there are some things that we may desire that will not affect our own well-being directly. For example, imagine meeting someone who tells you that they are heading to the hospital to visit an ill relative. You may briefly desire that their relative makes a full recovery and, thanks to the desire-satisfaction theory, your wish is fulfilled. However, you never meet either the person, or their relative again, so you never discover that the relative is well again. Has having your desire satisfied increased your well-being? We would argue that it hasn't.

Objective list theory

The objective list theory is like a tick list approach to well-being. Spend your life doing these things and you will be happier and fulfilled. But who decides which things go on the list?

Òran Mór, meaning the 'great melody of life' or 'big song', is a cultural centre and meeting place in Glasgow's West End. It was formerly a church – Kelvinside Parish Church – and it was here that, in 2007, Alistair attended and enjoyed a lecture given by Carol Dweck (and hosted by The Centre for Confidence and Well-being) on mindsets.

In this old church, positioned above what were the pews where the parishioners would have perched, are carvings of the heads of famous Protestant reformers – Calvin, Luther, Knox – and a sprinkling of figures from the Scottish enlightenment such as Francis Hutcheson, Adam Smith and David Hume. From where he was sitting, however, Alistair could not find Robert Burns. Imagine how intimidating it must have been for the many impoverished parishioners to have these great figures eyeballing them as the collection tin came around. Severe, worthy, moralistic and disapproving, these men would today be proud proponents of what has become the objective list theory. Except their list of what is good and right may not match yours or ours!

The objective list theory takes all good things that may add to our well-being but that are neither simply pleasurable experiences nor desire-satisfaction – things such as friendship, beauty, knowledge, health, creativity and virtue. The theory states that our lives will go best if we fill them with as many items from the list as possible. The main argument given against this theory is that it is elitist – why should Luther and Knox, or anyone else for that matter, decide what is good for us if we don't want it in our lives?

What happiness is

When we talk of happiness and the H Factor, we are not referring to the fleeting moments of joy or pleasure brought about by a purchase, a small success or by performing a one-off good deed, for example. Instead, we refer to the kind of long-term well-being that helps us feel content with our lot and that everything is in place. The feeling that protects us from the inevitable knocks and blows of negative life events. That is to say, our overall levels, or baseline levels, of happiness. Psychologists tend to refer to it as subjective well-being.

Being subjective, happiness and well-being are difficult to measure. Psychologists measure them from the perspective of the individuals themselves, rather than from standards that are pre-set by mental health professionals or researchers. Social surveys and studies into the subject tend to be based on how happy people report themselves to be. Professor of psychology, Ed Diener, argues that simply asking people to rate their happiness on a scale is effective and that people's self-reports tend to match what other people say about them. However, there are things that can get in the way of an accurate response. For example, a volunteer may have had a particularly negative experience immediately prior to the test, or may be feeling defensive about it.

The one thing that stands out as having the greatest influence on a person's subjective well-being is their temperament. That is to say that a person with a positive outlook on life will report higher levels of well-being than a person who has a negative outlook. We are as happy as we perceive ourselves to be. So, if we can change our way of viewing our own lives, we should be able to change our levels of happiness. Other factors that have been found to have an influence on subjective well-being are having goals and things to do that we see as important. That said, Alistair can't help but agree with Emma Thompson, who feels that happiness is 'hot weather in Scotland.'[100] (Thompson 2008)

Genetics

On Monday, 26 January 2009, Nadya Suleman gave birth to healthy octuplet babies. How happy will they be? Will they all be different or, given similar upbringings, will their levels of happiness be similar?

There have been several studies of twins that have attempted to discover how much of our well-being is defined at birth. They have shown that our genetic make-up does indeed make a difference to our subjective well-being.[101] One psychologist has even gone so far as to state that happiness is 50 per cent genetic (inherited), 10 per cent circumstantial (to do with our health, location, etc.) and 40 per cent intentional (meaning that we can influence this 40 per cent).[102]

> Half of your predisposition toward happiness you can't change. It's in your genes. (Lyubomirsky 2008)

Set point

It has been found that our happiness is mostly immune to life's events. Generally, two years after an extremely negative life event, such as being made redundant, getting a divorce or losing a partner, a person's subjective happiness will return to similar levels as those prior to the event.[103] The same applies for positive events such as getting a pay rise, or even winning the lottery! 'Set point' is the term used by psychologists for our fairly stable level of happiness – a bit like a thermostat, this is the level we work at on a daily basis, although life's events may cause this level to rise or fall temporarily. In the end, they say, we will return to somewhere near to our set point levels of happiness.

However, there is general agreement among psychologists that we can do something about our levels of happiness and move up from this set point to a higher level.

Whichever way you look at it, just because our happiness levels may be, in part, pre-programmed does not mean that we can't do anything about them. If we accept that 50 per cent of our happiness is genetically inherited and our circumstances account for 10 per cent, then that leaves a huge 40 per cent that we can change. Our happiness is also shaped by our relationships, by how we view ourselves and by our thinking processes. Consequently, our happiness levels are largely self-defined and we can increase them if we wish to do so.

How we view the world and the way in which we explain the things that happen to us can have an enormous influence on our feelings. This is known as our *explanatory style*. For example, if you get the dream job you applied for do you put it down to being in the right place at the right time, or to the fact that you have the right experiences for the job and you prepared really well for the interview? Did someone damage the rear bumper of your car because they weren't concentrating, or because things like that always happen to you? Did the vast majority of your exam group do well because they worked hard or because you taught them well?

A pessimistic person will personally take the blame for any negative events and will put good things down to luck. If the bad luck is blamed upon factors that are global and stable ('It's the way it is in my life and there's just nothing I can do about it') then hopeless depression can occur. Here the emphasis is not so much on one's own capacity to control the situation but the factors that appear to be outside one's control. It is an important point to note that children learn their explanatory style from their parents. It is the view of some academics that repeated exposure to controllable events may play a part in inducing an optimistic explanatory style, whereas repeated exposure to uncontrollable events may contribute to a negative or pessimistic explanatory style.

An optimistic person will see the positive events as something that he or she deserves and negative ones as bad luck. Someone with an optimistic explanatory style is far more likely to persevere at a task or challenge and, therefore, succeed thus confirming their own view that they deserve the good things that happen to them: 'What people think, believe and feel affects how they behave.'[104] (Bandura 1986)

How we view our ability to cope with situations, problems or tasks is known as 'self-efficacy'. Self-efficacy is not the same as self-esteem. As opposed to self-esteem, which is our general view of ourselves and our abilities, self-efficacy is our view on our ability to cope with something *specific* or to reach a *specific* goal. Someone who has high levels of self-esteem generally may not be blessed with self-efficacy with regard to a particular activity such as swimming. Because they have little faith that they will have any success in the swimming pool, they are likely to avoid diving in!

Psychologist Bandura's research showed that people with high self-efficacy feel that they have control over their own lives, while those who have low self-efficacy believe that there is not much they can do to change the things that happen to them. Our levels of self-efficacy predict how we think, how motivated we are and how we perform. People who have a level of self-efficacy a little above their ability are likely to take on challenging tasks and to gain valuable experience because they have a chance of success.

> Perceived self-efficacy not only reduces anticipatory fears and inhibitions but, through expectations of eventual success, it affects coping efforts once they are initiated. Efficacy expectations determine how much effort people will expend, and how long they will persist in the face of obstacles and aversive experiences. The stronger the efficacy or mastery expectations, the more active the efforts.[105] (Bandura 1977)

Our happiness is very much influenced by the way we see ourselves. Psychologists call this our 'theories of self' or 'self-theories'. Like self-efficacy, our self-theories are what define and shape our thoughts, feelings and behaviour. Why is it, for example, that some children in our classrooms are motivated to work hard and achieve success, even if a task is challenging, while others are more easily defeated and resort to avoidance tactics? (Avoidance tactics could be any or all of the following; going quiet, avoiding eye contact, dumb insolence – 'I dunno, do I?', poor or aggressive behaviour and poor attendance.)

Social psychologist, Carol Dweck, describes two views on ability. The first, the 'entity view', is held by people who see intelligence as something fixed; something that cannot be changed. The second, the 'incremental view', is held by those who believe that intelligence is something that we have power over; something that can be changed and developed. Children who fall into the first category are likely to want to be seen as clever and will, therefore, find techniques to avoid tasks that they perceive to be too difficult. They wish to avoid 'failure' at all costs. In contrast, children who hold an incremental view will see a challenge as an opportunity to learn and to improve their skills.

Consider the following two children. As you read, think about what views they have of themselves, of life and of intelligence. What may have contributed to these views? What can be done in a classroom and/or school situation to encourage, develop or change their views?

Adil

Adil is nearly 5. He is sociable and cheerful. He comes from a highly supportive home. His mother is a doctor and his father is a manager in a large firm. Both parents want Adil to succeed academically. Adil can read fairly fluently. His mother noticed that, at three, he was picking up books that they had read together and 'reading' them out loud. She felt he was trying to match the words he could remember to the letters on the page.

One Saturday, when Adil was playing outside at a friend's house, he noticed that her bicycle had no stabilizers. When he got home, he insisted that his bike's stabilizers were removed and spent the remainder of the weekend practising riding it. On Sunday evening he joyfully ran into the house, wiping the blood from his knees, and shouted, 'I can do it. Come and watch.' Thrilled at his persistence, his parents raced out to watch.

Adil's birthday is in November, putting him near the top of his class age-wise. His teacher is positive, calm and encouraging. She has put him on the Gifted and Talented Register and constantly consults with his parents over the books Adil brings home and over his progress. When Adil is unwell, he begs his mother to take him to school anyway.

Adil will sit for hours building Lego creations. He often asks his big sister to write down sums for him and to help him use a number line. He also loves to swim and to play football. When his big sister won a swimming award he cried because he hadn't been given one. His father explained that, if he wanted one, he would have to swim one width of the pool (5 m) without putting his feet down. Within three weeks, Adil had done this and was proudly taking his award into school to show his teacher.

Adil goes to football coaching every Sunday. There are lots of older children, and plenty of children who are better players. Adil gets highly frustrated that he has never won an award for scoring the most goals or dribbling the fastest. Sometimes he tells his parents and friends that he has won an award, even though this is untrue.

Maya

Maya is Adil's big sister. She is 8 years old and is a sociable child, although she is cautious around new people. She has two very close school friends and is well-liked in her class. Books have always been a big part of her life and she has a reading age of 11. She loves to write creative stories and her writing and spelling are also of a high standard.

When Maya was little, she always enjoyed doing the same jigsaw puzzle over and over. She loved to be called clever each time she finished it, but would not be persuaded to try a different one. She refused to practise writing her name, but then one day simply wrote it correctly.

Born in August, Maya is one of the youngest children in her class. In her first year at school, her teacher was an extremely lively, dramatic lady, who was also very strict and tended to shout a lot. Maya often said that she didn't want to go to school. She showed a great talent for reading but, despite progressing very quickly, had to move through every book and every level in order. Her parents felt that her reading was never challenged – she rarely came across a word that she needed help with. Now that Maya is allowed to choose her own reading books, she always selects one that is below her reading ability.

Maya can be reluctant to try new things – when she was learning to ride a bike, each tumble was accompanied by tears and shouts of, 'I hate this thing!' Maya doesn't like to play tennis because, she says, 'I tried it at school and I couldn't do it'. When she does so, her mother laughs and says, 'Just like me. I was rubbish at sport at school'.

What has contributed to Maya and Adil's different personalities?

Being siblings, Maya and Adil have had very similar upbringings. However, many things have made a difference to how their personalities are developing. Below are some of those factors:

- Birth order: Maya has had to make her own way while Adil has a lead to copy – or compete with.
- The gender difference: Perhaps being a boy has made Adil less risk-averse.
- Modelling: The children's mother can be self-deprecating, while their father is quietly confident.
- Challenge: In the early stages of education, Maya was not pushed to the edge of her comfort zone. Because her reading talents were not recognized, she wasn't challenged. Being risk-averse, she avoids things she may not succeed in immediately. Adil, on the other hand, has been given work at school that challenges him, has achieved success, and this has deepened his belief that persistence pays.

- Praise: Maya was told she was clever for completing the same task over and over. Adil, on the other hand, gained recognition for trying hard and persistence.
- Age: Being among the oldest in the year has simply confirmed Adil's belief that he can do anything.

Both children need to be challenged. Maya, in particular, needs a safe environment for this challenge.

Strategies for Maya:

- scaffolded challenge
- rewards for the efforts that have led to incremental improvements
- comparison with her previous stages
- embed the idea that she is capable, patient and likely to succeed with effort.

Strategies for Adil:

- different sorts of rewards
- maintaining a progress diary
- drawing up performance charts
- embed the idea that he is capable, industrious and a reliable team player.

The life well-lived

Some cause happiness wherever they go; others whenever they go. (Oscar Wilde)

http://thinkexist.com/quotation/some_cause_happiness_wherever_they_go-others/157620.html date accessed 13.10.09

How we choose to live our lives has an impact on our happiness. And the key is that we always have a choice. What would you like to have written as your epitaph and what would you like to be remembered for? If you can look back on your life and feel that you have lived it well, then it must have brought you (and others) happiness. Sadly, our world today puts a great deal of emphasis on how successful we are and this success is measured by various things – money, possessions, power and popularity, to name a few. Yet, how about the happiness that comes from a simple life that is lived well? That's to say, a life in which our success is defined by our family, our friendships and our character. A life in which we have made a definable, positive difference to the lives we have touched.

The business man was very successful. He had a beautiful family and a large house, he dined with the rich and famous and he regularly appeared in *Hello* magazine. When he drove his expensive car down the main street people stopped and noticed him. He had it all – but he wasn't happy.

He went on a business trip to the Indian Ocean. His company was considering building a hotel on one of the smaller islands there and he had been talked into making an inspection visit. The journey turned out to be long and arduous, with the last part involving a seaplane followed by a short boat trip. Eventually, the boat turned around the bottom corner of the island and, as a hot mid-morning sun beat down, it moored in the most beautiful cove the business man had ever seen. The beach sparkled silver and white, a small village stretched up onto the side of a hill and the only sounds were those of the waves lapping and the birds singing in the trees. The businessman thought it was a perfect spot for his hotel.

It was his habit when taking a business decision to take a walk, clear his head and begin to work out the figures. That is why he found himself right at the edge of the small village down by the beach. He took the chance, with no-one around, to sit on a chair left on its own by the water's edge. After he had been there a while, lost in his thoughts, he noticed a man sitting under a tree nearby. He tried to avoid eye contact with the man but – too late – the villager saw him, smiled and ambled over.

'Morning to you', said the man. 'It's a good idea to take a rest. The sun is fierce.'

'Agreed, I'm not really used to it', replied the businessman.

'I've got just what you need', said the man. 'Give me a minute.' And he disappeared off into a nearby hut that was surrounded by nets and a jumble of fishing equipment. A moment later, the man returned with a broad smile on his face and a can of beer in each hand. The beers looked cold and very inviting. The businessman accepted the offer with good grace.

'Here's to health, wealth and happiness', said the local, as he took a long slow drink. The businessman copied him and immediately felt the better for something cool inside him.

'Do you live here?' asked the business man.

'All my life, like my father and my father's father before me', he replied.

'And what do you do?'

'I do whatever I need to. I fish, mostly. There's enough for everyone here. Some days I just sit here and think.'

'Do you have a boat?'

'I do. It was my father's boat. It's over there.' The local man pointed to a small, rundown boat that looked to be in need of repair.

The business man glanced at the boat. He wondered how safe it would be on an open sea. Immediately he began to work out in his head how the boat could be made to be more profitable. If he built his hotel, his restaurants would need a steady supply of quality assured fish products from the local fleet.

The two men got to talking about life locally, about the village and about the fishing. The business man had grown to like this villager in the short time they were together and felt he could help him.

'Can I offer some advice?' asked the business man and, without waiting for a reply, launched into a speech:

'I'm a business man from Europe. I know business. If you were to paint that boat and build a small jetty here you could fish in the morning and offer tours of the island to tourists in the afternoon. You might want to consider putting an extension onto your house and running the operation from there.'

The man nodded and smiled as the business man continued;

'Once you have got some capital together you could put in for a bank loan and get a second boat. Now, a second boat would allow differentiation. You could employ someone full time on the tourist side to maximise your returns. Once you had a season or two under your belt, you could then acquire another, even bigger, fishing boat. Increased capacity might allow you to get an exclusive deal with the hotel and then, beyond that, operate a bigger fleet.'

The man nodded and smiled some more.

'With a bigger fleet, then you are really in with the big boys', the business man continued. 'Within ten years it would all be self-contained. It would run itself. You'd be able to sit back, put your feet up and relax.'

'Another beer?' asked the local man, leaning back in his chair. The sun shone down, the waves lapped against the shore and the birds continued to sing nearby.

Ralph Waldo Emerson defined success in a simple life well lived as:

To laugh often and much; to win the respect of intelligent people and affection of children; to learn the appreciation of honest critics and endure the betrayal of false friends; to appreciate beauty; to find the best in others; to leave the world a little bit better, whether by a healthy child, a garden patch, or a redeemed social condition; to know even one life has breathed easier because you have lived. This is to have succeeded.

Contemporary thinkers on happiness

Seligman

In 1998 psychologist, Dr Martin Seligman, who had been studying depression for 30 years, took a whole new look at how things were done. He suddenly realized that psychologists like himself had been looking at what was making people sad, and had aimed only to remove the negatives from their lives. By doing so, he felt, they were just being left empty. Seligman was also concerned that, by focusing on weaknesses rather than on strengths, psychologists were missing out on the opportunity to make the lives of average people fulfilling.

> I used to think that all you had to do to get a happy person was get rid of the
> negatives in their life, but if that's all you do you don't get a happy person, you get
> an empty person. You need the positives too.[106] (Seligman 2003)

Consequently, instead of looking at how very miserable people differ from the norm, Seligman began to study how very happy people differ from the norm. This led to the birth of positive psychology, which looks at helping people protect themselves from the negative events that life, inevitably, will throw at them.

Seligman's research over the last decade has led him to conclude that there are three different types of happy lives:

1   the pleasant life
2   the good life
3   the meaningful life.

The pleasant life is what he calls 'Hollywood happiness'. It is about laughter and joyful moments. To achieve the pleasant life, we should try to fill our lives with as many positive emotions and happy moments as possible. People can be taught a variety of skills and tricks with which to amplify these feelings of happiness. The problem with the pleasant life (as with hedonism) is that we tend to get used to these positive emotions and take them for granted. For example, the first time we treat ourselves to a really good bottle of wine it may bring us some pleasure. Do this every night and the pleasure is reduced and we may find ourselves wanting a box of chocolates as well!

> The biggest mistake that people in the rich West make is to be enchanted with the Hollywood idea of happiness, which is really just giggling and smiling a lot. (Seligman 2003)

The good life is about engagement in work, family and leisure and about achieving 'flow'. Flow is the state we enter when we are so involved in an activity and so concentrated upon that activity that we don't notice time passing. To lead the good life, says Seligman, we must identify the things that we are good at and the things that bring us this state of flow, then use these strengths in as many areas of our lives as possible (at work, at home and in our relationships).

The meaningful life is, again, about identifying our strengths (be they sporting, creative, leadership or a love of learning, for example) and then using them to the greater good.

With regard to which of the above three lives is most likely to lead to a prolonged feeling of well-being, Seligman has found that it is best to have a mix of all three. He warns that the pleasant life will not bring enduring happiness, but is more like the cherry on the cake for when we are leading a mixture of the good and the meaningful life.

> 'Nothing brings greater happiness in life than fighting for a cause that is greater than yourself.'[107] (McCain 2008)

Lyubomirsky

> Happy people construe the world, themselves and other people in more positive and adaptive ways than unhappy people do.[108] (Lyubomirsky 2001)

Professor of psychology, Sonja Lyubomirsky, moved to the United States from Russia when she was a child. She was struck by the fact that so many Americans seemed obsessed with happiness and with the number that bought (and sometimes read!) self-help books. Consequently, she went on to spend many years studying why some people are happier than others. Her research found that unhappy people tend to dwell on problems and react to them in a negative way, while their happy counterparts approach problems positively and are more flexible with regard to solving them. This led her to develop her Construal Theory of Happiness, which asserts that, 'Happy people construe the world, themselves and other people in more positive and adaptive ways than unhappy people do.'

Lyubormirsky's belief is that everyone can raise and sustain their levels of happiness beyond that for which they are genetically destined. In 2005, she outlined (with Sheldon and Schkade) a 'sustainable happiness model'. This states how people can increase their subjective well-being. To do this, she says, we must make an effort on a daily basis by practising a variety of cognitive, motivational and behavioural activities.

Fredrickson

Negative emotions have a very obvious use. They narrow our mindset in order to prepare us for a specific action. For example, fear protects us by urging us to run away and escape, and disgust will make us steer clear of the object of our revulsion. We need negative emotions to ensure our immediate survival. In contrast, positive emotions such as joy or gratitude do not appear to have any such immediate use. Barbara Fredrickson developed her 'broaden and build' theory after considering why it is that positive emotions have survived evolution despite this fact. Various experiments led her to conclude that positive emotions *broaden* our mindset – that is, they make us more creative and more able to think broadly. We then store this up and it helps us to *build* positive personal resources and character traits. So, while positive emotions are not needed for our immediate survival, we need them in hard times that we are likely to encounter at a later date. A positive emotion may be fleeting, but the benefits are, says Fredrickson, long term – they help us build personal strengths, abilities and relationships and they help us to lead fuller lives.

Barbara Frederickson conducted some interesting experiments to find the ideal emotional state for optimising creative responses. One such experiment involved deliberately evoking different emotional states in a control group. This was done by viewing short film excerpts which conveyed different emotions before asking participants to generate creative responses to a problem. The results are shown below.

Emotion evoked	Number of creative responses given to a problem
Joy	15 responses
Contentment	12 responses
Neutral	11 responses
Fear	8 responses
Anger	7 responses

We propose that positive emotions not only feel good in the present, but also increase the likelihood that one will feel good in future. That is, we suggest that positive emotions trigger upward spirals towards enhanced emotional well-being.[109] (Fredrickson and Joiner 2002)

Fredrickson also suggests that, to feel happier in the long run, we should start to take things one day at a time. We should register each positive emotion we feel on a daily basis so that we can store them up until we feel generally happier in the long run.

Gilbert

The fact is that human beings come into the world with a passion for control, they go out of the world the same way, and research suggests that if they lose their ability to control things at any point between their entrance and their exit, they become unhappy, helpless, hopeless and depressed.[110] (Gilbert 2006)

Daniel Gilbert argues that we constantly want to anticipate happiness but our capacity to predict our future happiness is poor. Nonetheless, we are habitually doing it. He claims that the uniquely human ability to simulate future experiences is one of the talents that got our species out of Africa and into Wal-Mart. Like eyesight and hindsight, foresight can be blind. And, in the last decade, psychologists and economists have discovered that people make systematic errors when predicting their future satisfactions. This may explain why our attics are full of junk that at one time in our lives promised to be so fashionable and life changing.

Gilbert suggests that we think of the more distant future in a way which is blurry and smooth like remote objects positioned on a distant hill, whereas we think of the near future in finer detail. When volunteers are asked to imagine a good day, they can imagine the good day in finer detail and with more variety of events if it is tomorrow than if it is a year ahead. The day a year ahead has all the lumps smoothed out and is described in bland terms. What's more, when people are asked how accurate the two descriptions are they claim that they are equally realistic.

Why do we do this? Our capacity for imagination includes a predisposition towards adding and removing details, filling gaps with unwanted or fabricated information or even removing whole scenes. Our fraud detectors are too often switched off when we imagine future experiences. If they are switched on, then they are influenced by 'presentism', which is a tendency for current experience to influence one's views of the past and of the future. That is to say that we project the present onto our future. The other thing that happens is that the things we may have anticipated would be really bad are never as bad in reality. Once we get there, our systems quickly adjust!

In the presence of a large bucket of sardines how you anticipate a mouthful of chips will be different to how it would have felt if you had been in the presence of a large bucket of chocolate. But actually, once you get the chips in your mouth they will taste the same anyway.

The significance of Gilbert's work won't be lost on politicians or large corporations who spend millions canvassing customers. It would suggest that, if we are poor at predicting what will make us happy in the future, we will not be the best barometers of opinion when it comes to political choices. Nor would it be lost on schools who invest heavily in canvassing student and community voice. Gilbert's answer to flawed prediction is to use surrogates. We should use other people's experiences to predict the future, instead of imagining it. People are surprisingly similar in much of their experiences, he says.

What does our research say?

Life would be infinitely happier if we could only be born at the age of eighty and gradually approach eighteen. (Mark Twain)

http://thinkexist.com/quotation/life_would_be_infinitely_happier_if_we_could_only/181597.html date accessed 13.10.09

There are five components that researchers have found to contribute to our happiness. They are best described in Alistair's acronym – SPICE.

1) Sociability

A proven major component of happiness for the individual is the ability to tap into a supportive infrastructure. For most of us this is the family, for some it is the workplace, for others it's those we meet through a hobby. Schools that actively encourage social activities among a wide range of staff and others provide supportive infrastructures that will increase well-being and, in turn, productivity.

A major longitudinal survey begun in the UK in 1958 found that those who exhibited sociability in childhood were significantly and consistently happier much later in adult life.[111] For a child, social competence is a greater predictor of success in adult life than exam grades. The child who can be self-deprecating, who can empathize and who has a playful approach to life is set up to become successful at building and maintaining friendships. To some extent, social competence can be taught.

2) Positivity

People are about as happy as they make their minds up to be. (Abraham Lincoln)

http://www.quoteb.com/quotes/1973 date accessed 13.10.09

Our second contributor to happiness is a positive perspective on life. A positive person sees the doughnut; a negative person just glares at the hole. Individuals with a positive perspective are often those who look forwards and outwards rather than backwards and inwards. They are less likely to dwell on negative experiences and misgivings. Because they avoid unnecessary comparisons, they can live in the moment and they are likely to have a high concern for others. Positive people share a sense of life getting better. This helps them respond positively to adversity. In schools, these individuals are the heroes of the staffroom; they are people magnets! Their optimism makes them attractive. They find time to listen. Negative people, in contrast, drain the energy of those around them. These are the cynics of the staffroom – those who have given up, but haven't yet shut up! Think about who you would prefer to sit with in the staffroom!

Being blindly optimistic, however, is not helpful and having unrealistic goals can corrode self-confidence. Children with authoritarian parenting are more likely to set unrealistic goals and have a self-concept that is vulnerable to failure.

Children whose parents are authoritative rather than authoritarian are more likely to have realistic goals and fewer anxieties around their achievement. Task-related feedback (goals which are all about specific improvements to the skill) rather than ego-related feedback (goals that are about the person) are much more likely to yield improvements and much less likely to have an inhibiting effect on self-esteem.

Similarly, schools that are authoritarian in character are less likely to foster innovation and creativity than those that combine high expectations with a caring culture. A positive perspective does not mean a Pollyanna perspective. It means that there is an underlying belief that things will get better, progress will be made and the general trend is favourable. Schools with a positive perspective, like individuals, put setbacks into context and are galvanized.

3) Integrity

Integrity is about doing the right thing when no-one is looking. It is what helps us sleep at night. If you really care about others, you do what is right.

Integrity at work can be shown by an experiment carried out by researchers at Halloween.[112] Psychologist, Dr Cialdini, filled a huge bowl with sweets and, when children came knocking, he brought it to the door and told them that he was really busy so he would just leave the bowl. The children were asked to just take one sweet as lots of other people would be along later and would want some too. Then he went inside and left them to it. Of course, thinking they weren't being watched, the children stuffed their pockets full of sweets. With the next group of trick or treaters, Cialdini did the same thing, but this time he had left a huge mirror at the back of the bowl of sweets. Faced with their own reflections, most children took less.

Those who operate with integrity are those who can hold a mirror up to their actions. They are less plagued by self-doubt and, as a consequence, can do what's right consistently. To outsiders, the seeming ease with which hard decisions are made again and again is admirable. Happier individuals don't have to shift through the integrity gears or deal with the anxieties of having to do so. They bring the same certainties to really hard decisions and their consequences as they would to the mundane. Moreover, they are often resolute without being dogmatic and, as such, are better equipped for dealing with failure.

The next way in which integrity contributes to greater all-round happiness is in minimizing unhelpful comparisons with others. The more an individual is clear about what matters to them and is resolute in pursuit of that, the less they feel the need to compete with others to get it. Their resolution is unlikely to be driven by self-interest or fuelled by invidious comparisons with others. To this end they are more likely to buy a new car just to keep the salesperson cheerful than to edge ahead of their neighbours! In many ways this is counter intuitive, because we are a species where serotonin (a neurotransmitter associated with feeling good) is boosted by success. Arguably, we are set up to compete, but happier people seem to feel less wounded by failure.

A happy school is one in which everyone acts with integrity and is able to hold a mirror up to their behaviour; a school in which everyone is working towards the same, agreed cause or core purpose. People who don't act with integrity should be encouraged to change their ways.

4) Cause

Our third happiness category is cause. Happy people have a sense of life's direction. They also have a set of longer-term goals. They enjoy, and regularly find, challenge. The challenge may be large scale like changing jobs, moving house or starting a family. It may also be small scale like trying a new skill for the first time. In either case, happy people are not likely to see challenge as on overbearing imposition. They are able to separate and manage their wants and their needs.

For young people, discovering that wants and needs are two different things can be a bruising experience. I may want the latest mobile phone, but I don't need it! I may want beauty, but I don't need it! I may want fame, but I don't need it! This can be made even harder by having peers who do get many of the things that they want but don't necessarily need.

Individuals who report themselves as happy say things like, 'Everything feels in place' and 'I'm content with my lot'. For a school to be a happy place it needs to feel stable. This does not mean that there is little or no change year on year nor that traditions go back through generations without regard to their impact on learning and self-esteem. It is more likely that there is a shared certainty about the school's core purpose and the values which underpin that core purpose. Our happiness category uses the heading 'cause' – it could be equally served by the heading 'core purpose'.

5) Efficacy

Our fifth happiness category is efficacy. Efficacy is the feeling of being in control. It is the ability to recognize and manage emotional response, particularly those negative emotions that threaten to hijack us. Finally, it is about making a contribution and having that contribution recognized in some way, either by others or by alignment to a perceived greater good such as a religious faith.

A major cause of stress among all large primates is a feeling of loss of control. It doesn't need to be real – it just needs the conviction that, despite all of your efforts, things are out of hand and there's nothing to be done about it. Such a conviction ultimately leads to what Martin Seligman calls 'learned helplessness'; in other words, a victim mentality. Happier people do not end up exhibiting these traits. They are more likely to be able to adjust their circumstances and thus how they respond to those circumstances through some intervention. Happier people have niches in their lives over which they can exercise control. The exercise of such control provides its own reward. They may be put upon at work but they run a youth group on a Sunday enjoy every minute and hour that goes into it. The old saw is, 'If you find a job you love doing you never work again'. Happier people are more likely to find themselves there.

An obvious corollary is the school where the culture is one of being put upon. Would a happier school, by our definition, be more likely to niche control and find areas to exercise enterprise and vision where it was less susceptible to the agendas of others? Instinctively, we think yes. Schools, like any other large organizations, have their share of learned helplessness. Some schools, through impoverished leadership, have become channels of learned helplessness waiting to be rescued from initiative fatigue. They bemoan their lot. Others stride ahead, confidently discounting initiatives that don't align with their core purpose and taking each challenge on with ease.

Making a recognized contribution is an aspect of efficacy which is about being valued. Humans like the affirmation of other humans. This may be eye contact, the use of a name, the touch on a sleeve, the note in a pigeon hole, the recognition in a thank you speech, promotion, knighthood or a seat in the House of Lords. Recognition and affirmation is important for many of us. Happy people get lots of it but not always in formal and public ways. How satisfying is it for a dog lover to be recognized upon arrival home and then greeted with a wet tongue? If it happened with a dog you didn't know it would be highly distracting! Happier people are often those for whom modest moments of recognition accumulate and are given freely in return.

Happier people do not seek out recognition. It comes as a consequence of their willingness to contribute whatever. Absence of recognition does not have the catastrophic effect for these people that it can have for others. Happier people are better able to manage negative emotions. Failure to manage negative emotions or see-sawing between emotional states is stressful. Stress itself is a major killer. Extended periods of stress lead to loss of appetite and libido, reduced growth, inhibited decision making and apathy. Happier people exhibit control in some, or all, aspects of their decision making and emotional response.

We began by suggesting that maybe we should take happiness more seriously. We think that the work of positive psychologists offers something for schools. Already the Every Child Matters agenda is at the heart of the new inspection process and is a focus for how we engage with young people. By studying what makes individuals, families, communities and nations happy we hotwire straight into the core purpose of learning and of schools.

2   Defining the H Factor

In this section we focus on the following topics:

> **The development of our happiness model**
> **Our recommended methods for individuals and schools**
> **The stories of four schools that place the happiness of their students at the centre of what they do**

And answer the following questions:

> *How did we arrive at the H Factor?*
>
> *How do schools begin to become happier places?*
>
> *What is meant by build, broaden and balance?*
>
> *What practical and immediate steps are possible to increase happiness?*

- How we arrived at the H Factor
- Build, Broaden and Balance
- Four schools by schools

How we arrived at the H Factor

In what seems a lifetime ago Alistair remembers visiting a school in Gillingham, Kent at the behest of the local authority. He was there to begin some work on school transformation. Alistair was to be involved in helping move the learning and teaching forward. His first day was set aside for meeting some key staff.

On arrival, there was a constant bustle of people in the reception area. Most of the limited space available was taken up by a large vending machine which made a lot of noise and had an unnerving habit of shooting the cans out across the floor. Opposite this machine was a hatch in the wall. On a shelf below this hatch sat a bell. This was Reception. Close to the bell was a handwritten sign that stated, 'Don't ask for change here'. The sign proved to be strangely prophetic. Change was not high on this school's agenda.

Our starting point for *Winning the H Factor: The Secrets of Happy Schools* is an interest in change; in what defines it, what drives it and in what can prevent it. We do not position ourselves as experts in this field – though we do have an accumulated 72 years of schools experience between us – but we do claim to know something about working with, around and through significant change. In every case the drivers of change have been located deep within the organization's culture. Creating happier schools is not and never will be about happiness lessons, positive thinking weeks or Red Nose days – it will be about achieving cultural change across the whole organization.

To create a happy but ineffective school is for us a contradiction because identifying, agreeing, delivering and evaluating core purpose is one of the key drivers of happiness. If you are not creating a culture wherein achievement is nurtured, developed, released and enjoyed then you are not putting core purpose at the centre of what you do. We very quickly realized that, like many of the happiest people, the happiest organizations are shaped by integrity and cause.

Spending so much time in and around schools focused our interest on some of the drivers of success. When we came to discuss our experiences of those schools we were quickly able to give labels to those drivers. Some (like leadership and classroom teaching) were obvious, others (such as system rigour, accountability, monitoring and evaluation) were expected, but some of the others made us sit back and ask questions. There were common strands to be seen in the positive and purposeful schools:

- There seemed to be a balance – which was not formalized – between working hard and playing hard.
- There was often a strong development culture going beyond continuing professional development (CPD).
- Among the staff community there were fewer energy sappers – there were more radiators than there were drains!
- On a daily basis there were less moments which sapped energy from the system and the people who operated within the system. For example, there were fewer trivial incidents with pupils.
- There appeared to be more sophisticated coping strategies in individual staff.
- People regularly went over and above what might have been expected in their efforts to support each other.

As part of a national programme, Alistair and Sir John took *Winning The H Factor: The Secrets of Happy Schools* out onto the road. In a series of public programmes around the country the pair offered to explore the how and why of happiness. Over 1,000 adults have taken part in the programme. In the first few sessions Alistair and Sir John used hand-held voting sets to build a profile of their audiences. They were asked about their gender, their role, their regional location and then their overall levels of happiness: very happy, happy, so-so, unhappy, very unhappy and, finally, none of your business! The questions were then broken down into three components: head, heart and health. The database they assembled is growing and beginning to show some clear patterns.

Some of the patterns of their research include:

- Primary practitioners reported being happier than any of the other groups (primary senior manager, secondary practitioner, secondary senior manager or other).
- The happiest regions were the north east with the midlands and the south east feeling the least happy.
- Well-being scores were considerably lower than any other aspect and these were lowest among senior managers.
- Empathy and affinity scores were the highest of all the components. These were higher in females than in males and highest in primary senior managers.

Through Alistair's company, Alite, it is our intention to create an online version so that we can continue to build a useful database and allow individuals, departments and schools to compare themselves with national and regional norms. Watch this space!

Happiness in schools hit the headlines in the UK when Anthony Seldon, Principal of Wellington College, championed its teaching in schools. When someone of Sir Anthony's status puts weight behind a cause the press and others listen. This, despite the fact that at his school it was taught discretely, in fortnightly lessons, and as part of a PSHE programme not dissimilar to that which has been taught in state schools for many years. We felt, and still do feel, that it is an ineffective model.

Prior to this, the SEAL (Social and Emotional Aspects of Learning) programme had been trialled in English primary schools and begun to be used in secondary schools. We also have concerns about SEAL; not about the intent but more about the methodology. Separating activities out from the everyday relationships within the school is less effective, especially if what is being 'taught' is not married to what is being experienced in other aspects of school life. Exploring how positive relationships are established, developed and sustained, especially across the whole school community, is for us a better starting point.

In many ways SEAL is a deficit model, over-reliant on one interpretation of emotional intelligence and too focused on feelings. Martin Seligman argues that it is the fixation with the self which, paradoxically, increases the likelihood of depression and anxiety. In this we would agree with Carol Craig of the Centre for Confidence and Well-being who wrote a detailed report on SEAL's 'potential dangers' and concluded: 'It is because there is no evidence that anything like SEAL has been shown to be beneficial for young people that we are claiming that SEAL is a large-scale psychological experiment.'[113] (Craig 2007)

The Centre for Confidence and Well-being is a Scottish project which looks at the impact of positive psychology in education, business and sport. It draws a lot on the work of Professor Martin Seligman and also Professor Carol Dweck, arguing that, 'Where schools want to undertake interventions which address psychology we believe these should be more about thinking styles, beliefs and cognitions than emotions or emotional expression'. So, for example,

> Professor Dweck's work on mindsets could be helpful as this is about views of intelligence and achievement. Optimism and explanatory style may be useful as this is about how people see adversities and successes. Teaching young people about flow (engagement in activities), and its rewards, could also help in encouraging young people to seek fulfillment through activities.

It is possible to model positive and happy behaviours in and around the classroom. You can describe happiness and what the academics and others say causes it. You can teach specific tools and techniques which may work, if rehearsed sufficiently, for some individuals in some contexts. You can use happiness as a backdrop to teaching about what makes us unique and as a prompt for respecting otherness. None of this will necessarily make your students or your school happier! There are other models.

One such model is to use signature characteristics or traits. Alistair's work in learning to learn led to him identifying the characteristics of the great learner – following Ellen Langer, Art Costa, Guy Claxton and others – and to identify five attributes which he called the five R's: resilience, resourcefulness, responsibility, reasoning and reflection.[114] Each of these attributes can, to some extent, be developed in learners.

- Resilience:
  - persist
  - stay positive
  - stay involved
  - set targets and practise.

- Resourcefulness:
  - show initiative

- learn in different ways
- ask good questions
- involve others in your learning.

- Responsibility:
  - know right from wrong and make good choices
  - manage yourself
  - help others
  - plan ahead.

- Reasoning:
  - explain your thinking
  - consider all the evidence
  - choose the best tool or method
  - take your time.

- Reflection:
  - remain curious
  - explain your progress
  - listen to and act on feedback
  - learn from experience.

We develop them by isolating and defining the attribute, creating awareness of it among our learning community, giving opportunities for it to be expressed, evaluating progress against a development profile and sharing that progress across the wider school community including parents and carers. If you want more of it, you catch it and reinforce it; give it status – big it up. As a major change agent in shifting a school culture away from preoccupations with effort and behaviour this is a powerful, yet subtle, tool.

So the process involves locating what attributes lie behind the effective learner or, in this case, what signature characteristics lie behind a happy school, defining those attributes or characteristics, capturing them in the moment, reinforcing them where possible, revisiting, promoting and supporting them. Then standing back.

Build, broaden and balance

We felt that time was needed 'on the balcony as well as the on the dance floor'[115] if schools were to be the sorts of places where high-quality learning could take place amidst a culture of self-scrutiny. Preparation, delivery, evaluation and improvement of high-quality learning experiences has to be the core purpose of our schools with the leadership role central to creating the conditions for this to take place. Very few leadership models deal directly with how to create the right climate to allow high-quality learning to take place. We aim to do so here.

Our premise is that there is sufficient research around what constitutes individual happiness, the extent to which it can be developed and the benefits of a happier workforce for us to pull it together in a model that means something for schools. Having done so, we suggest that our model provides a template for a more positive all-round learning and working environment and so can contribute to shaping the climate needed for high-quality learning to take place. A happy school is an aggregation of happy individuals in a school.

We take our model to operate at three levels; individual, unit and organization. In other words, the teacher, the classroom and the school community as a whole. The three levels:

- individual
- classroom
- school.

To that end we explored what our happiness model may look like at each level. What we offer is a tool for a cultural shift and not a set of lesson plans for happiness.

Our model suggests that improved happiness involves understanding how we think, how we relate to others and how we take care of ourselves. We talk in terms of head, heart and health. Our three domains are:

- head – how we think
- heart – how we form and sustain relationships
- health – how we keep ourselves safe and healthy.

We then broke each of these domains down and identified signature characteristics which we believe can be applied across all three levels of individual, classroom and school or organization.

- Head – how we think:
  - empathy
  - self-knowledge
  - integrity and purpose.

- Heart – how we form and sustain relationships:
  - openness
  - efficacy
  - affinity.

- Health – how we keep ourselves safe and healthy:
  - security
  - well-being
  - cooperation.

Then, for each signature characteristic we identified development opportunities, italicized below, and these form the basis of our suggested interventions to build, balance and broaden.

- Head – how we think:
  - Empathy:
  - • *develop curiosity*
  - • *listen appreciatively*
  - • *be capable of forgiveness.*
  - Self-knowledge:

- – • minimize comparisons
- – • know strengths and weaknesses
- – • understand the difference between wants and needs.
- – Integrity and purpose:
- – • be honest
- – • prioritize
- – • behave according to values and beliefs.

- Heart – how we form and sustain relationships:
  - – Openness:
  - – • show feelings
  - – • laugh and smile more
  - – • sustain relationships.
  - – Efficacy:
  - – • cope optimistically with setbacks
  - – • exercise control
  - – • have purposeful aspirations.
  - – Affinity:
  - – • enjoy the act of giving
  - – • say 'thank you'
  - – • maintain friendship networks.

- Health – how we keep ourselves safe and healthy:
  - – Security:
  - – • have a sense of worth
  - – • feel safe
  - – • have a voice.
  - – Well-being:
  - – • enjoy a hobby or interest
  - – • choose a healthy lifestyle
  - – • manage time.
  - – Cooperation:
  - – • make a worthwhile contribution
  - – • look after someone or something
  - – • achieve together.

We wanted our development interventions to increase the flexibility with which action meets thought so that we can be more robust. We must also be able to deploy our growing flexibility in as wide a variety of situations as possible. We must at the same time keep things in balance and maintain perspective. Our interventions are to build, broaden and balance.

The three Bs:

- Build – build up our repertoire of positive strategies.
- Broaden – broaden the opportunities to use those strategies.
- Balance – balance (and maintain the balance) of the areas of head, heart and health.

Build

Build up our repertoire of strategies for head, heart and health, particularly positive strategies. For example, can we learn to reframe negative interpretations of our experiences into more positive alternatives? Can we change our self-talk to include more positive phrases? Can we practise thinking through plans for dealing with difficult and adverse situations? Can we give ourselves advice in the style of a counsellor in order to develop a mechanism for managing impulsivity? At an organizational level, can we get better at distributing decision making and responsibility? Can we use what we know about flourishing ratios to improve the quality and timing of feedback?

Building more positive responses extends our capacity to think flexibly and so be more creative, notice more opportunities and attend to more detail. It's surely impossible to experience positive and negative emotions simultaneously so building the likelihood of a positive response diminishes the vestiges of negative thinking.

By practising strategies to help us cope and then help us flourish we increase our repertoire of responses.

Broaden

Broaden the opportunities to use those strategies. A novel way of thinking about or relating to an issue or problem requires lots of subsequent opportunity for trying it out, getting it wrong, making micro-adjustments and then trying again. Having built our cognitive and emotional base we need a more extensive playing field on which to try things out. This playing field needs to be safe. The consequences of making a mistake with our enhanced repertoire of strategies ought not to lead to a rapid retreat to our default mode.

By applying our strategies in a number of very different contexts, we broaden our ability to deal with both the fore- and the unfore-seen. And so we enrich our lives.

Balance

Balance (and maintain the balance) of the areas of head, heart and health. Perhaps work–life balance is a term whose 'balance' ought to be questioned? If we start afresh and ask ourselves to consider which dimensions of an individual's life he or she ought to hold in balance we could come up with lots of suggestions, but work and life surely wouldn't be among them! We think that our model of head, heart and health is a better way of describing the areas an individual should aspire towards balancing. Our questionnaire and wheel will help you to do this.

In summary, to win the H Factor we would ask you to increase the different ways in which you can think, relate to others and take care of yourself. Then we would ask you to try them out in different and increasingly challenging situations – as an individual, in your classrooms and in your school – and reflect on any differences you notice. That's it!

Four schools by schools

> Before we set our hearts too much upon anything, let us examine how happy they are, who already possess it.[116] (de La Rochefoucauld)

Context 1

When we talked to schools about our model, we found some where much of what we see as great practice was already evident. Take Sandringham for example.

Sandringham School is a large, over-subscribed comprehensive school in a relatively advantaged part of Hertfordshire. The children start at the school with higher than average levels of achievement and the number of children with learning difficulties is low. In 2005, Ofsted deemed the school to be 'good with outstanding features'. You may think that the senior leadership team would quietly settle for that. But at Sandringham School settling for something is never good enough. The head teacher, Alan Gray, and his team are constantly looking for ways in which they can push the boundaries of achievement and make the school an even better, happier place. This is reflected in one of its promises to students: 'We will not only judge your achievements against some agreed average but will also measure it against your previous personal best.'

Learning and achievement are at the forefront of everything that is done at the school. Yet this drive for educational excellence is combined with an atmosphere of respect, responsibility and positive relationships. Sandringham School aims to be like a big primary school, in which everybody is cared for, learning is personalized and standards are high. The school's mission statement is, 'Everybody can be somebody'. And they do mean everybody. No-one is overlooked.

So how do they make sure that everybody gets a taste of the H Factor?

For staff

What About Us? At the start of every year, a booklet entitled 'What About Us?' is passed around members of staff. In it are listed all of the events and activities that staff can take part in that term. These include aerobics, street dance, football, golf and also non-sporting activities such as a reading group, music lessons and pampering evenings.

Random Act of Kindness Day. Every year members of staff are encouraged to take part in a random act of kindness day. At the start of the day, they pull a name out of a hat and for the rest of that day they try to do something kind for the person named. This is left to their imagination but has included making cups of coffee, offering a lift home, doing a cover lesson and supporting children in the recipient's class during their own non-teaching period.

Discounts. The school has negotiated discounts with local shops, restaurants and fitness centres for members of staff.

Secret Admirer's Week. Prior to this day, members of staff fill in a questionnaire giving information such as their favourite drink, chocolate, flowers, etc. Each completed questionnaire is given to another member of staff who has a week to prepare to be that person's secret admirer for the week leading up to Valentine's Day. During the week itself, the secret admirers use the information to do as many kind things as they can for the person they have picked.

My Day Out. Every teacher is entitled to one day off school per year to visit another school or educational establishment of their choice to pick up new ideas and share good practice.

My Night. All members of staff are encouraged to leave work by 3.30pm at least one day a week so that they can find some quality time to pursue hobbies.

Staff Conference. Each year the school takes all the staff on a two-day staff conference. In 2009 the themes were, 'Challenge and questioning in the classroom' and 'How to support the "easy to miss" students and build relationships'.

Thank You Raffle. A pile of slips with the message, 'I just wanted to say ...' is kept in the staffroom. At any point in the year members of staff can write a thank you message to someone else onto a slip and put it in a box. It could be that they want to thank someone for doing some photocopying for them, for listening to them or for helping them with a challenge. At the end of each half-term, six slips are read out and the six members of staff that they refer to win a bottle of wine or similar prize. The remaining slips are placed in pigeon holes so that all staff can see what people have been grateful for.

For students

Year 7 Learning Area. To make the transition to secondary school easier for new students, they are all housed in the same learning area for tutor time. This is a safe place where they can go at breaks and lunchtimes if they need to.

Pin on the Positive. For one week every half-term a large photograph of each of the heads of year is displayed in the staffroom. Nearby is a pile of post-it notes. Whenever a member of staff has something positive to say about a student, they write it on a post-it and stick it onto the photo of the relevant head of year. The head of year then passes the good news to the tutor who passes it on to the students. The use of this is particularly encouraged for catching positive things about the children who come at neither end of the academic spectrum and who could otherwise be overlooked.

Reward System. The reward system is comprehensive and thoroughly embedded in the school's ethos of positivity and celebration. Students are rewarded at every opportunity for excellent learning and for making a positive contribution to their community. It includes merits at the back of diaries, postcards and phone calls home to parents, head of year and head teacher commendations, and end of year prize-giving assemblies.

Roll of Honour. Every faculty has a role of honour board and each half-term star students are nominated in each year group. Their photos appear on the board and they receive a certificate that is presented to them in assembly.

Awards Evening. Year 11 and Year 13 students return to the school after their exam results to receive their certificates in an Oscar-style celebration of both academic and non-academic successes. It is a great opportunity for students to return to the school after one term at university or in employment and celebrate their success with all staff, governors and parents.

Learning Quote Competition. Every year, the school runs a competition for students to say why they are proud of their school. The winning comments are displayed around the school and used in the weekly school newsletter. The competition also encourages students to say why they love learning and to generate their ultimate question.

Students as Lead Learners. Every year, a group of 12 students from Year 7 are trained in leading plenaries for their peer group. It is their role then to approach their teachers at the start of the lesson and see if it is possible to lead the plenary at the end of the lesson, using a range of techniques. After the lesson, the students get feedback from the teacher and their peers and complete a log book. Once students have completed their log book they receive a certificate and then they go on to train other students. Recently, students have been involved in what is called the 'Big Switch' – they have gone into another Year 7 class to lead a 'switch plenary' without having any prior knowledge of the topic and work that has been covered. This develops higher-order questioning skills as well as leadership and communication skills.

Bully-Free Status and Girls' Bullying Project. All Year 7 students go through a programme called 'Protective Behaviours' when they arrive at the school so that they know how to be safe and who to turn to if they don't feel safe. Each Year 7 tutor group then has the opportunity to apply for bully-free status by working through a six-week scheme of work in lifelong learning lessons, preparing a portfolio of evidence and reflection logs, leading a year group assembly and then making a presentation to a panel made up of the head teacher, deputy head teachers and governors. If they can demonstrate that they understand what bullying is, that they have taken steps to make everyone in the form feel safe and, most importantly, that they can demonstrate it has had a real impact on their behaviour and relationships they are awarded bully-free status and are each presented with a lapel badge. These students then work with the Year 6 students during their transition to Sandringham and act as e-mentors to them over the summer holidays, answering their questions and reassuring them about the move to secondary school.

In Year 9, all girls follow a six-week Girls' Bullying programme to help develop self-esteem, assertiveness, friendships, awareness of body image and body language. This is supported by a parent information evening.

Interest modules. In Key Stages 3 and 4, students take interest modules that are not exam subjects. These are chosen on the basis of their own interests and the modules include sports and dance leader awards, Young Enterprise and Duke of Edinburgh award schemes.

Right Child, Right Course. To be sure that all children end up studying the best subjects for them in Key Stage 4, every single Year 9 student has an interview with a member of the senior leadership team prior to making their choices. All Year 11 students have a meeting with the head teacher after the trial exams to give them advice and guidance ahead of their Level 2 exams.

Meet the Head and Student Focus Groups. Every Thursday, two students from each year group are nominated by their head of year to meet the head teacher for a 20-minute discussion on what works well at Sandringham and how the school could improve further. In addition, head's of year hold half-termly student focus groups to gain feedback on a wide range of topics such as the behaviour policy, reviewing schemes of learning and careers education.

As a consequence of the dedication, hard work and commitment of the staff, along with a thirst for becoming ever better (the school website states that the aim is to be 'world class'), the school has received Specialist Arts and Science status and is a Leading Edge and a High Performing Specialist School. The number of students gaining five A*–C grades at GCSE (with English and maths) has increased from 55 per cent to 77 per cent in three years. In the December 2008 Ofsted report the school was judged to be 'outstanding'.

Yet, when praised for this glowing Ofsted report deputy head, James Heale, smiles and says, 'Oh yes, but there are still plenty of things we are working on ...'

> Happiness depends, as Nature shows, less on exterior things than most suppose.
> (Cowper 1779)

Context 2

Another school, Harrop Fold in Manchester, starts from a very different context and its story shows just how great the influence of school culture can be.

In 2004, Harrop Fold was a school in trouble. Following the merging of two schools, GCSE results and attendance plummeted, pupil behaviour was described by Ofsted as 'intimidating, rowdy and unruly' and staff morale was incredibly low.

Yet, less than two years later, the school received a letter from the then Prime Minister, Tony Blair, congratulating everybody involved on the progress the school had made and, by 2007, the school had been awarded specialist art college status.

So what turned the culture around from one in which the glass of three fire doors was broken each day to one in which students walk around 'with huge smiles on their faces' and staff believe that 'all of our children can do well and all of them have a chance in life'?

Of course there are many things that contributed to the change of culture. The new head teacher gathered a team of motivated individuals around him and they started from what deputy head, Drew Povey, calls the school's moral purpose to 'make sure that all of our students achieve'. With the building blocks of a strong leadership team in place, they set about taking on the challenges. As the senior teacher in charge of behaviour, Drew immediately began to tackle the issue of the broken fire doors. Not only was replacing them costly, 'At £300 per pane of glass, this was costing the school almost £1,000 per day', but they were also a symbol of the bad behaviour and lack of respect for the school and for learning. So he decided to throw the responsibility for this over to the students:

> It wasn't exactly rocket science. We knew they wanted a basketball court, so we told them that they could have one – when the breakages stopped. And, funnily enough, they stopped right there and then. I think we had one pane of glass broken that term. So the students got their basketball court.

Now, students have a school council that has its own budget and that is really listened to. Students truly feel that they have ownership of what goes on in their school: 'Students are part of all decisions that take place at the school ... we are encouraged to express our views' (A Year 7 student).

Of course, this same ownership has been given to all stakeholders. All parents, governors, members of staff and the community are involved in major decision making. To the point that, symbolically, when offered the chance of 'fresh starting' the school and giving it a new name, they voted overwhelmingly to keep the old name as they were 'proud of how far we have come'.

In the early days, it was essential to turn around staff morale. Unsurprisingly, there was bitterness between members of staff from the two original schools to deal with, along with the stresses of knowing that they were part of this 'failing' school. At that time between ten and 12 teachers were leaving per term. Today there are no difficulties in recruiting new staff members. 'Staff want to be here now', explains deputy head, Janice Allen. 'At times when we know they may be feeling low, we do what we can to help. We want them to be at their best when they come into school. That's why, as a direct result of Alite's H Factor conference, we had a staff well-being day in January.' Nowadays, staff members are seen laughing together, communicating with each other and sharing ideas. They have become a team working together towards a common goal.

'The Senior Leadership Team leads by example', Janice says.

> We are there ALL the time. We go into every classroom at least twice a day. We are there in the morning when the children come to school, in the evenings when they are leaving and we talk to them. One of the things I was worried about when I was promoted to deputy head was that I would lose contact with the children I went into teaching for. Not so; I know the names of every single child in the school and I talk to them at break, lunchtimes and as they move about the school.
>
> It is better to be happy for a moment and be burned up with beauty than to live a long time and be bored all the while. (D. Marquis)
>
> http://www.paradise-engineering.com/quotation/index.html accessed 14.10.09

Context 3

If you ask parents what they want for their children at school, the outcomes do not vary – irrespective of the school context. Right at the top will sit 'happy' and 'safe'.

At one primary school we work with in Worcestershire there are around 270 pupils, with three classes in each year group. Most children come from an advantaged social background, and 30 per cent of parents have had further education. Many work in professions that require university degrees and expectations for children's academic achievements are high.

Each spring, the school asks parents of children who will be joining Reception in September to complete a form giving information about their child. The final question on the form is, 'What are your hopes and aspirations for your child and of the school?'

With permission from the parents, we looked at 78 responses to the question for the 2008 intake. We divided the forms into three groups. The first group included those responses that only mentioned their child's happiness or well-being (these included words such as happy, enjoy, social development and self-confidence), without referring to any educational goals whatsoever. The second group included those responses that solely mentioned academic success and/or learning (we looked for words such as SATs, reading, writing, numeracy, literacy, educational/academic development and learning). The third and final group included reference to both happiness and to academic potential and/or success. The results are outlined in the grid below:

Group 1 (happiness/well-being only)	Group 2 (academic potential only)	Group 3 (both happiness and academic potential)
38	3	37

Interestingly in group three, when happiness and academic success were both mentioned, it was happiness that was written first in every case except one. When the words 'learn' or 'learning' appeared, they were nearly always coupled with 'enjoy', 'confidence to', 'passion for' or 'interest in', rather than with specific subjects or exam success.

66 per cent of the responses included either the word 'happy' or 'enjoy', or both. Words that appeared regularly included 'friendship', 'fun', 'confident' and 'safe'.

Learning to read and write came low in their priorities (on more than one occasion, these words were coupled with 'and secondly'). SATs were not mentioned on a single form.

The table below shows the key words that appeared on the forms (if a word was repeated on the same form it is only counted once. Each form may have included several of the words):

Happy/happiness	39
Friendship/friends	18
Enjoy	17
Reach potential/learn to best of ability	15
Confident/confidence/self-confidence	15
Learn/learning	13
Flourish/thrive	6
Safe	5
Read/Write	4
Academic success/develop educationally	3
Numeracy/maths/sums	2
Structured learning	1
SATs	0

Below are some individual comments of note:

- 'If the social side is happy, then this should make for a good school experience and happy children.'
- 'We want her to have a happy experience of school.'
- 'Ben is so full of hope and optimism for school.'
- 'School should become a key positive part of his life.'

- 'If Carly is happy, we have no doubt that she will achieve her full potential.'
- 'If I can get him really interested in learning now, I feel it will be a lifelong habit.'

> It is not in doing what you like, but in liking what you do is the secret of happiness.
> (J. Barrie)

http://quote.robertgenn.com/getquotes.php?catid=133 13.10.09

Context 4

Filing into class, a group of Year 4 children are greeted by their teacher at the door. Every child looks up, makes eye contact, smiles and says, 'Good morning' as they shake their teacher's hand. In return, he greets them all by name, making the odd comment to individuals.

The children quickly settle down and the register is taken but, instead of the usual 'Yes, sir', children give a number and an adjective:

> 'Ten; high spirits.'
> 'Five; indifferent.'
> 'Seven; excited.'

This is not an exercise in language skills but a means of letting their teacher and their peers know how they are feeling at the beginning of the day. The children all respect the feelings of others and also know how to behave according to their peers' state of mind.

For two or three minutes, their teacher now talks the children through their breathing exercises so that they are calm and reflective. Their minds are set up for a session of learning.

And, at Latchmere School in Kingston upon Thames, learning is a serious business. SATs results are consistently excellent. The curriculum is broad and rounded and standards of attainment in reading, writing, maths and science are higher than those of local schools and than national results. This school also has a high dose of the H Factor. Yet, back in 2005, conversations in the staffroom were probably not terribly different to those in staffrooms across the country. Teachers worried about what society is doing to young people today. They noticed the stress of children preparing for SATs. Some parents had reported that their children found it hard to sleep prior to tests and other stressful events at school.

Then a book bought in an airport lounge made them take action. Advanced skills teacher, Kevin Hogston, was about to head off on holiday, when he spotted *Teaching Meditation to Children*[117] by David Fontana and Ingrid Slack.

'Forget the kids, I could do with that!' he told his partner, who encouraged him to buy it. By the end of his holiday, Kevin had devoured the book and, when he returned to school, he began some breathing and calming exercises with his class. As he saw the benefits, he began a meditation club. Membership increased, staff noticed improved concentration among the children involved, parents reported increases in their children's self-confidence and children talked of being able to get to sleep more easily and to deal with problems better. Meditation was helping the children achieve the H Factor.

The H Factor is nowhere more evident than in the Blue Room. Especially designed and renovated with the children, this loft space that used to be a store cupboard is a place for reflection, meditation and calm. As you follow the blue lights up the winding stairs, you are aware that you are about to enter a place that is found rarely in educational establishments. Everything about this room is welcoming, from the soft carpets and cushions to the framed pictures and paintings on canvas. Lava lamps bubble and music plays. There is room for 30 children, whose maturity and respect for this room and for each other is overwhelming. They demonstrate peer massage, with one boy talking through the movements and explaining how you must keep asking your partner how they are feeling so that you do not hurt them.

The Blue Room is timetabled to be used by every class and every child in the school. It has massive amounts of support from children, from parents ('Self-awareness and the value of reflection are very important and a wonderful thing for them to be introduced to at school') and from members of staff who often take advantage of its calm atmosphere to relax and reflect after a hard day. And here's what Ofsted said about it when classing the school 'outstanding' in every category:

> The Blue Room is characteristic of the Latchmere ethos. It provides an excellent facility for personal, social and health education (PSHE) activities as well as a lunchtime relaxation club for staff and pupils. Pupils describe how its soft carpets, soothing music, calming blue walls and a magnificent sunset mural, help them to learn how to cope with their worries, gain in self-confidence and be ready to learn.

But the final word as to its effectiveness must go to a Year 6 pupil, who said:

> The moment I started meditation I knew it was going to help me, mostly with my sleeping problems. At bedtime I used to feel stressed and hassled. Controlling your mind is a very powerful and useful skill, this is what was stopping me from

sleeping, my mind was always thinking of the negative, nerve-racking things that I just wanted to get out of my head. I never used to stop and think of the things that made me feel calm and proud of myself. Now when I go to sleep I imagine being in the relaxation room. I can see the blue colour of the room and the big smiley face picture. I focus on these as part of my meditation.

3

Happier individuals

In this section we focus on the following topics:

Tools and techniques for shifting expectations
The importance of building and sustaining positive relationships
Changing the way we think
Monitoring well-being

And answer the following questions:

What's the true worth of an optimistic approach?
Is it possible to learn to be better at building and sustaining relationships?
What should we do to change the way we think?
What are the important elements of well-being?

- Changing expectations
- Building better relationships
- Changing your thinking for the better
- Looking after yourself

Changing expectations

Jim Stockdale was an American navy pilot who was shot down and captured in 1965 during the early years of the Vietnam War. In total he spent eight years in captivity, many of those in solitary confinement. He tells of the ordeal in his book *In Love and War*, the book which he co-wrote with his wife.[118]

Stockdale's personal background and his military training combined to give him particular advantages during those years. He saw himself as being in command and therefore having to epitomize to all around, through whatever means, how to behave with honour and dignity. He felt that for him to do so would increase the number of prisoners that would survive their ordeal unbroken. All the while he was fighting his own private battles, he also had to fight against his captors and their attempts to use their prisoners for propaganda. At one point, he beat himself with a stool and cut himself with a razor, deliberately disfiguring himself, so that he could not be put on videotape as an example of a 'well-treated prisoner'.

Through coded letters with his wife, built around mutual knowledge of shared places, including towns where they had lived and golf courses where he had played, he passed on secret intelligence information. Discovery would mean more torture and perhaps death. He instituted rules that would help people to deal with torture. No-one can resist torture indefinitely, so he created a stepwise system – after x minutes, you can say certain things – that gave the men milestones to survive towards.

Stockdale instituted an elaborate internal communications system to reduce the sense of isolation that their captors tried to create. This system used a five-by-five matrix of tap codes for alpha characters. (Tap-tap equals the letter a, tap-pause-tap-tap equals the letter h, tap-tap-pause-tap equals the letter f, and so on, for 25 letters, c doubling in for k.) At one point, during an imposed silence, the prisoners mopped and swept the central yard using the code, swish-swashing out 'We love you' to Stockdale on the third anniversary of his being shot down.

What helped Stockdale was an unquestioning faith, belief in the system he served and, as he put it; 'I never doubted not only that I would get out, but also that I would prevail in the end and turn the experience into the defining event of my life, which, in retrospect, I would not trade.' When asked about the difference between himself and some of the others who did not cope, he responded by pointing out the difference between optimism that is often unfocused and a form of blind faith and the need to deal with current reality.

> The optimists were the ones who said, 'We're going to be out by Christmas.' And Christmas would come, and Christmas would go. Then they'd say, 'We're going to be out by Easter.' And Easter would come, and Easter would go. And then Thanksgiving, and then it would be Christmas again. And they died of a broken heart. This is a very important lesson.[119] (Stockdale 1984)

As Stockdale began his eight years of captivity, he adopted the Stoic philosophy of keeping separate files in his mind for those things that were 'up to him' and those things that were 'not up to him'. Things which he understood were 'within his power' and those things which were 'beyond his power'. He controlled the controllables.

When life gives you lemons, stick 'em in your bra. Couldn't hurt. Might help.[120]
(Mathews)

In life, there are optimists and there are pessimists. When something good happens, an optimist sees it as personal (i.e. brought about by themselves), permanent and pervasive. In contrast, when something good happens to a pessimist, they are likely to see it as something external (i.e. caused by something other than themselves, such as luck), temporary and as an isolated event. However, should something bad happen, this is turned completely on its head. An optimist sees something bad as caused by external influences, as temporary and as an isolated event. This is the type of person who might stick Matthew's lemons in their bra! A pessimist, on the other hand, will blame themselves for it, consider it a permanent state of affairs and see it as something that is typical of their lives.

Twin studies suggest that how happy you are at this moment in time is the best determinant of how happy you will be in the future. If that is not a good enough reason to make a concerted effort to be (even) happier, we don't know what is. If you are a positive person who always looks on the bright side, then the chances are you will continue in that vein. If you are more negative and are constantly looking to the future for something better, then the chances are that you are missing out on spotting and enjoying the good things that are about you right now.

Optimist	Pessimist
When good things happen	
Personal	External
Permanent	Temporary
Pervasive	Isolated
When bad things happen	
External	Personal
Temporary	Permanent
Isolated	Pervasive

Pessimists report more negative experiences in their lives and are likely to talk in terms of thwarted ambitions and missing out. ('I would've been a professional basketball player, but I twisted my knee the day before the trials.' Or, 'I'd have got that job, if only I hadn't missed the bus.') Optimistic people are more likely to be able to live in the moment, to talk in terms of making their own luck and are able to focus outwards, not just inwards on themselves. Because they are able to move on, they can forget about any negative things that may have happened to them. If they can laugh about and see the funny side of life's negative events, then other people are likely to warm to them. Consequently, in times of difficulty, they will have a network of friends and family to support them.

> When bad things happen, I try to see the funny side. It may not be immediately that I am able to do so, and I never do it when someone is hurt. But I try to come back and think, 'How will I tell this story to make people laugh? How many times can I dine out on this story?' By focusing on the entertainment value it will have when I tell my friends, I can lift myself out of a bad mood. After all, it has happened and I can't change it, so I might as well get something good out of it! (Sian, company director and mother of three)

So how do you see yourself? How do others see you? Will the turnout at your funeral depend on the weather? How will history see you? Do you see the doughnut or the hole?

Your mood rubs off on other people. Happy people become magnets for other happy people. Professionally, as well as personally, getting the H Factor will help you. People (colleagues as well as pupils) will respond to you positively. Think about who you like to be with in the staffroom and why. What is it that makes them good to be around? Copy their good behaviours. Don't be the cynic of the staffroom.

Of course, most of us have doubts and worries; maybe things that keep us awake around 3 a.m. in the morning. Sir John quotes an estimate that we each have around 50,000 thoughts per day. There is a little voice inside our heads working 24/7, and it is reading from a script that we didn't write.

In Chapter 1, we talked about psychologist Sonja Lyubormirsky's belief that 40 per cent of our happiness is under our own control. We want you to use that 40 per cent to win you the H Factor, which will in turn help you win the H Factor in your classroom and school.

You will never be happier than you expect. To change your happiness, change your expectation.'[121] (B. Davis)

Challenging your explanatory style is one of the most effective ways in which you do this. Catch yourself at the times when you are explaining things to yourself and, if you are looking at things that happen in everyday life in a negative way, try to put a positive spin on it. Of course frustrating things happen in our everyday lives. That is natural. But how we explain those negative things to ourselves greatly affects how we feel about them.

Here are some examples:

1) You couldn't find your car keys so you left for work ten minutes late. Now you are stuck in traffic that isn't moving because of an accident up ahead.

You could sit there and fume about the fact that your 2-year-old daughter got hold of your keys and, if only she hadn't, you wouldn't be in this jam. You could put your hand on the horn and vent some frustration that way. Then, once the traffic has eventually cleared, you could drive fast and aggressively (risking your own safety and that of others on the way) until you get to work still feeling mad and take your frustrations out on your colleagues and pupils.

Alternatively, you could be grateful that you are in the jam and not in the accident that caused it, which you may well have been if you had left home on time. You could resolve to keep your keys out of your daughter's reach in future and, at the same time, thank your lucky stars that you have both credit and battery life in your mobile phone so that you can (safely and legally!) let people know why you are running late. When you get to school, you will feel calmer and thank the person who took your first class profusely, promising them that you will return the favour in future.

2) It is Sunday, your partner has gone to a rugby match and you are at home with the children. You really need to get the ironing done for work the next day, but one of the children is not very well and is whining at you. The other two are arguing about a toy they both want to play with.

You could shout at all the children, tell them to behave and put them in front of the television while you get on with the ironing. Of course, they won't sit still even in front of the telly and they keep asking for food and drinks, so you are never going to get the ironing done. When your partner gets home you can have an argument about the horrible time you had on your own when they were having fun and make them do the ironing as some kind of punishment.

Alternatively, you could ring a friend and ask if they wouldn't mind taking your well children for a couple of hours until your partner gets home. Then you could snuggle up on the sofa with your ill child and think about how lovely it is that he still wants cuddles at his age. You could watch a film together until your partner gets home, giggle at some Disney antics and maybe doze off a bit. Yes, the ironing is still there, but you will feel in a better mood about tackling it.

Most of life's small, everyday annoyances can be looked at positively if you try and, if they can't, it helps if you view them as something temporary that will pass with time. This story of Hasty the farmer illustrates how a negative explanatory style can change the way life treats you.

> Hasty, a farmer, needed to plough his field before the dry spell set in, but his own plough had broken.
>
> 'I know, I'll ask my neighbour, farmer Steady, to borrow his plough. He's a good man; I'm sure he'll have done his ploughing by now and he'll be glad to lend me his machine.'
>
> So Hasty began to walk the three or four fields to Steady's farm.
>
> After a field of walking, Hasty says to himself, 'I hope that Steady has finished all his own ploughing or he'll not be able to lend me his machine ...'
>
> Then after a few more minutes of worrying and walking, Hasty says to himself, 'And what if Steady's plough is old and on it's last legs – he'll never be wanting to lend it to me will he?'
>
> And after another field, Hasty thinks, 'Steady was never a very helpful fellow, I reckon maybe he won't be too keen to lend me his plough even if it's in perfect working order and he's finished all his own ploughing weeks ago ...'
>
> As Hasty arrives at Steady's farm, Hasty is thinking, 'That old Steady can be a mean old fellow. I reckon even if he's got all his ploughing done, and his own machine is sitting there doing nothing, he'll not lend it to me just so he can watch me go to ruin ...'
>
> Hasty walks up Steady's front path, knocks on the door, and Steady answers.
>
> 'Well good morning Mr Hasty, what can I do for you?' asks Steady.
>
> And Hasty says, with eyes bulging, 'You can take your bloody plough, and you can stick it up your rear end!'

Meet your if-onlys

Thinking back on the things we wish we had done with our lives is counter productive. So is dwelling on the things we wish we had never done. The following exercise should help you to take one last look at these things and begin to get over your if-onlys. On a piece of paper note the things that you wish you had (or hadn't) done in the past. Things that may have made a difference to your life now. Spend no more than ten minutes considering these.

Now put your if-onlys into two categories – those you can change, and those you can't change. You can use the table below:

Those I can change	Those I can't change

Once you have done this, get your pen and put a line through those you can't change. Forget them. Now is the time to move forward. More importantly, look at the things you can change and make an action plan. What will you do to change them? How will you do this? When will you do this by?

What can I change?	What do I need to do to change it?	How will I do this?	By when?

You may notice at this point that the things that you would like to change relate to times when your actions or words did not match your values and beliefs.

The difference between a rut and a grave is the depth of the hole.[122] (Burrill)

When our values or beliefs do not tie in with our actions, or when we have two contradictory beliefs, we experience what is known as 'cognitive dissonance'. This is an uncomfortable feeling that we have not quite got something right. Smokers may have a feeling of dissonance because, on the one hand, they see themselves as sensible human beings who want to live as long a life as possible while, on the other hand, they are doing something that may kill them. Someone who likes to be environmentally friendly may feel dissonance when they jump in the car to make a short or unnecessary journey. Happy people can deal positively with dissonance, either by reframing their beliefs or by changing their actions. A less happy individual is more likely to make excuses for their behaviour: 'I need a cigarette, I'm stressed', 'I'm less likely to get Alzheimer's if I smoke' or 'I don't have enough time to walk today'.

When you are making changes, it may be the case that you will have to question your beliefs, some of which may be long held. Sometimes people get so tied into habitual behaviour that they are unable to be creative. In order to come up with creative solutions, it may be necessary to change your thinking. The diagram below shows two different ways of thinking.

Ways of thinking

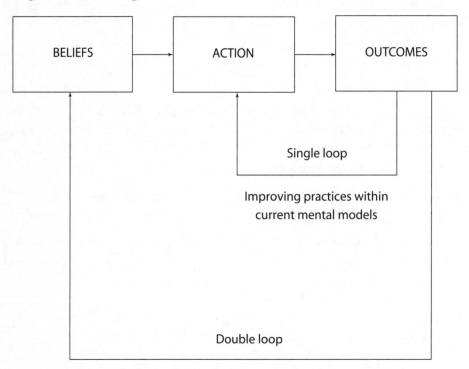

Changing mental models and reframing problems

Most of the time, we act according to our beliefs. This leads to an outcome. Usually, this outcome will serve to strengthen our original belief. Take, for example, Hasty the farmer from p. 88. His belief is that his neighbour is selfish and won't lend him the plough. He acts accordingly (by swearing at his neighbour). The outcome is likely to be that his neighbour, understandably, acts as Hasty had expected and does not lend him his plough. This, in turn, confirms Hasty's belief that his neighbour is selfish.

Hasty is involved in single loop thinking. He believes, acts, gets a result and then goes straight back to acting without considering his beliefs. What he needs to do is some double loop thinking and to go from the outcome back to his belief. If he

were to stop believing that his neighbour is selfish and start believing that maybe, if he were nice to him, his neighbour might lend him the plough then it is likely that he will act differently and, in turn, the outcome will be different.

The diagram shows that it is sometimes not enough to simply tinker with an action in order to get a different result. It may be that we have to be more creative and, to be more creative, we have to challenge our views and rethink our ideals.

> I think my capacity to change has given me tremendous happiness, because who I am today I am completely content to be.[123] (Curtis 2009)

Elizabeth is a teacher in a rural comprehensive school in Hertfordshire. She has been teaching for 20 years and has a lot of experience. About five years ago, she was very tempted to leave teaching because she felt disillusioned with her job.

> I had been a classroom teacher for 15 years. Things began to get on top of me. The children in school seemed to be getting more and more badly behaved. We had had a change of management, and most members of staff (myself included, I'm afraid) put the change in behaviour down to this. The talk of the staffroom was, 'She's just too soft. Bring back the days of the old head – he may have been unapproachable, but he kept the children in line.' When I got home, I'd moan to my husband about how the school was going to the dogs (sometimes I saw my own children's eyebrows raise when we started on the topic, but even that didn't make me sit up

and think). He, ever supportive of me, would agree and we'd launch into a rant about how young people today just don't seem to have enough rules and guidance.

Elizabeth had got herself into single loop thinking. She held two beliefs. The first was that teaching and children were no longer what they used to be and the second that the new head teacher was ineffective with regards to discipline.

One evening, my partner and I launched into our usual discussion about what could be done with the youth of today. My son, who was 16 at the time, put down his knife and fork and said, 'Could you two just stop for a moment and think about what you are saying. If all young people are so bad, what does that say about me and Mickey? Are we out of control? And what about our friends? You know what, they're all OK too. And something else you might like to think about – in our school we only ever mess around in lessons when they're no fun'.

It hurt. But he did have a point. It made me question my beliefs. Were all children that bad? And what about my pupils? Did they all misbehave, or just some of them? And when they did, why did they misbehave? I went back into school with fresh eyes and began to look for the good things. I thought about my lesson plans and found that I had become a bit stale. On the days when I taught really exciting stuff, my pupils behaved better, so I made sure that I did more of the exciting stuff. Because their behaviour then got better, I could praise them more and they responded accordingly. I also made sure that I avoided the negative conversations in the staffroom and I looked for the good in the way the new head was handling the pupils. What I saw was that things were different – not worse.

Elizabeth's son made her venture off the path of single loop thinking and move to double loop thinking. His comments made her consider the fact that the outcomes she was experiencing (poor behaviour of her pupils) were because of her beliefs. When she reconsidered those beliefs and began to change her thinking she could change her actions accordingly (she made her lessons more interesting and she interacted with them in a positive manner). The outcome was that the behaviour of pupils improved.

We all have power over our own actions and reactions, even in the most dire of situations. Viktor Frankl, a holocaust survivor, wrote about his experiences in a Nazi concentration camp. There he lost everything – his loved ones, his home, his possessions, the manuscript of a book he was writing – and daily he coped with brutality, humiliation, hunger and fear of death. In his book, *Man's Search for Meaning,* Frankl noted that, no matter how dire a situation, a person's ability to choose how they act and think cannot be taken away from them.

> We who lived in concentration camps can remember the men who walked through the huts comforting others, giving away their last piece of bread. They may have been few in number, but they offer sufficient proof that everything can be taken from a man but one thing: the last of the human freedoms – to choose one's attitude in any given set of circumstances, to choose one's own way.[124] (Frankl 1946)

The other thing that Frankl noticed was that there was a discernable difference between the people who managed to survive the ordeal and those who gave up on life. This difference was that the survivors managed to maintain some kind of meaning in their lives, despite their losses. That meaning could have been having a small task to carry out every day or simply maintaining hope that one day they would meet up with a loved one again.

> Ultimately, man should not ask what the meaning of his life is, but rather must recognise that it is he who is asked. In a word, each man is questioned by life; and he can only answer to life by answering for his own life; to life he can only respond by being responsible.[125] (Frankl 1946)

Maintaining meaning in our lives is essential if we are to win the H Factor. That meaning can come from anything; from a long-term goal we set ourselves professionally or personally to a short-term goal like laying a patio in the garden. It can come from raising a family to learning to cook, from winning an Olympic gold medal to completing a sponsored walk. The main thing is that we constantly find something that is important to us to give our lives meaning. Singer-songwriter, Ayo, talks of music as her 'medicine' when she is feeling down or ill. As a child, her parents divorced, her mother was a heroine addict who took her along to drugs parties and she found herself in and out of care. Yet she still manages to look on her life positively, talking about the fact that she can laugh with her siblings when they look back together on all that they experienced. Her music and her optimistic outlook gave her what she needed to get through very difficult times.

In summary, the things that researchers, scientists and psychologists have found include the following:

Things that happy people often do:

Take part in a shared interest
Exercise regularly
Keep a diary
Count their blessings
Laugh and smile a lot
Show their feelings

Sing (alone is good, in a choir is better)
Pray
Go to a religious service regularly
Sleep well
Things for other people
Charitable giving
Eat well
The gardening
Avoid comparing themselves to others
Meditate
Reframe problems to come up with creative solutions
Join a club

Things happy people are heard to say:

'Thank you'
'I'm really well, thank you!'
'I can do this'
'When I reach the end of this task successfully, I will feel ...'
'I shall dine out on this story!'

Things happy people often have:

A group of close friends and family who they see often
A positive attitude
Integrity
A hobby
Goals
The doughnut, not the hole!
Time for themselves
Lots of roles
A project

I mean, the things that make me happiest in the whole world are going on the occasional picnic, either with my children or with my partner. Big family gatherings, and being able to go to the grocery store – if I can get those things in, I'm doing good.[126] (Winslet 2008)

Individual

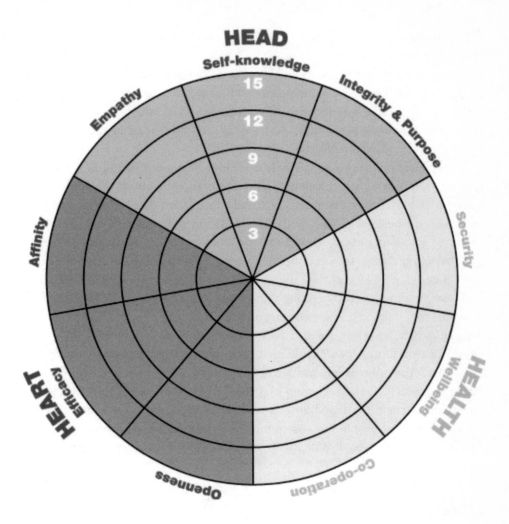

Building better relationships

HEART is about building better relationships. Maintaining contact with family and friends is essential for both our own and their well-being. It is also worth cooperating with acquaintances who are neither family nor close friends as this has been found to promote happiness and to prevent people from comparing their status with others.[127] Maximizing contact with people who are themselves positive and happy will rub off on your own happiness. Equally, minimizing contact with people who are always negative can help – avoid the staffroom cynic like the plague and don't let them poison your own positive attitude.

Openness

Openness is about letting other people know and understand you – what you see is what you get. Think about the people you know who are open and honest – it makes it very easy for you to know where you stand and you don't have to spend time second guessing what they are thinking. Being open makes life easier for yourself and for those around you.

Open people find it easy to show their feelings, both positive and negative. This does not mean that they constantly burst into tears or shout at the top of their voices in public if they are upset – generally, they don't feel the need to let off steam because being able to show their feelings means that they are not a pressure cooker of emotions. Instead, open people can confidently say, 'Sorry, you are wrong and that is hurtful' if they feel upset by something or someone. Showing their feelings does not mean that they always have to act them out – strong feelings like anger can be diminished by voicing them calmly and then there is no need for a dramatic, foot-stamping, wall-punching outburst!

Open people let others know if they are not happy or comfortable with their behaviour or actions. Open people light up a room when they arrive – not when they leave! They also laugh and smile a lot. And laughing is good for you. In 2005, scientists[128] showed a group of people clips from funny films and found that laughter made the blood flow faster around their bodies. In contrast, when the same group of people was shown a highly stressful part of a film (such as the opening scenes to *Saving Private Ryan*), the blood flow around their bodies slowed by around 35 per cent.

Efficacy

Efficacy is about what you believe with regard to your abilities – if you think you can, you can. If you think you can't, you're probably right! People with high levels of efficacy see a setback as a challenge that they can overcome, rather than as a barrier that prevents them from moving on. They have meaning and a purpose to their lives, be it because they are visiting every DIY store in the land to find the right tiles for their bathroom, or because they teach in a poverty stricken school in India. Instead of talking about what might have been, they are able to turn their dreams into action. People with high levels of efficacy don't just imagine what they could do; they go for it and do it.

Affinity

Affinity is about our relationships to others. Relationships are important both at work and in our personal lives. People who appreciate this have a broad network of friends and a mixture of old and new friends. They also keep in touch with their family members and take pleasure from making gifts to others and from giving their time to help and support others.

Sir John suggests that everyone needs a) a connector (someone who knows everyone) b) a mover (someone who knows everything) and c) a listener (someone with whom you can be vulnerable). He would also add a fourth person to this and that is someone who hates everything to do with teaching – preferably not someone in the profession! – so that you can occasionally go out and have a conversation that has absolutely nothing to do with work.

Happier individuals questionnaire: Heart section

The following activities will help you to come up with an action plan for winning the H Factor on an individual level. A key to making changes is to follow these steps:

Think about where you are now.
Identify what things you need to improve.
Plan how you will make changes.
Act by setting a timetable for action.
Reflect by setting a date to come back and reflect on what you have achieved.

Firstly, **think** about where you are now with regard to your own personal happiness by completing the first part of the Happier Individuals Questionnaire below. Use the descriptions given above to help you with this. Score one point if the statement **never** applies to you, two points if it **rarely** applies, three points if it **sometimes** applies, four points if it **often** applies and five points if it **always** applies. Then add up your score for each section (you will have a score out of 15) and write it in the total boxes.

	1	2	3	4	5	Total
Openness – what you see is what you get						
I find it easy to show my feelings						
I laugh and smile a lot						
I manage difficult conversations						

	1	2	3	4	5	Total
Efficacy – whether you think you can or whether you think you can't you are probably right						
I cope optimistically with setbacks						
I feel that life has meaning						
I turn dreams into action						
Affinity – no man is an island						
I enjoy the act of giving						
I sustain relationships						
I have a broad network of friends						

Next, turn to the Winning the H Factor Individual wheel on p. 95 and shade in the Heart area so that you have a visual picture of how you have scored. This visual picture should make it easy for you to **identify** any areas in need of improvement.

You will complete this wheel later.

Next you need to **plan** any improvements you may need to make. Spend some time considering ways in which you could increase your scores in the Heart section of the wheel. If you need some ideas, there are plenty of suggestions on the following pages.

When you have completed all three sections of the questionnaire (Heart, Head and Health), you will be given an opportunity **act** and to **reflect** upon the changes you have made.

Openness – What you see is what you get

I find it easy to show my feelings.

Calm preparation

If you currently have feelings that you are unable to express spend some time thinking of the potential benefits of calmly doing so. Once you have begun this thinking process you will find that you are prepared to do so the next time you are in a similar situation.

Label the emotion

Go through your last week. For each significant event or moment, identify your prevailing emotion. Label the emotion. For example: sadness, fear, anger, envy, frustration, admiration, joy. Now attach a score out of five to each emotion based on how helpful the emotion was to you at that point in time. Score five out of five for emotions that were really helpful. Score zero out of five for emotions that were not helpful in any way. Score up to minus five for emotions that were damaging. Ask yourself what could have been different if you had been able to adjust your score up or down. What would the consequence have been? Consider now how you could let go of the emotions that were not helpful to you and maybe express more of the emotions that were helpful.

Own your feelings

When you have strong feelings you would like to express, the first step is to admit them to yourself. Name them to yourself: 'Right now I feel …' Next, consider the consequences of showing them. Then think about how you will express your feelings; the language you will use, the tone of voice and your body language. How will others react to you? You are not aiming to intimidate or upset anyone else, but to calmly inform them of your feelings. Simply verbalizing feelings can help make them less intense. Saying 'I feel really angry about that' can diminish the strong feeling of anger and make it more manageable.

Talk to a trustie

If necessary, start showing your emotions with people you trust. Don't try it at work until you are comfortable with it! If you find expressing your feelings difficult, perhaps you can find one or two people you trust with whom you can share your vulnerabilities.

Express yourself

People who can calmly express themselves find less need to explode with dramatic force because they have got things off their chest. Train yourself to show feelings when necessary. Prepare some phrases to help you with this. For example: 'When you do/say …, I feel …/It really helps me when you …/I would like to be able to …/Could we work out a way for this to be possible?/Personally, I don't want to have this conversation, but professionally I feel that I must/One of the things I like about you is …'

Deal with it

Know that expressing your feelings alone is not enough. If a situation that makes you angry or sad occurs repeatedly, you have to deal with that situation. Otherwise you are damaging your integrity by saying, 'I don't like this situation, but I will accept that it can continue without change.'

I laugh and smile a lot.

Internal jogging

Laughter is a language understood by us all and it connects us to other people. Laughing lowers our blood pressure, releases endorphins and is good for the heart.[129] As such, it could truly be the best medicine! It has been called 'internal jogging', because it gets the blood pumping round the body and opens up blood vessels.[130]

Read a funny book, watch a funny film, go to see a stand-up comic or spend time with your funniest friends. Browse the comedy section of a card shop.

Buy some comic CDs or cassettes to listen to in the car. Go to a funny video clip website, type in some key words and download two or three short clips that amuse you personally and keep them on your computer. Play them when you need a giggle. Joanna's top two can be found at http://www.funny–videos.co.uk/videogermancoastguard.html and http://www.youtube.com/watch?v=o6P2w5GkXmU.

You must be joking

Try not to take yourself too seriously. Can you see the funny side of things that have happened? (Even things that don't seem at all funny at the time!) Stress and upset are not caused by the situations themselves but by the way in which we choose to view those situations. Seeing the humorous side of something stressful can help prevent it from becoming too much to cope with.

Universal languages

Like laughter, a smile is a universally recognized form of human currency. It activates recognition structures in the brain and begins the release of endorphins. With high levels of endorphins we feel less pain and we are better equipped to cope with stress. Smiling makes people warm to you immediately. Look people in the eye when you pass them, smile and say, 'Good morning'. (Yes, even strangers you pass in the street!)

I manage difficult conversations.

Control what's controllable

Start by managing the difficult conversations you have with yourself. What is it that keeps you awake at night? What are the things you beat yourself up over? Your looks, your weight, your income, your ability to be a good friend, your ability at work? Then consider which of these things you can do something about. Make a list of them and start doing something about it. Be aware of the times and situations when you start your mental self-battery. The next time that you are in a similar situation turn off the voice in your head. Tell it that it has no cause to be there. It can help to deliberately think of something else that is positive to divert your mind away from the negative.

Difficult conversations

Face up to the difficult conversations you need to have with other people. If there are things that you feel need to be said, decide when and how you will say them and go for it. Very often, the things that have been bothering you are much less of an issue when you face them than you ever imagined.

Health check

Ask yourself, 'How am I doing?' Check regularly that you are meeting your goals. Ask others how you are doing to create a culture of openness and feedback. If you do this, you have to allow them to be honest with you and be prepared to accept criticism.

Efficacy – Whether you think you can or whether you think you can't you are probably right

I cope optimistically with setbacks.

Setbacks

A setback as exactly that – something *you believe* has moved you backwards temporarily. Examine the beliefs you have formed around the setback. Are you using it as a reason not to move on? If you view setbacks as temporary and as opportunities to learn, you will find it easier to start to move forwards again.

Contingency planning

Top athletes plan for the possibility of setbacks. It may be the loss of form going into a championship, arriving at the stadium with the wrong kit, being late for an event or feeling a twinge in the warm-up. The idea is not to rehearse the problem but to rehearse the solution.

Take responsibility for rehearsing solutions to potential problems. Remember that the key is to move on. Plan what you would need to do to move forward again. If it helps, think about how it will feel when you have overcome the setback and are back on track. Visualize the problem but always do so with a solution attached. For example, athletes would see themselves in the arena dealing with the challenge and performing to their potential once again.

Don't dwell, get well

When we dwell on something that has gone wrong it makes us far more likely to stop progressing or even to hit a further setback. For example, someone who is giving up smoking may slip up, buy a packet of cigarettes and smoke half of them on Friday evening. If they dwell on this and beat themselves up for wasting money and for failing to give up, they are more likely to feel bad about themselves and to finish the packet on Saturday morning. Better to think, 'That was a setback and I'll move on' and to throw the remainder of the packet away.

Positivity ratios

Think positive. Talk positive. Think about the impact of the way you talk on your feelings and on those of others. Learn to reframe problems; talk about challenges and solutions rather than problems. Then, rather than focusing on the challenge, think of at least two solutions. If you are stuck for ideas, ask other people for help.

I feel that life has meaning.

Set personal goals

Set yourself goals and a time in which to reach them. They can be physical goals, goals to do with work or personal goals. They can be completing a DIY project, getting fit enough to run a marathon or writing that book you know you have in you.

Write them down

Write down three personal goals. Use positive language. For example: 'I will clearly express my opinions' as opposed to 'I will stop being too frightened of looking stupid to say what I think'. Now write down at least three ways in which you aim to reach each goal. For example: 'I will look at meeting agendas in advance, decide what it is important for me to say and make sure that I prepare to say it.' Refer back to your list on a regular basis to remind yourself of your goals.

Flow diagrams

Make a list of all the things that you like doing. Think of all the things that get you into the state of FLOW. These are the things that you become so involved in that you don't notice time passing. Cover every area of your life – at home, at work and at play. The chances are (although it is not always the case) that these are also the things that you are good at. Once you have done this, try to plan how you can do more of these things. It may be, for example, that you love telling funny stories to your classes. So how about offering to take a whole school assembly once a week? Perhaps you love going out for a cycle at the weekend, so how about cycling to and from work?

Now think of the things that you really don't like doing. Try to find a means of doing less of these things to make time for the things you do enjoy. Maybe you hate doing the vacuuming, but you can really relax when you get a chance to do the ironing with the radio on in the background. Could you offer to do someone else's ironing for them in return for them taking on a job that you don't enjoy so much? Or could you actually afford to pay someone to do the things you don't like? If not, could you earn money doing the things you do enjoy in order to be able to do so? For example, if you love to paint could you make some cards and sell them? Or if baking is your thing, perhaps you can make cakes for friends' children's birthday parties? If you're great at DIY, how about offering to do some odd jobs for other people?

I turn dreams into action.

Meet your if-onlys!

Make a list of all the things you wish you had done but, for some reason, haven't yet achieved. Now cross out the ones you can't possibly achieve any more, or wouldn't want to because of a change of life circumstances. (For example, it may be that in your teens you dreamt of doing a parachute jump, but now you wouldn't want to because you have a young family or a health problem.) If you can't do it, get over it!

Look at the remainder of the list and make sure that they turn from 'if-onlys' to 'I did its'. If you've always wanted to learn to cook, sign up for a cookery course. If you wished you had taken a gap year to travel, visit some of the places you would like to have seen. Have you always wanted to try stand-up comedy, writing a book, learning to do magic tricks? Well stop making excuses ('I can't afford it, I'm too old, I'm too young, I haven't got time') and get on with it. You may have to plan and save, but make sure that you set yourself a time limit and go for it!

To do or not to do

Maintain a to-do list AND a stop-doing list. Make sure that your to-do list has something on it that you really want to do personally. Review it weekly. Have no more than four things on your to-do list.

Urgent versus important

Complete the urgent versus important matrix on p. 258. This will help you to plan which things to tackle now and which to leave for another time. Include your dreams on this and use it to help you plan when you will turn them into action.

Affinity – No man is an island

I enjoy the act of giving.

Give and go

Theories of reciprocity suggest that should one person give another a gift then the chances of the receiver returning the favour are increased.[131] It is for this reason that sales websites often offer free gifts or entry into prize draws – as well as attracting the customer to the website in the first place, it also makes them feel more generous and more likely to spend money. If you do something for someone else, without expecting anything in return, the chances are that you will get something back for your troubles. And even if you don't you will have had the pleasure of giving or of knowing that you have helped someone out.

Simple gifts

Volunteer to do cover for someone at a point when they have a particularly high workload.
Help a student teacher prepare a fantastic lesson.
Make the teas and coffees in the staffroom and make sure you know who takes milk and sugar.
Offer to pick up a friend's children from school or a club.
Offer to baby-sit for someone so that they can go out for the evening.
Cut some flowers from your garden and give them to someone for no reason.
Offer to do someone's photocopying.
Show someone how to use a new programme on the computer.

Share your inspiration

A study[132] has found that people who read fiction tend to have better social skills, such as empathy, than those who read non-fiction. While in this chicken and egg situation the scientists do not yet know which came first, the empathy or the fiction, they suggest that getting involved with the characters in books and escaping from real life for a while could help us empathize. Feel good about sharing books!

Give others the chance to read a book you love with the added interest of seeing where the book might travel to! If you go to http://www.bookcrossing.com/ you can register books and track them as they are passed from person to person.

Random acts of kindness

Buy a coffee for the person behind you in the queue of a coffee shop.
Go up to a stranger and GENUINELY give them a compliment (tell them you like something they are wearing, ask where they got their hair done as it looks nice, etc.). If someone did this to you, you would never forget it.
Give up your seat on the train or bus.
Let another car pull out in front of you. Yes, even the aggressive driver! Smile as you do so, because you know their aggression can't affect you.
If you are waiting to pay for a lot of shopping and you aren't in a hurry, allow the person behind you in the queue to go first.
Give someone some small change for the parking meter.

Wired for giving

Our brains are wired to do good for others. MRfI scans of the brain have shown that the areas that react to receiving money, eating sweet food and positive social contact also light up when we willingly give money to charity. In fact, they even light up when we see the money transferred to pay tax![133]

Choose a charity to support and do so regularly. At http://www.microloan-foundation.org.uk/ you can make a donation to loan to women entrepreneurs in sub-Sahara. If you wish to choose a specific person to loan your money to, visit a website such as http://www.kiva.org where you can loan any amount of money to a variety of entrepreneurs across the developing world. Help lift someone out of poverty, get reports on their progress and, if they are successful and pay you back, you can use the money to make a loan to someone else.

If you don't have spare cash, why not clear out your cupboards and fill one of the charity bags that are put through your door? Alternatively, join your local Freecycle group (www.freecycle.org/groups/) where you can advertise pretty much any unwanted item for others to collect from your home.

How would this feel?

The Dalai Lama talks to inanimate objects. He claims that he gains 100 per cent benefit while he doesn't know if they gain any benefit. Would you feel better without the recipient of an act of your generosity knowing it was you? We think you would …

Practise spontaneous giving and/or random acts of kindness without the recipient knowing it was you who did it.

Scrape the ice from the windscreen of a neighbour's car.

Leave a bar of chocolate or pot plant on a neighbour's doorstep or in a colleague's pigeon hole.

> When we feel love and kindness toward others, it not only makes others feel loved and cared for, but it helps us also to develop inner happiness and peace. (HH the Dalai Lama)

I sustain relationships.

Find time for friends

It is relatively easy to make friends, but you have to work to keep them. Allocate time to see your friends. Be systematic about it if it helps. Agree with a group of friends that you will all go out on the first Friday of every month. That way it is in everyone's diaries and you all plan ahead for it. If evenings are difficult, agree to meet for brunch on the fourth Sunday of the month. If money is tight, have a games night (Pictionary, Trivial Pursuits, cards, Twister, etc.) once a month – rotate the location from house to house, bring a bottle and the host can provide nibbles and choose the games.

> One night a month, all my girl friends meet up and we share our 'What my boyfriend/husband did' stories. These are never nasty but always funny. It's good to know that I'm not the only one who thinks a *Lord of The Rings* Gandalf mug isn't a good Valentine's Day gift. (Gemma, Teacher, Gloucestershire)

Family time

Again and again, research from different scientific disciplines shows the value of positive family relationships to the emotional well-being of individuals.

Organize time to spend with your family. If you don't actively organize it, you will find time slipping away. Plan to have specific mornings, days or afternoons free for doing something with your direct family. For example, make every Saturday morning a 'board game' morning, a 'going for a walk/swim/cycle' morning or a 'visiting family' morning. Organize one evening meal a week with your partner during which you will not be interrupted by the door/phone/children. Make sure that you keep the allocated time free and don't allow work or something else to eat into that time.

Socialize together

Actually go on that work meal or out for drinks with colleagues. Don't find an excuse not to and then end up watching Casualty on your own. If you keep saying, 'Maybe next time', the invitations will stop coming. If no-one at work already goes out for drinks, organize a night out yourself – send an email, put a note in pigeon holes or a poster on the wall. Organize a regular meeting immediately after school on a Friday at the local pub or coffee shop. Make it the same time and same place every week and everybody is invited.

Six degrees of separation

In what became a famous experiment Stanley Milgram, a Harvard professor with an interest in social networks, asked, 'How many acquaintances would it take to connect two randomly selected individuals?' He sent 160 letters to randomly chosen residents asking them to send a postcard either to a target person directly – if they knew the person – or to someone they already knew who was more likely to know the target person. Based on the replies, Milgram worked out the median number of people the card was sent to before reaching its target as 5.5. In other words, we are all separated by no more than six relationships!

Keep in touch with the people who are important to you. Group emails, texts and round-robin Christmas letters don't count! Cut out the middle man and actually pick up the phone for a chat or, even better, pop around to see the people you care about.

Remember birthdays. Have a stock of cards and a supply of stamps and make sure that you write birthdays in your diary.

I have a broad network of friends.

Re-connect

Build up a network of friends in different areas of your life. If you have lost contact with old friends from school, college or university perhaps it is not too late to get in touch again?

Accept invitations. Don't use tiredness or can't-be-botheredness as an excuse to avoid making new friends.

Make an effort to talk to and listen to all the people you meet.

Sit with someone different in the staffroom for a change.

Invite a neighbour over for drinks.

Morale hoovers

Limit contact with people who are negative and/or unsupportive. They can very quickly drain you, and all other people who are around, of energy. At the same time, distinguish between negative people and those who are just being true to themselves and honest with you.

Safety net

Try to agree with at least one person in your life that you will never talk about work.

Changing your thinking for the better

HEAD is about patterns of thought. To feel happier, it may be necessary to change your thinking for the better. Take control of your thoughts and banish any negative thinking. Most thoughts such as; 'I never could draw', 'I am so clumsy' or 'I have ridiculously large feet' were put there by other people when you were a child. By teachers, parents and other adults who didn't know any better than to put down young people. You know better. Don't fall into the trap of negative thinking. If you are positive about yourself and the things that happen to you, you are more likely to be positive towards other people.

Empathy

People with high levels of empathy are interested in other people and remember things that they have been told in the past. In order to be in a position to remember things that they are told, they have an ability to listen effectively – a skill that many of us lack, but one that is easy to improve. Empathy also requires being able to forgive others. Being unable to forgive is a short-cut to unhappiness, as holding grudges causes us to focus on a negative event or situation rather than to move on with our own lives. Robert Enright said that genuine forgiveness occurs when 'one who has suffered an unjust injury chooses to abandon his or her right to resentment and retaliation, and instead offers mercy to the offender'.[134] The point being that we have a choice – we can choose to abandon negative feelings. Choosing not to forgive someone does not hurt them as much as it hurts you.

Self-knowledge

Social comparisons can lead to discontent and unhappiness as there will always be someone, somewhere who has more than us. Happy people minimize comparisons with others and rarely feel the need to make them. Happy people are also aware of their own strengths and weaknesses and they fill their lives with as many things as possible that maximize their strengths (both at work and at play). They know the difference between things that they want and things that they need and recognize the fact that, if they want to achieve something, they are the one who is responsible for achieving it.

Integrity

People with integrity do the right thing, even when no-one is looking. Two separate events in February 2009 show how much easier it is to do the right thing when we are being watched than when no-one is looking. At the beginning of the month, a book supplier vacated its warehouse in Bristol leaving thousands of books behind. When it was made public that people could come along and help themselves to whatever they liked, people came with trolleys and crates and climbed and stamped over fallen books to get their hands on as many items as possible. Little restraint was shown and, although no-one was doing anything illegal, the whole affair was a bit of a scrum.

In contrast, during an art project in the Manhattan district of New York people showed far more restraint. When two artists, Stein and Robles, opened a 'free store' within walking distance of both Wall Street and Ground Zero, 'customers' were invited to take whatever they felt that they needed from the shop and no payment was expected. On this occasion, nobody pushed and shoved, nothing got broken and Stein commented, 'Almost everybody has bartered with us – they brought us something in and took something that they thought was of equal in value'.[135] (Stein 2009)

Do we conclude from these two events that Bristolians are greedy, impolite and undisciplined whilst New Yorkers are generous, polite and restrained? Unlikely. The Bristolians were not doing anything that they had been told they couldn't do. So why did they act differently? Well, there were some key differences to the two situations. One was that in New York stress was put on the word 'need', and people were actually asked only to take what they felt they needed. The other was that New Yorkers were asked to check out and get a receipt for their goods before leaving. In New York, someone was looking so it was easier to do the right thing.

What people with integrity do and say matches their values. They are able to tell the truth even if it is not easy to do so. If there is a difficult conversation to be had or problem to be solved, they do not lie awake and worry about it at 3 a.m.; instead they have the conversation or sort the problem out. People with integrity give time to the things that are important to them, rather than talking about the things that are important but doing something completely different.

Happier individuals questionnaire: Head section

Now complete the second section of the Happier Individuals Questionnaire below and score as with the previous section:

1 = This statement **never** applies to me.
2 = This statement **rarely** applies to me.
3 = This statement **sometimes** applies to me.
4 = This statement **often** applies to me.
5 = This statement **always** applies to me.

	1	2	3	4	5	Total
Empathy – put yourself in others' shoes						
I am interested in other people						
I am a good listener						
I find it easy to forgive						
Self-knowledge – if it's to be, it's up to me						
I minimize comparisons with others						
I know my strengths and weaknesses						
I know the difference between my wants and needs						
Integrity – to yourself be true						
I tell the truth even when it is hard to do so						
I give time to those things that are most important to me						
I behave in ways which are consistent with my values						

Write your totals in the boxes, turn to the Winning the H Factor Individuals wheel on p. 95 and shade in the Head section of the wheel.

As you did previously, once you have identified where you would like to make improvements, start to think about how you can do this. There are suggestions below should you need some more ideas.

Empathy – Put yourself in others' shoes

I am interested in other people.

Names

A simple way to sabotage a relationship is to get someone's name wrong, to forget it or to not be interested in it in the first place. Dale Carnegie wrote *How to Win Friends and Influence People* in 1936. It became a bestseller and still is. One of its core messages was that to influence someone else you have to show interest in that someone else. Start by remembering people's names.

Actually listen when someone gives you their name. If you don't catch it, ask them to repeat it. Then repeat it back to them; 'Hi, Katie, nice to meet you.' Try to use their name several times during the rest of your conversation as a means of ingraining it on your memory, then use it when you say goodbye; 'It was really nice to talk to you, Katie. See you again.'

It is said that Franklin Roosevelt remembered names by imagining them written across a person's forehead. If you have a visual memory this technique could help you. Alternatively, imagine writing it down – move your index finger to spell it out as you do so.

Word association can also help. Imagine someone called 'Hattie' with a silly hat on, Holly with a sprig of holly on her head, Felix as a cat or Martin with a tinny voice. Or think of someone else with the same name, for example if you meet a Michael, think of how he is (or isn't) similar to Michael Douglas.

Write the name down – have a book in which you can note names and when/where you met people. Obviously, only write in or refer to this book in private!

Ask

Ask people about themselves. Don't feel that you have to do all the talking in a conversation – stop worrying about the impression that you want to make on them and start wondering about them. That way, you will be sure to make a good impression without trying. Ask questions about their jobs, hobbies and family. Remember things about other people. If someone tells you that they are going on holiday, the next time you see them ask them how it was. If they were preparing for a job interview, ask them how it went. Use your notebook to add details about people if it helps you to remember.

I am a good listener.

Be present

Firstly, think about your motives for listening to someone – do you want to hear about them, to learn something new, to listen to some different opinions or are you just waiting for the chance to tell your own anecdote or to give them your opinion? Are you already preparing your response before they have finished speaking? If you are, you are very unlikely to hear all that they say. Before you enter your next conversation make a conscious decision to 1) listen without thinking of a response; 2) clarify what the other person has said and only then 3) respond.

Eye contact

Make eye contact when someone is talking – it helps you actually listen to the words. Nod and respond to what they are saying ('Really?', 'Uh, huh', 'Yep, go on') as this will also remind you that you are supposed to be listening! Avoid talking over them, getting distracted by something else that is going on or thinking of your counter argument while they are still talking. If you find yourself starting to do this, change your body position and refocus on the speaker to bring your attention back.

A and A

Absorb and appreciate what is said before you reply. Be more reflective when having conversations. For example, clarify that you have understood by saying: 'If I'm right, what you are saying is …' or 'What do you mean by … ?'

Build on contributions that have been made to a conversation: 'Sam, just now you said … Do you think that could be applied to … ?' or 'I agree with you when you say … and, if we take your argument further, you could say …'

Wait first

Wait until the speaker has finished before you respond. Make any counter arguments clear, precise and honest.

I find it easy to forgive.

> The weak can never forgive. Forgiveness is the attribute of the strong. (Gandhi)
>
> http://www.quotationspage.com/quote/2188.html 13.10.09

Say it

Research shows that finding forgiveness actually lowers your blood pressure and your heart rate.[136] How you have learned to cope with frustration will also correlate to physical changes in your body. The better adapted you are to dealing with negative events and to focusing on positive events, the less you put your health at risk. There are all sorts of things we find it hard to forgive – a hurtful remark, being cut up by another car, feeling put-upon, infidelity, etc., but harbouring grudges does not help our own well-being. In some situations, simply saying it how it is and telling the person involved can help you start the forgiveness process.

Write it down

Of course, there will be some situations in which it is impossible to speak to someone who has hurt you as you will not or do not wish to see that person again. In which case, try writing a letter expressing how you feel and then tearing it up and putting it in the bin. Alternatively, write your feelings in your diary or in a blog. Writing things down can be very cathartic, although how you write events is important. Recent research has found that people who focus on the positive that arises from being treated unfairly are more able to forgive and move on than people who focus on how they feel or on something completely different.[137]

Walk a mile in my moccasins

The old saying goes, 'Don't judge me until you have walked a mile in my moccasins'. The old joke goes, 'Do so especially for someone you don't like – then you will be a mile away and you'll have their moccasins'. Author, Robert Byrne, prefers, 'Until you walk a mile in another man's moccasins you can't imagine the smell'.

Seriously, however, if you feel you have been treated badly, put yourself in the other person's shoes. Why may they have done what they did? What is happening in their lives to make them behave in that way? Have you ever behaved in a similar way? If you can understand their motives it may be easier to forgive them and move on.

Protect yourself

Forgiveness is not the same as condoning an action and giving someone carte-blanche to continue treating you badly. If someone continually treats you badly, then you must put into place a means of protecting yourself. It may be as simple as saying something like, 'Please stop putting me down in public, it makes me feel bad and you look unpleasant'. It may mean cutting that person out of your life, speaking to someone in a senior position at work or moving jobs. If you find yourself in a position of continually having to find forgiveness for the same thing, consider how you can prevent the initial behaviour and take action.

Self-knowledge – If it's to be it's up to me

I minimize comparisons with others.

Invidious comparison

Minimize comparisons with others. There will always be someone, somewhere who has more, has done more, who earns more or who is more attractive, fitter or funnier than you. Forget them and focus on yourself. Strive to be the very best you can be and to do the very best you can do. Keep other people's achievements out of the picture.

Gratitude diary

A gratitude diary in which people wrote down things for which they were thankful once a week significantly increased their overall satisfaction with life over a period of six weeks, whereas a control group who did not keep journals had no such gain. Keep a diary!

What's on your list?

> Perfect happiness is ... 'Being aware that I am experiencing it'.[138] (Simon 2007)

Construct a happiness inventory. Regular recording of the things for which people are grateful has been found to improve alertness, determination and energy levels.[139] If you wish, you could do this online as a blog. It could be a simple list of the things you are happy about and grateful for, or you can write in as much detail as you like. Alternatively, when you go to bed each night think of the things in your life for which you are grateful. Then think of the things that have happened during the day that have added to your happiness. Include the really small things like the bus arriving on time, for example!

> I have a rule that during every day I try to find a little ray of sunshine. Sometimes it's obvious and heart-swelling like watching my children, sometimes it's as simple as laughing at a joke. I invented this rule when I got to a New Year's Eve and couldn't think what had been good about the year. By making sure each day has an acknowledged highlight it means a whole year seems like a rich tapestry of happy memories. (Indira, Actress, Gloucestershire)

The secret of happiness is ...

Focusing on the happiness of others. By externalizing your concerns – looking out of the window rather than constantly in the mirror – you grow your capacity to empathize. Rather than focusing on how others see you, focus on how you can make others happy. Start by thinking of one person who is important to you and aim to make them noticeably happier within the time frame of, say, the next week or two. Think about what small things you can do or say to increase their happiness. At the end of the time frame, reflect on how it made you feel as well.

> Happiness comes when your work and words are of benefit to yourself and others. (Buddha, circa 500BC)

I know my strengths and my weaknesses.

Acquire the reflection habit

Constantly living in the fast lane – whether it's a lane of your own or someone else's choosing – stops you learning from errors and robs you of the present. If you purposefully set your mind to deliberate over experiences, you will gain from the process. Make it a methodical and slow process and ask the hard questions like, 'Did I really do that?', 'How might I do better next time?' and 'What lessons can I learn from this?'

Buddy up

Have someone with whom you can regularly share your strengths and weaknesses. Make sure that this is someone you trust.

What's your skill set?

Think about the things that you are good at or have been successful in. Why is it particularly these things? What skills or personality traits make you good at these things? What about the things that you avoid or have not found the same levels of success in? Is there a common trait that would lead you to spot a weakness?

Ask yourself these three questions:
'What am I good at?'
'What can I improve upon?'
'How do I do so?'

Change the negative self-talk

Recognize the things that you do and say that undermine your self-belief. How do you talk about yourself and your abilities? Can you acknowledge your strengths, or do you constantly feel the need to put yourself down? If you do the latter, catch yourself when you do so and spot the times you do it – is it with particular people or in particular places (at work, at home, on the sports field)? Next time you know you will be in such a situation, don't allow yourself to do it.

I know the difference between wants and needs.

The big list

Make a list of all the things you want. Cross out anything you don't actually need.

The matrix

Use a want versus need matrix (see p. 258) to decide what you should pursue and what you should forget about.

Integrity – To yourself be true

I tell the truth even when it is difficult to do so.

Integrity ratings

Do you give back the money if you are given too much change, even if it is just a matter of a few pence? Would you hand in a wallet if you found it? In research using wallets that were deliberately left lying around, all wallets were returned in Stockholm, none in London. Do you tell people the truth when it is important that you do so? Do you tell yourself half truths to make excuses for your own behaviour? Being honest in small matters is as important as in big matters. Each time you fail to be honest with yourself or with someone else then you are eating into your own integrity. If you lie, exaggerate or cheat you are effectively telling yourself that you couldn't get the things you gain by honest means.

Score your everyday behaviours against an integrity rating. Consider everything you do in a day – even the small things – and score them on an integrity rating of zero to five, where zero shows no integrity and five shows extreme integrity.

Pick your truths!

Consider the value of telling the truth at a particular time. If you are already in a taxi on the way out and your friend or partner asks you how they look, it would only be hurtful and damaging to tell them that, in your humble opinion, they look like the dog's dinner. If, however, you are asked your opinion at the point of buying the outfit, then it may be a good time to suggest that the style, colour or cut is not perfect for them.

Choose the right moment for telling someone the truth. Do it in private. Don't try to point out someone's flaws by publicly humiliating them. Similarly, if it can wait, don't tell someone a difficult truth if they are about to go for a job interview, important meeting or if they have just suffered a bereavement. That said, don't wait for the perfect time either. Sometimes you just have to bite the bullet.

Salty wounds

Choose the right words and know when to stop. Prepare what you want to say, say it and stop. Don't keep on and on as this could seem like you are bullying or rubbing salt into the wound. When you are telling the truth, be prepared to give examples should you be asked to do so. Look the other person in the eye. This will show your own honesty and sincerity.

I give time to those things that are most important to me.

Go beyond fine words

Often we are good at saying what is important to us, but not so good at actually giving time to those things. Sit down and really question the important things in your life. What matters to you most? Your family, your friends, your job, your sport or hobbies? Then think about whether you genuinely spend time on the things that are the most important to you. If not, what encroaches upon that time and how can you prevent it from doing so in the future?

Try getting up half an hour earlier each day, or leaving work half an hour earlier once or twice a week. Consider how you can spend less time doing the things you don't enjoy so that you can spend time doing the things that are important to you. Perhaps you could trade a chore you don't like with someone who doesn't mind doing it.

Start early

We often waste a lot of time chasing around at the weekend. Do some of the 'weekend' jobs on a Friday night (fill the car with petrol, pick up some milk on the way home, collect the dry cleaning, etc.). Can you share some of the other weekend chores with somebody else – say by taking it in turns?

I behave in ways which are consistent with my values.

What's worth fighting for?

Consider what your values and beliefs really are. What is important to you? Make a list of the five things you value most. Here are some to get you started:

- money
- friendship
- love
- family
- status
- happiness
- control over others
- control over your life
- work
- honesty
- knowledge or wisdom
- truth
- respect
- freedom
- beauty or good looks
- physical fitness
- environmental protection
- power
- kindness
- independence
- charity
- trust
- ambition
- integrity.

Try putting the list above into a rank order. Which are at the bottom and which are at the top? If a partner or someone who knew you well were asked to do it on your behalf would they come up with the same list? If the list is markedly different, what does it say about how you express your values? What can you do to change this?

Best value

Check that everything – and we mean absolutely everything – you do and say is consistent with your values. Think back over the last day, week or year and consider whether you have lived up to your values. If not, consider how could you have changed your behaviour? What could you do in the future to match your actions to your values?

Joanna, for example, realized that she often moaned about the amount of litter dropped outside the shop opposite her house, but that she never picked it up. So she began by consciously looking for litter when she walked past the shop, picking it up and putting it in the bin. What she has found now that her awareness is raised is that other people do the same – on several occasions she has seen her neighbours picking up litter. And seeing this has had a positive effect on Joanna's own view of the local area and the people who live in it.

When you experience dissonance (that uncomfortable feeling you get when your actions don't quite match up with your beliefs) think about how you can change your actions. So, for example, if you believe in being honest but don't tell someone when they give you the wrong change, you may experience dissonance. You have a choice. You can make an excuse such as: 'Well, it serves her right, she was chatting to her colleague when she should have been concentrating on serving me.' Or, you can tell them that they made an error and give them the money back. Consider which will make you feel better and act accordingly.

Challenge the guiding beliefs

Challenge your thinking – if you have a long-held belief, consider whether it still applies to your life today. If it does, great, but accept that change does happen and that sometimes we have to adjust our beliefs and change our way of thinking. Take a look at the example of the **ways of thinking** diagrams below and see if it can help you adjust any long-held beliefs of your own for the better.

Single loop thinking:

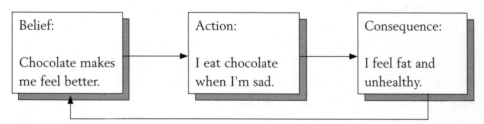

The single loop thinker above does not question their belief. So, they move from feeling fat and unhealthy to eating more chocolate because they believe it will help them escape those feelings. The double loop thinker below comes back to the belief and questions it and can then put changes in place.

Double loop thinking:

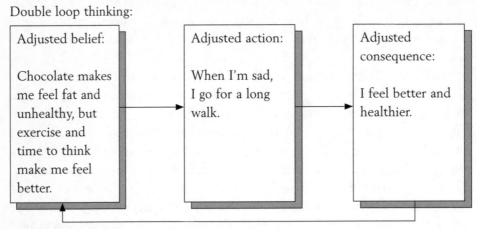

| Adjusted belief: Chocolate makes me feel fat and unhealthy, but exercise and time to think make me feel better. | Adjusted action: When I'm sad, I go for a long walk. | Adjusted consequence: I feel better and healthier. |

Looking after yourself

HEALTH is about looking after yourself and feeling good. Looking after yourself does not mean always putting yourself first, but it does mean being aware of your own needs (including the very basic need for healthy food, exercise and relaxation) and finding a way of meeting these. If you look after yourself, you will be more pleasant to be around and you will find that your good mood will rub off on those around you.

Security

To feel secure, we need to feel valued and safe. When we feel secure we are more likely to feel happy. In one experiment,[140] a group of mice were occasionally given an electric shock. However, they were never given this shock when a particular tone was being played in their cage. The mice began to associate this tone with being safe and, as a consequence, they behaved in a content manner whenever the tone was being played. But what was more interesting was that they behaved in an *even more* content manner than a group of mice that had never received an electric shock. The conclusion drawn from this is that, when the mice knew that they were absolutely safe from harm, they were at their most content. In another experiment[141] mice were given a shock when they stepped off a 'safe' platform. The mice didn't risk taking the step off the platform a second time!

Being secure is also about having the ability to exercise control in our lives. It is at the times when we feel that we are losing control that we feel the least happy. This loss of control can come from feeling that our space is cluttered and untidy, from not knowing how a colleague, friend or relative will react next, from not having enough information or from not being in control of our finances. The first thing people are taught when they learn to ski is how to stop – once you can do this, you have control. The same applies when we learn to drive; if we don't know where the brakes are, the chances are we won't put our foot on the accelerator. Nothing is more harmful to our feelings of well-being than feeling like our life is running out of control.

Well-being

To win the H Factor, you need to look after yourself both physically and mentally. Happy people have a hobby or an interest and they build in time for themselves. This is not always easy, especially with busy work and family lives, but it is essential to make a small amount of time for ourselves in order to reflect and to be productive at work and for our families.

There is evidence that meditation improves well-being. When it was used in several prisons in the USA, India and New Zealand, it led to prisoners becoming less likely to feel depressed, hostile and helpless. They also smoked less, behaved more reasonably and were less likely to take drugs.[142] Meditation has also been shown to improve feelings of well-being and, in one experiment, to help heal sufferers of psoriasis four times faster than those who did not meditate.[143]

Well-being is, of course, also about having a healthy lifestyle, eating well and taking exercise. People talk about the feelings of well-being they get when they are in green environments – that is in areas with natural vegetation, water and/or panoramic views. It has been found that living in an area with green spaces reduces the negative effects associated with income deprivation.[144] So, while it has been claimed that watching television enhances well-being and soap operas can make positive changes to society,[145] if the only fresh air you get is when you are watching Emmerdale and the only exercise you get is on your Wii, then we would advise you to get out and about a little more!

Cooperation

When it comes to basic instincts in the animal kingdom, there is plenty of evidence that the world can be an aggressive, dangerous place. However, it is also in the interest of animals that they care for their offspring and for their relatives, and this is very often done through social relationships. Shelley Taylor[146] talks of the how animals and humans do not just need 'fight or flight', but that equally important are 'tend and befriend'. Animals practise reciprocity in many ways – female ants who look after the queen rather than have offspring of their own, elephant 'families' who protect each other's young and the weak and vampire bats who will regurgitate food after a good night's hunting to help out less successful bats[147] to name but a few.

When people work together, they achieve more than the sum of the individual parts. Cooperative people say 'thank you' often. And they have more to say it for, because they often find that other people are cooperative in return. People who look after someone or even something (a garden, an allotment or a pet, for example) tend to have more of the H Factor than those who don't. The same applies to people who go to a religious meeting regularly, regardless of their specific faith. This could be because of the social support they give and receive and the feeling of belonging they get from attending the religious group.

Happier individuals questionnaire: Health section

Look at the third section of the questionnaire below. Complete as with the previous two sections. Just in case you need a reminder, here's the scoring system:

1 = This statement **never** applies to me.
2 = This statement **rarely** applies to me.
3 = This statement **sometimes** applies to me.
4 = This statement **often** applies to me.
5 = This statement **always** applies to me.

	1	2	3	4	5	Total
Security – the wind beneath my wings						
I feel valued						
I feel secure						
I exercise control in my life						
Well-being – I'm OK, you're OK						
I have a hobby or interest						
I have a healthy lifestyle						
I build in time for myself						
Cooperation – together everyone achieves more						
I say 'thank you' a lot						
I enjoy a challenge						
I look after someone or something						

Once you have completed this, add up your scores and shade in the Health section of the wheel on p. 95. Which are your weaker areas? What would you like to improve upon? Think up some ways in which you can improve your scores in the Health section. Once again, if you need some help with this there are plenty of tips below.

Security – The wind beneath my wings

I feel valued.

Start by valuing yourself

Until you do so, others are less likely to value you. People who value themselves do not feel a strong need to have other people point out their strengths or tell them that they are doing a good job. Valuing yourself is not arrogance. People who come across as arrogant are generally those who have low feelings of self-worth. Think of three things you really like about yourself. Make a list. Remind yourself of what they are and think about them regularly. Think of one thing you don't like about yourself. If you can change it, do so. If you can't, get over it!

Prompts

Think of your top three strengths – you are a loyal friend and/or an excellent listener, you are funny, sporty, happy, etc. Now take some tiny coloured stickers and stick them in four or five places in the house where you will regularly see them – on the kettle, the microwave, your wardrobe door, on the corner of a mirror. Each time you see them, remind yourself of your top three strengths. Say them out loud if you feel comfortable with it!

Accept complements at face value

It could be that you are more valued at work and in your personal life than you believe. Start by actually noticing when someone pays you a compliment and/or says 'thank you'. Don't play it down when someone does, but accept it graciously. If someone is kind enough to complement you or something you have done, don't shrug it off with a comment like, 'Lost weight? You're joking aren't you? I'm such a heifer!' or 'It's OK I suppose, but I'd have like to have had time to do it better'. A smile and a simple, 'Thank you' or 'Thanks, I enjoyed doing it' does not make you sound big-headed. On the contrary, you are more likely to receive further complements in future. If you have done something well but no-one complements you, then do it yourself. Actually verbalize it by saying, 'Well done, me. I did a really good job there'. Give yourself a pat on the back if you deserve it.

Playfulness

Be cheerful and fun to be around. People will value your presence if you have a sense of humour, a positive attitude and look on the bright side. There are some among us who are people magnets. If others are asked to characterize the behaviours of these people magnets, a sense of fun emerges every time. The quality of playfulness often accompanied by a sense of humour is so valued that we tend to remember not only those who had it but how we felt in their presence. So, if you have this sense of fun you will be bringing happiness to others.

When writing biographies of some of the worst villains – those who are not deemed to be known for their people skills – writers still feel compelled to find some evidence of their playfulness and humour. For example, Joseph Stalin liked to watch films and frequently invited actors who were playing him in one over for dinner. Once he asked an actor 'Stalin', 'How will you play Stalin?' The clever actor replied, 'As the people see him'. 'The right answer', said Stalin, presenting the actor with a bottle of brandy.

I feel secure.

Choose how you respond

Do not give others permission to upset you. Know that, whatever the situation, you choose your response. No-one can make you feel a particular way. They can say and do things that affect you, but you and only you choose your response.

Listen yourself calm

Download one of the podcasts on dealing with everyday stress from http://www.mhf.org.uk/information/well–being–podcasts/. Some are only five minutes long. Listen to them at break-time or on public transport.

I exercise control in my life.

Accept

Accept that there are some things that you cannot control. Forget them. Control what is controllable. Don't spend time worrying about the things you can't control.

Move on

Don't be defined by your problems. Focusing on the negative and dwelling on things that make you feel bad will prevent you from seeing solutions. Don't be the sort of person who complains again and again about the same things but isn't willing to take advice and move on. Take back control by seeing change as a solution. Move on and put problems behind you.

> The only way to maintain a moderate sum of happiness in this life, is not to worry about the future or regret the past too much.[148] (Gibson)

Check your bank balance

Not knowing how much money you have (or don't have) means that you don't have control. You don't know how much of the money you are spending is your own and how much belongs to someone else. Banks, being banks, will often let you go on spending even if you don't have the funds and then they will charge you for it. So, when your statement comes in, look at it. If it doesn't look good, take back control. Do this by establishing which of the things you buy are things you want and which are things you actually need. Complete the wants versus needs matrix on p. 258 to help with this.

De-clutter

Give everything its place and keep it there. Living with mess can make you feel that things are out of control. It is easier to avoid mess if you have less 'stuff'. Give the things you don't use, wear or need to charity. Make sure that everything you keep has its place. Avoid wasting time searching for keys, screwdrivers, spare change, etc. by putting them in suitable storage containers and giving them a place. The same applies to your desk at work. Get rid of what you don't need – including the unnecessary paperwork and jobs it would be 'nice' to get around to, but you know you won't.

Well-being – I'm OK, you're OK

I have a hobby or interest.

Hobby world

Develop an unexpected hobby or interest. It may be something that you've always wanted to try, or it may be something random that just pops into your head.

Below are a few suggestions if you want some help with making a decision:

- go dancing – any kind will do
- visit a spa
- take singing lessons
- learn to entertain others with magic tricks
- buy a dart board
- go to a karaoke night and actually join in
- climb trees
- go bird watching
- take an open-top bus trip
- research your family tree
- join a choir.

Find the time

Allocate time to your interests on a regular basis. Simply having an interest is not sufficient – you must give it enough priority to allocate time to it. You may need to fit it in by cutting back on something less desirable or interesting, by getting up half an hour earlier or going to bed a little later. Most days we waste a little time here and a bit more time there, so if you plan your time carefully you should be able to fit in the things that are important to you.

I have a healthy lifestyle.

Balance is all

Know what is good for you and tweak your diet accordingly. Have your five portions of fruit and vegetables per day.

Sleep it off

Get the right amount of sleep. Most adults need between seven and eight hours per night. If you don't get enough sleep your performance will be affected – you may find that you can't concentrate properly, that you can't make decisions, and that you aren't as creative as usual. In the long term, lack of sleep can lead to feelings of depression.

Do you really need to watch the 9 p.m. movie? Turn the television off and have an early night instead.

If you find it hard to get to sleep, here are some tips:

- Make sure your room and bed are comfortable (think about the temperature and levels of noise and light).
- Get some exercise each day
- Avoid caffeine after 3 p.m.
- Avoid excess alcohol – it may help you drop off but you won't sleep so well
- Eat between 6 p.m. and 7 p.m.
- Try simple meditation techniques
- Have a regular bedtime and getting up time,

Re-hydrate

Drink water. We need from 2 to 2.5 litres of fluid a day. Some of this comes from fruit and vegetables and it is OK to drink squash and juice, but the general advice is to try to drink 2 litres of water (still water is best) per day. Water aids concentration, keeps your skin looking healthy and can lower the chance of a heart attack.

Drink less alcohol

Monitor and limit your alcohol consumption.

Get moving

Up your heart rate daily for at least 30 minutes. Buy a pedometer and set yourself weekly targets. Get off the bus a stop earlier. Stop getting in lifts and use the stairs instead. Walk or cycle instead of using the car.

I build in time for myself.

Plan 'me' time

Plan to have time for yourself. It may be that you won't have time to do everything you want to, but by deciding what is most important to you, you can build in time to spend on yourself. You may have to make trades – every other day go for a run rather than read the newspaper (you can catch up on the news by listening to the radio on the way to work instead), or miss a crucial TV soap to go on a course at the local college (again, technology means you can catch up with the soap later if you wish). If you like to read, get up a little earlier in the morning and tell everyone else in the house that they are not allowed to join you until the normal time. Sit down with a cup of tea and read. Don't become distracted by jobs that may need doing. Create time in your day when you are not to be interrupted. It need only be 20 minutes, but it will make you feel so much better to have had that time. Make sure that everyone concerned knows that you are not to be disturbed.

Say 'no' more often

Learn to say 'no'. Don't be a slave to your work or to other people. Sometimes you may simply have too much on your plate to take on more. If your daughter asks you to take her to band practice and you don't have time, then it won't kill her if you say 'no' for once. Tell her you are sorry and you will try to help out next time, but right now you are too busy. Similarly, if something urgent comes up at work but you already have other priorities, discuss with your colleagues what order you should do things in. Try saying: 'I am very happy to take that on. However, right now I have X, Y and Z to do. Which order would you like me to do them in, or is someone else available to help with this?'

Relax

Learn simple meditation or relaxation techniques.

Find somewhere comfortable to sit. Close your eyes. Allow your body to relax. Feel each of your muscles relaxing – this can take a conscious effort. As you do so, notice how your body feels, any sounds and how you feel mentally. Think about your breathing rhythm. Try to keep your breaths even. If your mind wanders off, bring it back to think about your body and your breathing. Try to do this for ten minutes.

You will find links to websites and suggested reading on meditation at the back of this book.

Cooperation – together everyone achieves more

I say 'thank you' a lot.

Gratitude says it all

Research in the field of positive psychology points out the mutual benefits of expressing thanks. Being grateful helps people enjoy life more.[149] Expressing gratitude promotes positive feelings for both the instigator and the receiver.

Say 'thank you', 'please' and 'well done' more often. These small words are highly motivational and are likely to get other people to cooperate with you. People who feel appreciated are more likely to want to help and to contribute. They will feel that their input is valued. Surveys have shown that being thanked has a very positive effect on people's morale.[150]

Say it with cards

Make or buy a selection of blank cards to show your appreciation for small acts of kindness, gifts or offers of help.

Have a special set of post-it notes (if possible, try to find some in interesting shapes or with some with a picture – try www.euroffice.co.uk for speech bubble shapes or www.vistaprint.co.uk where you can design your own) on which you can leave messages of thanks.

Appreciation strategy

Plan how you will show others that you appreciate something about them or something that they do. To which of your relatives, friends or colleagues could you show appreciation? Include people you don't like! Sometimes a smile and a thank you will do. Make sure that you mean it, though.

At work, show other people that you value their contribution or effort. If a colleague makes an interesting contribution to a staff meeting, tell them afterwards that you appreciated it – irrelevant of your respective positions in the school. If a non-teaching member of staff helps you out with something (getting a phone number/contacting a parent/writing a letter, etc.), tell them that it saved you time and that you are grateful.

Letters of gratitude

In a study at Kent State University, researchers found that writing a letter of thanks to someone who means a lot to you was very beneficial both for the writer and the recipient.[151] Write a letter to someone to whom you are grateful. In a separate study it was found that, if the writer delivered the letter by hand and actually read it out loud to the person they were thanking, it was even more beneficial.[152] The researchers suggest that, ideally, the letter should be about a page long and should have concrete details of what the writer feels grateful for.

I enjoy a challenge.

Set yourself a challenge

No real learning ever took place within the middle of a comfort zone. There are few among us who are beyond being motivated by some sort of challenge, however modest. And with the challenge comes growth and learning.

Below are a few ideas:

- Get fit for a sponsored walk.
- Go for a promotion at work.

- Take on new or different responsibilities at work.
- Think of a class or child you could really help and make sure that you do it.
- Give up smoking.
- Learn to cook.
- Take up a new hobby.
- Write a poem.
- Write a book.
- Learn to drive.
- Decorate a room.
- Be more assertive.
- Say 'thank you' five times a day.
- Learn to dance.
- Look on the bright side.

Make sure that your challenge involves something that you want to do or that will bring you pleasure.

Get out of your comfort zone

Try teaching something that you are not at all comfortable with. Select a subject that you felt you couldn't do at school and offer to teach one or two lessons for a colleague. Because you will possibly have to start from scratch and because of your own lack of confidence, you will probably find that you:

a) prepare the lesson really well

b) teach it particularly well

c) learn something about the subject

d) see things from the pupils' perspective

e) enjoy it.

I look after something or someone.

Do the neighbourly thing

Talk to your neighbours. If you see that they are busy in their garden, offer to help them. If they are carrying in heavy shopping when you get home from work, help them fetch it into their house and have a chat as you do so. If you do some cooking or baking, make some extra and pop it around. When you go on holiday, give them the spare food from your fridge that would otherwise be thrown away. That way, they also know that you are away and may keep an eye on your house.

Adopt a pensioner

Look after someone. For example, 'adopt' an elderly person locally. Pop around once a week to check that they are OK, make them a cup of tea and have a chat. Offer to do their shopping/go to the post office for them or just drop by with some biscuits or home-made cakes.

Hug a tree

Look after something. For example, grow cacti or bonsai, get an allotment or do the gardening regularly. Gardening helps your fitness levels and removes you from the stresses of your everyday life for a while. While you are out in the sun, you are increasing the amount of vitamin D you get, which helps your body absorb calcium and is needed for healthy bones and joints. Gardening keeps you in touch with nature, which reduces stress and you can take great pleasure in creating a thing of beauty. If you are growing fruit and/or vegetables, then it will also help with your healthy eating and your budget!

Furry life

Get a pet. Having a pet gives us company when we need it, something we can talk to or think out loud to and often something to laugh at. What type of pet you get will depend upon your circumstances. Walking a dog will increase your fitness levels and is likely to increase your contact with other people who you meet on walks. Having a bird or an aquarium of fish requires a regular but not enormous commitment. Watching fish has been found to release stress and reduce blood pressure.[153] This could be down to the fact that it focuses our attention away from our problems and stressors for a while.

Build, broaden and balance activity

- Complete the questionnaire and fill in the wheel.
- Review the wheel for any obvious gaps and imbalances.
- Create an action plan to build, broaden and balance.
- Use your action plan.
- Look at the BBB strategies and note those which you have used or could use.
- Reflect upon the effectiveness of these strategies and set a date to come back to the questionnaire and complete the wheel again.

4   Happier classrooms

In this section we focus on the following topics:

> **The importance of classroom climate**
>
> **Teaching happiness**
>
> **A simple formula to create a positive climate for learning**
>
> **Applying the model to your classroom**
>
> **Maintaining a safe but challenging learning environment**

And answer the following questions:

> *Does the mood of the student make any difference to their learning?*
>
> *Can happiness be taught and, if so, how do we do it?*
>
> *What are the key things in any learning environment?*
>
> *How do we begin to apply the H factor to our classrooms?*
>
> *How do we make our classrooms safe?*

- Creating a positive learning environment
- Should we teach happiness?
- Getting the BASICS right
- Learning alongside each other
- Achieving together
- Safe to succeed

Creating a positive learning environment

George B. Dantiz studied mathematics at the prestigious University of California at Berkeley. His studies included a statistics class. One morning he arrived late for the class. He frantically copied the two problems he saw on the board, knowing that to miss homework was not going to be a good move so early in the course. He found the problems difficult and had to spend more time than he would have liked struggling with them. At the next class he handed them in. What he did not know was that they were not homework problems but examples of unsolvable challenges that the lecturer had been using to demonstrate the complexity and rigour of statistics in the lecture that day. Dantiz had approached the challenges in a completely different frame of mind to that of his classmates. As a result of his efforts he quickly became a celebrity. The story forms the basis of the plot of the film *Good Will Hunting*.

Students who feel positive about themselves, positive about each other and positive about their learning are more likely to be creative, willing to become involved, to take risks in their learning and be able to solve problems.

In his own experiment, Alistair showed a classroom of 10 year olds a series of pictures of sad faces accompanied by soulful music which had a depressing effect. The black and white photographs were of young people from a secondary school in Acton and were taken with all permissions and by a professional photographer recruited for the role. The experience of watching the faces to music was designed to lower the mood and to create a less than positive atmosphere.

Having shown the video, Alistair asked the ten year olds to complete a relatively simple task (a dot-to-dot picture) within a time limit. The children struggled. Some found it difficult to get started and those he had expected to do well underachieved. The children were debriefed and explanations sought for their lack of performance. Alistair asked about the pictures and the music and then led a further discussion about mood and how it affects how we go about doing things.

Shortly afterwards – and before the 10 year olds could get too depressed – Alistair repeated the experiment. This time the faces of the children and the music were positive, upbeat and happy. The pictures were of exactly the same children but taken on a different day. The join the dots task was repeated with a set that was only slightly different. This time the performance improved and the levels of completion went up. Alistair talked it through again and comparisons were made. Among the explanations offered by the children for their poor showing the first time were:

> 'The music got in my head.'
> 'I was feeling sad.'
> 'I forgot where to start.'

'It all went very quiet.'

'First time, I was thinking about what had happened to them.'

And, because there's always a rogue:

'The dots were closer together second time so it was easier'!

The experiment was an attempt to reconstruct a difference in mood. Its real purpose was to encourage reflection on what makes a positive classroom and whether there are any possible benefits in being in a positive or good mood when learning. What sorts of things might help create a good mood? What can we all do individually to help create a good mood?

Classroom climate is one of the three key factors that influence learning.[154] Yet, when the Hay Group asked teachers to predict how pupils would respond to a classroom climate questionnaire, most were unable to predict the response correctly!

From the pupils' perspectives, they are mostly looking to the teacher to create a sense of security and order in the classroom, an opportunity to participate actively in the class and for it to be an interesting and exciting place.[155] (Hay McBer 2000)

Aspire to make your classroom a happy place by making it secure and by building unity. Celebrate success! Make sure that everyone gets a chance to feel it and to experience it and encourage pupils to point out and celebrate each others' success. As Joanna explains:

I had asked my class to work in groups and to appoint roles within their groups. To my surprise, Marco, who has difficulties with spelling, had offered to scribe for his group. I took a look at what his group was doing and praised him for taking on the challenge. 'We all decided to do the job we like the least today, Miss', he explained. 'That's why Ahmed is going to present our ideas' (Ahmed has a lisp and is reluctant to speak in front of the class). When I asked Ahmed how he felt about it he said, 'If Marco's feeling brave today, so can I. I'm thinking about how proud we'll all be when we've finished'.

On another occasion, Alistair worked with a primary school in Richmond to create a series of learning experiences – assemblies, classroom work and home learning – around the topic of happiness. The intention was to show how to increase your own well-being but to do so by focusing on the happiness of others. The challenge for the children was to think of any three people who were not in the room or at the school at that time, but who were known to them. It could be a member of family, a neighbour, a friend or someone they had seen but had yet to speak to. The challenge, over a period of time, was to make these three people 10 per cent happier!

In a series of lessons called 'Acting on Happiness' ideas were pooled and then summarized before being made into a video featuring the children. In the video the children gave their advice to others who wanted to be happier. The children then had three weeks to make their targets 10 per cent happier using a combination of the agreed methods. The methods recommended were:

a   Build friendships: Happier people make and keep friends. Make friends with someone new.

b   Make a gift to someone: People who are happy give more to charity and are unselfish. Try giving something away.

c   Take regular exercise: Exercise releases chemicals in your brain which make you feel good. Get fit, stay fit and enjoy it!

d   Avoiding comparing yourself with others: Jealousy is the shortcut to unhappiness. Happy people avoid comparing themselves with others. Just get on with it.

e   Look after someone or something: People who are happier think more about others than they do about themselves. Taking care of someone else is good for you.

f   Achieve something of which you are proud: Why spend your life doing things that are a waste of time? Do something useful which you can look back on with pride.

g   Smile and laugh more: Laughing helps you relax and helps you learn. Smile more often. People who laugh more have more friends.

h   Turn dreams into actions: Some daydreams stop you from living your life. If you really want to do something or be someone get started!

i   Join a club: Research shows that people who join clubs with other people mostly live longer and healthier lives than people who stop in all the time. Get out and join something!

j   Catch yourself doing good: Don't beat yourself up! When you do something good give yourself a positive talking to. Happy people are positive about themselves.

k   Know the difference between wants and needs: Wants and needs are different. I might want an expensive toy but I don't need it. Happier people don't get obsessed about wants.

l   Count your blessings: Enjoy the good things in your life. When you feel down remember them all.

m   Say thanks: Say 'thank you' more often. You make someone feel good when you thank them.

n   Learn to forgive: Bearing a grudge is a shortcut to unhappiness. Get over it!

o   Deal with it!: Things will go wrong. Practise what to say and do to cope better.

You can watch the children's video at http://www.alite.co.uk/events/winningtheh-factor.html. The work with this and other groups of children is not yet complete, but there has already been excitement about the project and lots of anecdotal evidence to show that it has shifted the classroom culture towards openness and a willingness to share personal successes. Watch the video and judge for yourself if what the children say has wisdom. Then ask, 'Is it possible, or even desirable, to teach happiness?'

Should we teach happiness?

Should anyone have the temerity to argue that schools should teach happiness, journalists will start sharpening their pencils! In an article entitled 'Of Course Happiness Can't Be Taught'[156] one says:

> Our lives have been infected enough with this sort of clap-trap. Do we want to produce a nation of namby-pambies? This idiocy belongs to the realm of Susie Orbach, the feel good merchant, who said in the aftermath of that absurd communal breakdown that followed the sad death ten years ago of Diana, Princess of Wales, that Britons hitherto a repressed people had discovered a new 'emotional literacy'. (Henderson 2007)

So there we have it – clap-trap, which threatens the essence of our nationhood, peddled by feel-good merchants speaking twaddle about emotions. These feel-good merchants, deliberately misinterpreting the response to Diana's death, encouraged a form of 'emotional incontinence'. However, what suits us British best, the article goes on to say, is the 'stiff upper lip'. So, maybe the answer lies in stiff upper lip lessons?

Despite what the *Daily Telegraph* says, the facts behind the unprecedented outpouring of public grief do say something about our way of handling emotions in the UK. We are not great at it.

In the month following the death and funeral of Princess Diana there was a 17 per cent rise in suicides in England and Wales. The impact was greatest on women of a similar age to Diana herself, who died at 37. The rate of suicide in women increased some 34 per cent in the month following Diana's death, and in women aged 25 to 44 the rate increased by over 45 per cent.[157]

There are dangers in blaming all of society's ills on what we teach in schools and then expecting schools to react and pick up any pieces. The article spoken of above is typical of most that handle the topic of happiness. It deals with the headline and avoids the detail. It switches back to the idea that time spent on anything other than helping children read, write and count is time spent on destroying their life chances. This is reductive and single loop thinking. It presents the classroom as a simple place where only one mode of engagement is possible at any one time. So anything to do with understanding relationships, developing learning skills, motivation or respecting others is to be held in suspense while we get on with the real stuff of reading, writing and counting. It doesn't work that way! Classrooms are complex, dynamic, interactive environments where learning is simultaneously formal and informal, conscious and unconscious, directed and discovered.

When we go beyond simple eye-catching headlines and into the detail, we begin to understand both the 'what' and the 'how' of happiness teaching in schools. By breaking down happiness into component parts – how we think, how we build and sustain relationships, how we secure health and well-being – we can argue against the headliners. So is it possible or even desirable to teach happiness?

Let's start with a few questions:

- Should children be taught maths?
- Should the teaching of maths be taught from an early age?
- Is an understanding of maths and how to use it in one's everyday life a desirable thing?
- Should we employ specialist maths teachers?
- Should all teachers have some basic understanding and ability in maths?
- Is there a legitimate body of knowledge about maths that can be taught?
- In the world beyond school do children see evidence of the benefits of maths?
- Would there ever be an occasion in life when it would not be an advantage to have some knowledge of maths and how to apply it?

Few would argue that the answers would be seven 'yeses' and a 'maybe'! Now let's try the same questions but replace the subject:

- Should children be taught music?
- Should music be taught from an early age?
- Is an understanding of music and how to use it in one's everyday life a desirable thing?
- Should we employ specialist music teachers?
- Should all teachers have some basic understanding and ability in music?
- Is there a legitimate body of knowledge about music that can be taught?
- In the world beyond school do children see evidence of the benefits of music?
- Would there ever be an occasion in life when it would not be an advantage to have some knowledge of music and how to apply it?

What would you say – seven 'yeses' and a 'maybe'? This time let's use the original questions but replace the subject once more:

- Should children be taught how to behave?
- Should how to behave be taught from an early age?
- Is an understanding of how to behave in one's everyday life a desirable thing?
- Should we employ specialist behaviour teachers?
- Should all teachers have some basic understanding and ability in how to behave?
- Is there a legitimate body of knowledge about behaviour that can be taught?
- In the world beyond school do children see evidence of the benefits of how to behave?
- Would there ever be an occasion in life when it would not be an advantage to have some knowledge of how to behave?

How did you answer: six 'yeses', a 'no' and perhaps a 'maybe' for employing specialist teachers?

Keeping our original questions, let's make one last and final replacement:

- Should children be taught happiness?
- Should happiness be taught from an early age?
- Is an understanding of happiness and how to use it in one's everyday life a desirable thing?
- Should we employ specialist happiness teachers?
- Should all teachers have some basic understanding and ability in happiness?
- Is there a legitimate body of knowledge about happiness that can be taught?
- In the world beyond school do children see evidence of the benefits of happiness?
- Would there ever be an occasion in life when it would not be an advantage to have some knowledge of happiness and how to apply it?

How did you answer these last questions? Was there a fault line between the logic applied to the teaching of maths, music or behaviour and the logic of teaching happiness? The choice of school subjects we deem worthy of teaching is a combination of historical precedent; what already exists; what can be examined or assessed; what can be packaged up and 'sold' to so called stakeholders and what is thought to reflect the needs of the age.

We will not and do not make the case for the teaching of happiness as a discrete subject. We do not believe in, or endorse, happiness lessons for their own sake or, for that matter, behaviour lessons or lessons in emotions. We would say that it's the wrong way to go.

However, if we take care to define what it is we mean by happiness then we can ensure that in classrooms we do three things:

- model it in our everyday dealings with children
- teach through it, about it and with it
- aspire towards it for each and every person in our classrooms.

Getting the BASICS right

The BASICS model[158] outlined below is the model that we have found to be the most effective in building and sustaining a positive classroom climate.

> **Belonging:** There is a sense of **belonging** because everyone values the contributions of others. Participation is encouraged and appreciated. Involve your pupils in decision making and planning for the work that you will be doing. In 2002, researchers[159] compared different areas or districts of Switzerland with regard to the extent to which they involve the people in decision making and found that the people that were consulted in major decision making were happier than those that were not.

> **Aspiration:** Both learners and teachers have **aspirations** for high levels of attainment, both in the short and the long term. High teacher expectation has been found to be one of the three most important factors in pupils' learning (the other two are lack of disruption and encouragement to engage).[160]

> **Safety:** The class is a safe place to be. Everyone is free to take risks, to be creative and to contribute without fear of ridicule. There are high expectations of behaviour and children can learn in **safety**. Make your classroom free of put-downs. There is no room for fear in our classrooms, because fear inhibits learning by releasing stress hormones which travel to the hippocampus (the part of the brain responsible for memory and learning). Fear evokes in us the fight or flight syndrome – pupils who fear being put down are likely either to behave badly (fight) or withdraw from participation (flight).

Identity: Everyone recognizes each other's individuality and there is no pressure to conform. Everyone is allowed his or her own **identity** and differences are respected and valued. There is no favouritism.

Challenge: There is a **challenge** to the learning for everyone. Engaging in challenging activities helps children to develop strategies to cope with life. With each challenge they overcome, they increase their belief that they can overcome the next one. Learners should be brought to the very edge of their comfort zone. Keep in mind the need for challenges to be made within a progression. Every success that comes from being challenged will add to your learners' self-esteem and positive attitude towards the next task. Look out for the children who seem to simply sail through everything. They too need a challenge so that they don't come up short when they are one day challenged in a less secure environment.

Success: Both the adults in the classroom and the children's peers have an opportunity to share in each other's **success**. Make sure that you catch everyone being successful and point out the reason why they were so successful. For example: 'That piece of writing you have done is excellent. You obviously listened well when we discussed the use of adjectives. You have used the word "slovenly" in exactly the right context.' In a class where success is celebrated, everyone wants to achieve and mistakes are seen as a necessary part of the learning experience.

Now we come to your core purpose. In order to make your classroom a happy place, it is essential for you to know why you are there in the first place. What is your core purpose as a teacher? At this point you may be thinking that this is ridiculously obvious and that we have lost our marbles even to be asking this question. But sometimes there are aspects of our lives and jobs that get in the way of our core purpose, and it never hurts to remind ourselves of what we are here for. So, take some time now to consider why you are a teacher. What is the point of you being in your role? What is your core purpose? What do you want for the people you teach and what do you want them to remember you for?

Below are some of the responses we were given by our colleagues:

'To make sure that every child I teach learns to the best of their ability.'

'To make learning real and exciting and to instil a love of learning in my pupils.'

'To make a definable, positive difference to the lives of every single child I meet.'

'To show them that they can do whatever they set their minds to and to help them to be the very best that they can.'

Once you are very clear on your own core purpose, hold a mirror up to yourself. Does everything you do in the classroom match up to your core purpose? (Do you treat all children equally? Are you always positive? Is learning at the centre of *everything* you do?) Do the beliefs you hold about the children in your classroom tie in with your core purpose? (It is no use, for example, saying that your core purpose is to give everyone the opportunity to succeed then excluding a child from your lesson for bad behaviour.)

Consider the times when you feel that you lose sight of your core purpose – for example, when you have paperwork to produce and consequently less time to spend on preparing fantastic lessons. Be aware of these times and remind yourself of your core purpose during them. Write your core purpose in places where you will often be reminded of it – on a sticker on your desk, intermittently throughout your diary or planner, at the back of your classroom under the clock.

Think also about what preoccupations you are bringing in to your classroom. Do you need to do some double loop thinking? Challenge yourself by taking some of your long-held beliefs and apply some double loop thinking.

Single loop thinking

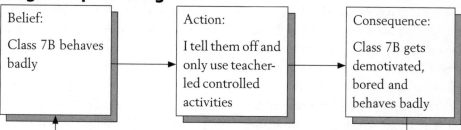

A single loop thinker will go back to the action again and again, and the belief will be reinforced by the fact that Class 7B does indeed behave badly. However, a double loop thinker will go back to the belief and question it. They will ask themselves, 'Why does Class 7B behave badly and what can I do about it?' Below is what they may come up with:

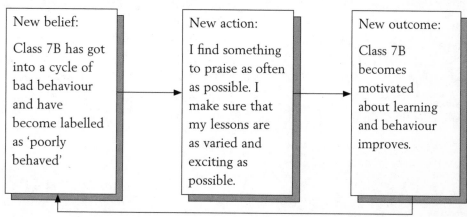

In the classroom, just as in life, we tend to get more of the things we expect to get. If we focus on bad behaviour, we will get more of it. If we focus on good behaviour, the chances are we will see more good behaviour. Sometimes it can help us to move away from a preoccupation with control – keeping children in their seats, quietly filling in worksheets and appearing to behave well, while not necessarily learning as much as they could – and to move towards a preoccupation with learning. Ask yourself, 'What will they learn today? How will they do this?' If children are really motivated by learning and discovering then they will behave – it may be noisier if they are working in groups and questioning each other about what they are doing, but it doesn't mean that you have lost control.

Modelling the H Factor is also about how you behave as a teacher. Consider how you use your voice and your body language. Do you react differently to one pupil than to another, even if their actions may have been the same? Do you allow things that have upset you outside the classroom to make your behaviour less than consistent? Take a child's-eye view – consider how the children in your classroom see you and what they may believe matters to you. It is essential that you model the behaviour that you want to see in them.

Spend some time thinking about who and what are the focal points of your attention. If it helps, ask a colleague to sit in your classroom with a seating plan and to tick each child as you address them. See who you tend to focus on and who you may miss out. Adjust your behaviour accordingly. Keep a list of names of children who you aim to give attention next time, or have all of the children's names on pieces of card and choose them at random for questioning.

In a review of feedback studies conducted by Professor John Hattie et al. in 2007, he found that 'Feedback is one of the most powerful influences on learning and achievement, but this impact can be either positive or negative'.[161] Feedback needs to be timely, relevant and focused on improvement. The evidence for the effective use of formative assessment approaches is overwhelming. Show your pupils how to give feedback. Make sure that it focuses on the task not the person. Find two things that are great about a task and then two things that can be done to make it better. Talk about the effort that has been put in that has led to the success. Avoid praising children for being 'clever', otherwise they will think that cleverness is what helps you achieve, not persistence.

So, how do you begin to measure the H Factor in your classroom? In order to measure it, we have defined it by breaking it down into our three categories – heart, head and health. We have then broken these three categories down further and explained them on the following pages.

Learning alongside each other

HEART is about building better relationships and thriving together. To foster good relationships, there needs to be trust. Investigations and surveys have shown that the happiest countries are those with a high level of trust. Build trust in your classroom by ensuring that all children are treated equally and that it is a no put-down zone. A happy classroom has no-one who is invisible. Learn everyone's names, remember them and use them. Speak at least once to every child in every lesson. Keep a particularly keen eye out for the average children – the ones who always behave, who always do OK, but who could easily become invisible.

Classroom

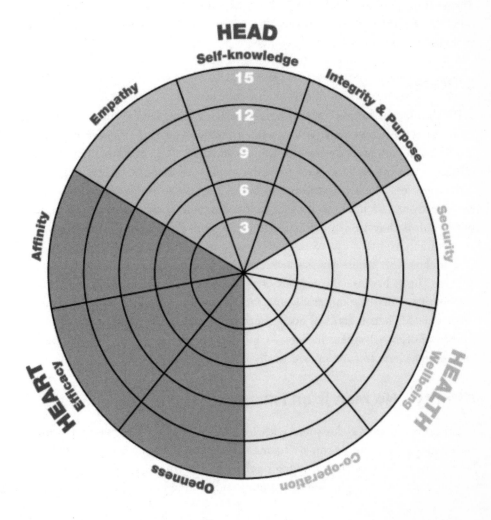

Openness

What children think does matter and should be valued, as the American press discovered in 1976 when a group of children reporters went to the Democratic National Convention. The children were there to talk to the hotdog sellers in Madison Square Gardens, but one 13 year old slipped into a lift with some of Jimmy Carter's senior aides. Because he was young, he was ignored and they continued to talk around him. The 13-year-old and his colleagues were able to publicize Carter's running mate before the remainder of the world's press!

Consider how open your classroom is – in an open classroom, the teacher is happy to give something of him- or herself. He may tell stories about his family, or about something that has happened to him in the past. Pupils are able to share their feelings easily without fear of ridicule. They enjoy being together and there is a sense of pulling together as a team. Everyone is encouraged to express their opinions and differences are valued. There is no need for anyone to hide feelings or thoughts – what you see is what you get.

Efficacy

Why should we bother increasing our classes' efficacy? Children with high levels of self-efficacy will persist with a challenging task. Consequently, they are likely to be rewarded with success and this will, in turn, increase their efficacy still further. The exact opposite applies to those with low self-efficacy – they are less likely to persist, will believe a task to be harder than it is and are, therefore, less likely to be successful. This will then confirm their negative self-belief. If they think they can, they can, and if they think they can't, they are probably right!

In a classroom where levels of efficacy are high, children have aspirations and dreams. This is because the teacher often explains how the learning is relevant to the children's dreams and ambitions and they are encouraged to have goals and to 'go for it'. Their individual goals (both short and longer term) are meaningful, readily understood and achievable. Children are shown (both by example and explanation) how to cope optimistically with setbacks.

Affinity – No man is an island

Relationships within a classroom with high levels of affinity are good. No man is an island – in fact, pupils enjoy working together and helping each other and they know how to be good friends. One of the ways in which to increase the affinity in your classroom is to have home groups and away groups. These work with the same principle as home and away sporting fixtures. Children learn regularly and comfortably in their home groups, in which they know and trust every member. They also learn 'away' with other children in order to increase the challenge for them just as away matches do for sports teams.

Happier classrooms questionnaire: Heart section

The following activities will help you to come up with an action plan for winning the H Factor in your classroom. The key to making changes is to follow these steps:

Think about where your classroom is now.
Identify in which areas you need to improve.
Plan how you will make changes.
Act by setting a timetable for action and making the changes.
Reflect by setting a date to come back and reflect on what you have achieved.

The next pages will help you do this.

Firstly, **think** about where you are now with regard to the levels of happiness in your classroom. You will do this by completing the Happier Classroom Questionnaire, the first section of which is below. Score one point if the statement **never** applies to the members of your class, two points if it **rarely** applies, three points if it **sometimes** applies, four points if it **often** applies and five points if it **always** applies. Then add up your score for each section (you will have a score out of 15) and write it in the total box.

Happier classrooms questionnaire: Heart section

	1	2	3	4	5	Total
Openness – what you see is what you get						
They can share their feelings easily						
They enjoy being with each other						
They are encouraged to express their opinions						
Efficacy – whether you think you can or whether you think you can't, you are probably right						
They are shown how to cope optimistically with setbacks						
They know how their learning has relevance to their dreams						
They have meaningful individual goals						
Affinity – no man is an island						
They appreciate the worth of giving						
They learn how to be a good friend						
They learn how to sustain a network of friends						

Once you have added up your scores, turn to the Winning the H Factor classroom wheel on p. 143 and shade in the Heart area so that you have a visual picture of how you have scored. This visual picture should make it easy for you to **identify** any areas in need of improvement.

You will complete the other two sections of this wheel later.

Now you need to **plan** any improvements you may wish to make. Spend some time considering ways in which you can increase your scores in the Heart section of the wheel. If you need some help with these ideas, there are plenty of suggestions on the following pages. Some of the suggestions detailed can be used in any classroom, no matter what age the pupils or what subject. Some lend themselves better to primary school classrooms or to tutorial time. Others can be adjusted to suit the age group and/or subject you teach.

You will be given an opportunity to set dates for **action** and to **reflect** upon the changes you have made when you have completed all three sections of the questionnaire.

Openness – What you see is what you get

They can share their feelings easily.

Register emotions

While you want your classroom to be a happy place, the children entering it will do so with all sorts of emotions. When you register students, take the opportunity to ask them to answer by telling you how they are feeling. Provide them with a comprehensive list of adjectives and meanings beforehand.

Emotions gauge

An emotions gauge is a visual representation of how pupils may be feeling at any time during a lesson. You could design this using different types of faces (happy, sad, frustrated, excited, etc.) and encourage pupils to stick their name or photo onto it if they feel the need to. Alternatively, you could hang the words on a string and pupils could peg their name to the appropriate word.

Label it

Talk about emotions yourself. Label your own emotions and talk about why you feel the way you do. That way, you will be giving a name to an emotion and modelling a means of handling difficult emotions. Modelling behaviour is important, as children tend to do what we do rather than what we say!

Acknowledge it

Acknowledging your pupils' feelings will help them deal with them and move on. Consider this situation; you give a class back their assessments and 12-year-old John, who hasn't done too well, mutters something under his breath, screws his paper up and throws it on the floor in front of him. Consider the following two responses: 'For goodness sake, John, don't throw things around my classroom. If you'd only tried harder you wouldn't have done so badly' or 'John, I guess you're feeling disappointed at that mark? Let's talk about what can we do to help you do better next time'.

The first response is highly likely to confirm to John that he is rubbish at learning (in fact, he knows that he tried really hard), to make him feel more aggressive and to get him into further trouble in the rest of the lesson. However, by acknowledging the fact that he must be disappointed, you are already making a move to help him. Talking him through what went wrong and how he can improve will make him see where he went wrong and understand that he can do better.

What about this situation? At morning-time tutorial Year 11 Rebecca, who has a poor attendance record and has been known to 'do a runner' from school, stomps into the room, shoves her chair, sits down with her coat on and loudly announces: 'I hate this place. I'm going home at break.' Here are two possible responses:

Response 1: 'Rebecca, I've told you 100 times not to make such a noise when you come into the room. Now, take your coat of like everyone else in this tutor group … And where is your tie, young lady?'

Response 2: 'Hey, Rebecca, did something happen on the bus to make you feel angry? Is there anything I need to know so I can help you?'

Putting yourself in Rebecca's shoes, how would the first response make you feel? Would it not confirm the fact that you hate 'this place'? Would you be inclined to stay in school, or would you disappear from the site as soon as you could?

The second response may not lead to her immediately opening her heart to you, but it is the beginning of negotiations. It is not confrontational and should take the wind out of her sails and help her calm down. At least she may stay in school for the day and do some learning without disrupting other lessons.

Deal with it

Visit http://www.partnershipforchildren.org.uk/resources/activities/activities—feelings.html. This website has a series of ten-minute exercises for dealing with emotions. It is primarily aimed for the use of parents with their own children, but can be easily adapted.

They enjoy being with each other.

Names

To enjoy being with each other, your pupils need first to enjoy being with *you*. Greet them all at the door. Use their names and make eye contact. Getting names wrong is about as de-motivating as a teacher can be. For tips on how to remember names, see p. 111.

Core values

Show your excitement about learning. Remember why you became a teacher. Display your core values as a teacher on your all about me board (see p. 166) so that your pupils can see them too. Remind yourself regularly of why you are doing what you do.

Laughter

Restore your sense of humour. Use laughter to relax everybody and put them in a positive frame of mind for learning. Laughter reduces levels of stress hormones such as cortisol in the body, it distracts us from other worries and, if we all laugh together, it connects us and improves relationships. However, never be tempted to use laughter at someone else's expense.

Model behaviour

Show pupils how to behave towards each other. Model the behaviour you want to see in them. If you shout, your pupils will think that is acceptable behaviour. If you put them down, they will do the same to each other. Be positive about them and about yourself. Say, 'One of the things I like about you is …' or 'You are a really good friend/listener/helper/support' more often and encourage them to say such things to each other.

They are encouraged to express their opinions.

Be present

It is easier to express your opinion when you know that your audience is listening. Model good listening skills. When you are listening stop whatever else you are doing and give 100 per cent attention to the child in front of you. Avoid the nodding dog syndrome! Look them in the eye and acknowledge what is being said. Find ways to recognize children's contributions – make eye contact, smile, use their names, touch their sleeve and paraphrase to show that you have understood. By modelling good listening it will be easier to encourage your pupils to listen properly. You should expect attentive listening from everyone else in the class too and point it out when someone is listening well.

Home then away

Home groups are groups of four or five children who often work together on tasks – they can feel very safe in this group because they get to know each other well and can trust each other. Away groups are made up of different people and can be used for giving and receiving feedback on home group tasks. It is useful also to use away groups when you would like children to pass on what they have learned to someone else or when they need an extra challenge.

Allow children to test their opinions by talking first to a trusted partner, then maybe moving around to other individuals or to the rest of their home group. They can then give feedback to another group or to the whole class, possibly with revised opinions, but definitely more confident to discuss what they have found.

Philosophize

Have a regular philosophy lesson in which you ask pupils questions to get them thinking. Philosophy is about teaching them how to think, not what they should think, so as a teacher you just ask the questions and let the discussion come from them. This is a fantastic opportunity to have child-led learning as there are no right or wrong answers, so you are not the one 'in the know', so to speak. Encourage pupils to continue the discussion with their families when they get home.

'If David Beckham wore a dummy, would you?'
'If you could change places with anyone for one day, who would it be?'
'What makes you laugh?'
'What would you like to be able to do really well?'
'Why are people born?'
'Do you always do what you are told?'
'Should we always tell the truth?'
'Is it OK to eat meat?'
'Can life be fair to everybody?'
'Should charity begin at home?'
'Does money buy happiness?'
'How much money is enough?'
'Is it ever OK to tell a lie?'
'Are people born to be good?'

Social persuasion

Social persuasion is a great way in which to get people to do their best. Involve all members of your class in giving positive feedback and encouragement to each other. Do this by asking them to help judge other pupils' work and achievements. Ask, 'What was great about this piece? What have they done really well? Why do you like it? How can they make it even better? What could be tried differently?' Giving their own opinions and feedback has the added bonus of helping pupils improve their own work.

Efficacy – Whether you think you can or whether you think you can't you are probably right

They are shown how to cope optimistically with setbacks.

Build positive self-efficacy

Efficacy is the level of belief a person has in their ability to complete a specific task. Build it up by using praise which rewards the attributes or qualities you seek more of – for example, persistence reflection or responsibility. Have a persistent person in every home group so that they can model persistent behaviour for the others to copy.

Catching moments

Make sure that every single pupil has a regular opportunity to experience success. However, don't let the success come too easily – they must be challenged. Spot the moments when pupils are successful, point it out and make sure that they register what it feels like. Actually ask them, 'How does it feel to have done that so successfully?' or say, 'You must feel proud that you stuck at that difficult task'.

School for setbacks

Ensure that levels of stress when faced with a challenge are reduced by having a classroom climate in which setbacks are seen as a learning opportunity. Talk about them as such. Say, 'OK, so that's set us back a bit. What skills will we need to use to overcome this? What will we have learnt when we've got over this challenge?'

Go wobbly

Give all children in your class a Weeble (these are wobbly, plastic toys that bounce up when they've been knocked over), with a laminated photo of themselves stuck onto it. If they hit a setback, get stuck with their work or feel that their self-esteem has been knocked they can knock it over and watch it bounce back up again.

Visualize success

Challenge anyone who shows a negative explanatory style. If a pupil is finding it difficult to be persistent, get them to think about how it will feel when they succeed. Get them to imagine being at the end of the task or challenge. Talk them through the feelings they will have, who they will tell what they have achieved, how those people will respond, etc. Talking about what success looks and feels like will help your pupils focus on their goals. Use a timeline. Lay a piece of string on the floor. One or more children stand at one end and their goal is at the other end. Get them to walk along the timeline. Ask them, 'What will it feel like in 20 minutes/a month/on exam results day?' Say, for example, 'Imagine what you are working towards. You come to the school, open your letter, the press may be here and you have got the results you need. Who will you call? What will you say? How will it feel? What will you do?'

Post-a-reminder

Have motivational posters in your classroom and talk about their meaning with your pupils. Put the phrases on a PowerPoint and run it while your class is completing a challenging task. Here are a few to get you started:

It is hard to fail, but it is worse never to have tried to succeed.[162] (Roosevelt)

Everyone I box now is going to be after me, but that's what I want – to be tested to the full.[164] (Khan 2004)

In the middle of a difficulty, lies opportunity. (Einstein)

Failure? I never encountered it ... I just stumbled over a few temporary set backs.[165] (Walters)

To borrow a simile from the football field ... success can only come to the player who 'hits the line hard'.[163] (Roosevelt)

It is a rough road that leads to the heights of greatness.[166] (Seneca)

Tap in

Show them how to **TAP IN** to their ability to move on from setbacks:

1 **T**ake stock (look at the setback, consider what has gone wrong).

2 **A**ccept responsibility (laying the blame on others won't help you move on).

3 **P**lan improvements (think about how you can get over the setback).

4 **I**magine success (visualize how you will feel when you get past it and reach your final goal).

5 **N**egotiate a new path (move forwards again and put the setback in the past).

They know how their learning has relevance to their dreams.

Ambitious display

Have a display of the ambitions of the children in your class. Refer to them with regards to the learning they are doing. Have a wall display of children's aspirations (this is especially effective in primary schools). Refer to it. For example, in a numeracy lesson you could say: 'Fred, you want to be a builder like your dad. Can anyone think why counting in tens could be useful to Fred in this job?'

In a language lesson you could say: 'You want to be a ski instructor don't you Oliver? Listen carefully to this grammar point as we are learning how to give instructions today.' When a group of children have given a confident presentation, you could point out, 'That argument needed great organization, which you'll need if you want to be an accountant, Elizabeth. And, Carly, your clear voice and confidence are that of the actress you intend to be. And what teamwork – you need that in pretty much any job, don't you?'

The facts of life

Talk to your pupils about the facts. Display them if it helps. Here are some to get you started:

The odds of winning £10 in the main lottery are 1:57. At the minimum UK wage an adult would have to work only two hours to earn this.

The odds of winning £100,000 are 1:2,330,636. Here are some professions where you could earn that amount every two years, or less: cabinet minister, air traffic controller, broker, chief executive, doctor, lawyer, financial manager, chartered secretary, prison officer (senior manager), area manager for the fire service, IT strategy professional, advertising manager, marketing manager, mining manager, purchasing manager, police inspector.

The odds of winning the National Lottery jackpot are one in 14 million. That means, if every single person living in Wales bought three or four tickets each, and every ticket was different, only one person would win the jackpot.

They have meaningful individual goals.

Meaningful feedback

The challenge with feedback, of course, is to make it effective! When tutoring a very able pupil, Joanna looked back through the girl's German book and found that the teacher had written at least ten times, 'Remember capital letters on nouns, Hannah'. But Hannah had never remembered. Not once. At their next tutorial, Joanna asked a simple question: 'Hannah, what's a noun?' Hannah looked embarrassed, 'Um, a doing word?' No wonder that Hannah had chosen to ignore what the teacher was telling her to do. What a waste of the teacher's time to write the same thing again and again but to no effect.

Involve pupils in their own target setting. Ensure that they understand their goals. Get them to talk to a partner or their buddy about what they will do to reach their targets. Ensure that your feedback gives your pupils information on how they can improve next time. Avoid just marking and giving a number out of ten. Instead try underlining errors and asking home groups to discuss what went wrong and how to improve.

Marks for effort and achievement are no help for improving outcomes. Say a child gets a four for effort because they put some beautiful pictures on their work, but a one for achievement because they didn't include all of the information that was asked for. What does this tell them? 'You tried hard, but this was still rubbish.' However, change this to, 'Beautiful pictures, you have gone to a lot of trouble. Next time you do this task, aim to make a list of all the information asked for and tick it off when you have included it. You can get the information from a book, the internet or by asking someone else' and the child knows where to go next. Don't mark work for the sake of it or to show that you have looked at the books. Before you write anything, ask yourself whether it will help the child do better next time.

Be honest when you are giving feedback. Pupils should know that a mark or grade is a sign of how they are doing at a particular point in time. It is not an indication of how well they can do in the future. Make sure they understand that with effort they can improve and that their intelligence and abilities can be developed.

Make sure any feedback you give is related to the task and not to the individual. You could, for instance, mention two things that are good about the piece and one thing that could be done to improve it. For example if a child has done an imaginative piece of writing but the spelling is inaccurate, you could say: 'I can see that you have used some really imaginative language, here. Your simile really helps us imagine what the character looks like. Where do you think you could look to get help with spelling the tricky words?'

Goal-setting sheets

Go to http://www.activityvillage.co.uk/goal_setting_for_children.htm for free-to-download goal-setting sheets for younger children.

Go for goals

Teach pupils how to set their own goals. Get them to write down one long-term goal (for example, a profession they wish to join or an exam result they wish to obtain). Next, they should consider at least three steps to set themselves on the way to achieving their goal (for example, they will organize some relevant work experience, revise hard or buy some revision books). The next step is to make these steps even more achievable (they will write a letter to specific companies, organize a revision timetable, ask their teachers' advice on which books to buy). Now encourage them to consider possible setbacks (the company can only offer work experience in school time, they may not feel like revising on occasions, they can't afford the books) and how they could overcome them (speak to the head teacher, do something else and come back to revision later, get some second hand books from another pupil). Once they have written the goal down and considered how they will get there, then they can formulate a timeline and see how they are moving towards their goals.

Map it out

Get pupils to create a goal mind map. Encourage them to consider all the areas of their lives (home, school, friends, sport, hobbies, etc.). They can then use any type of media (drawing, cut-outs, writing, PowerPoint) to depict their goals in each of these areas. As they are doing this, make sure that they know the difference between wants and needs (see p. 163).

Affinity – No man is an island

They appreciate the worth of giving.

Buddy systems

Giving is not just about giving a gift or something tangible. Giving your time and expertise are of very great value. Have a buddy system in your class. Buddies should know that they are there to support each other and to give help if needed. That help can be through supporting each other with learning or in social situations. Buddies are there to keep an eye out for each other and to give each other their time and advice should it be needed. That way, pupils learn that the more you give, the more you get back. It is important that the relationship is mutual, so don't simply put a good reader with a poorer reader, without the poorer reader being able to offer anything in return.

Celebrate together

Celebrate achievements as a class. Encourage pupils to give each other a pat on the back or to shake hands and say, 'well done' when they have done something good. Clap groups and individuals when they do something that they have never done before. Have a class celebration song that you sing when everybody has done well and tried hard. Have 'golden time', which is a time when pupils can choose an activity because they have achieved what they set out to achieve and more. Have a birthday wall. Sing 'Happy Birthday' and think of things to make that child feel special for the day. Give them a card, a birthday badge or a birthday hat. Allow them to take a birthday diary home in which they can record something about their special day.

Charitable giving

Have a charity that your class or tutor group supports. Agree what it will be with them – discuss whether it should be local/topical/big/small, etc., get them to do some research and come up with suggestions. Older children could prepare presentations for their chosen charity and then vote on which one they will support. Discuss ideas for fundraising with them – it need not always be financial, many charities make money from clothes, old foil, stamps, etc. Put the pupils in charge of the decision making. Display a tally of how much support you have provided.

They learn how to be a good friend.

Good friends

Talk about what it is to be a good friend. What does a good friend do or say? What should we avoid doing to be a good friend? What can we do if it goes wrong? How do we deal with having different groups of friends? Many opportunities for this will simply come up in the everyday life of the classroom. If you praise one pupil when you see him doing something for a friend, ('Thanks for helping out there, Jon, you are a good friend') the others will start to emulate that behaviour.

Point it out

Happiness is catching. Good friends know how to be happy. Catch your pupils being happy. Point it out to them. Let them get used to knowing what it feels like. When they achieve something or when something happens that should make them feel happy say, 'Wow, you must feel happy about that'.

Give due credit

Have a 'ray of sunshine' award. Hand it out whenever someone does something kind, or is a good friend. Give pupils 'I am a good friend' stickers when they do something to help someone else out or when they show concern for a friend.

Have a 'good friend of the day/week' badge or award. Award it to the person who has shown that they are a good friend and explain what they have done to win the award.

Yearbooks

Create a yearbook with your class or tutor group. Include comments about why people are good friends.

They learn how to sustain a network of friends.

A bit of magic

Learn to do magic tricks then teach them to your pupils. Alternatively teach them solely to those who may need some extra help to develop their social skills. Imagine the benefit to a child with low self-esteem if he or she can pull a £2 coin from behind someone's ear!

If you don't fancy magic, then try some stand-up comedy or performance poetry.

Ready language

Have some phrases ready to praise pupils at the appropriate moments:

'Wow, Beth, you are a good friend.'
'That was really trustworthy/honest/kind/thoughtful.'
'You always share so well.'
'You always say what you believe.'
'You are very polite/have very good manners.'

Achieving together

HEAD is about ensuring that everyone has an agreed set of values, that they respect each other and that they take pride in their own achievement and in that of others. The class works as a team and shares victories and accomplishments. Defining ourselves purely against others makes us negative and can de-motivate us. How sad that the politician and writer, Gore Vidal, believes: 'Whenever a friend succeeds, a little something in me dies.'[167] In a class with the H Factor, the opposite is true – when a friend succeeds we celebrate with them. Winning the H Factor is about everyone achieving together, it is never the case that a child's sense of worth and status depends on contrast with others. Instead, their friendship and sense of belonging are two keys to their happiness.

> The best way to cheer oneself up is to try to cheer someone else up. (Twain)

> http://quotationsbook.com/quote/6227/ date accessed 15.10.09

Both happiness and unhappiness spread within a social group. This applies to relationships that are three times removed – that is to say to the friends of our friends' friends! Happiness is not only for isolated individuals, but it rubs off on those around us. If we are surrounded by happy people, we are more likely to be happy in the future.

> People's happiness depends on the happiness of others with whom they are connected.[168] (Fowler and Christakis 2008)

The importance of a teacher and of how they value pupils' achievements was illustrated to Joanna recently when she watched a dance festival for local schools. At the end of each performance, the children held their poses and, as the applause clattered around the room, they prepared to take their bows. It was evident from the clapping that they had done well, but in that split second before they would allow a smile to cross their faces, who did most of them look at to see if they had done well? Their teacher. The teacher's approval was what meant most to them at that moment of completing their performance.

Teachers should never fall into the trap of labelling a class (even in their own minds) as unteachable, badly behaved or in any other such negative way.

A teacher who sees a group only in terms of the negative will just get what they were expecting. Equally, negative thinking on the part of the pupils should be corrected. Do not allow talk such as, 'We're rubbish at this' or 'It's just too difficult'.

Empathy

It should be an expectation that is well understood by everyone in the classroom that the opinions of others are valued. It may be acceptable to disagree with them, but others must be listened to. Children in a classroom where there are high levels of empathy are encouraged to put themselves into other people's shoes and, when things go wrong, are able to see things from another perspective in order to help them forgive.

Self-knowledge

In a classroom with the H Factor, children do not compare themselves to each other, and the teacher does not make comparisons either. Knowing our strengths and weaknesses is important but, more important, is knowing how to maximize our strengths and overcome our weaknesses, for example by knowing how to find information or how to get help. If you want the children in your class to have high levels of self-knowledge, it is important to tell the truth when giving feedback. Don't be tempted to tell them that they are clever to boost their self-confidence.

Instead focus on the fact that, with the right amount of effort and support, they will be able to improve and to do their very best.

Integrity

Sometimes it is difficult to tell the truth, but in a classroom with the H Factor children can tell the truth even if it is difficult to do so. Children with integrity know the difference between right and wrong and do the right thing even when there isn't a teacher watching! Having integrity is empowering, as it helps children stand up for what they believe in, even if their peers may be putting pressure on them to do otherwise.

Happier classrooms questionnaire: Head section

Complete the following section of the classroom questionnaire and score as with the previous section:

1 = This statement **never** applies to the members of my class.
2 = This statement **rarely** applies to the members of my class.
3 = This statement **sometimes** applies to the members of my class.
4 = This statement **often** applies to the members of my class.
5 = This statement **always** applies to the members of my class.

	1	2	3	4	5	Total
Empathy – put yourself in others' shoes						
They learn to value each other's opinion						
They listen to each other with sensitivity						
They show a willingness to forgive						
Self-knowledge – if it's to be, it's up to me						
They minimize unhelpful comparisons with others						
They know their strengths and weaknesses						
They know the difference between right and wrong						
Integrity – to yourself be true						
They tell the truth even when it is difficult to do so						
They have an emerging set of values						
They know the difference between right and wrong						

Write your totals in the appropriate boxes, turn to the Winning the H Factor classrooms wheel on p. 143 and shade in the Head section of the wheel.

As you did previously, once you have identified the areas in which you would like to make improvements, start to think about how you can do this. There are suggestions below should you need some more ideas.

Empathy – Put yourself in others' shoes

They learn to value each others' opinions.

Thinking hats

Edward De Bono's *Six Thinking Hats* provide a good, easy to understand tool for students to see a problem from different starting points. Six distinct starting points are identified and represented by different coloured 'hats':

- white hat – neutral fact-based thinking
- red hat – emotional and instinctive responses
- black hat – critical appraisal of the question or issue
- yellow hat – benefits to the approach or issue
- green hat – provocative and creative thinking
- blue hat – thinking about processes used and thinking applied.

By organizing a challenge around teams who adopt one or more hats it is possible to work though to a quality learning outcome. This is also a good method for staff problem solving. Let's say on difficult issues such as changes to the length of lessons, modifications to the curriculum offered, the adoption of new qualifications or the abandonment of tests!

They listen to each other with sensitivity.

Children's parliament

Organize a children's parliament or take part in an existing one such as the Scottish 'wee democracy' at http://www.childrensparliament.org.uk/. By introducing debating protocols such as party divisions, prepared position speeches, turn taking, responding to submitted questions, speaker of the house and voting we encourage children to listen constructively.

Pay per question

Create vouchers with nominal values. It could be in Euros or Sterling or an imaginary currency such as the 'query'. The idea is that students have a budget from which they purchase the right to ask questions. This can be organized as an auction or as a straight transaction. It could be linked to the type of question asked with higher-order questions costing more or it could be a simple payment per question. For example, asking questions of an 'expert' in role:

- a creative application of the information (*30* querys)
- an opinion about the worth of something (*25* querys)
- a synthesis of things that we should know (*20* querys)
- a comparison that helps us understand (*10* querys)
- a fact relating to the topic (*5* querys)
- a basic item of information (*1* query).

For younger children, give a small budget in real denominations and ask them to think carefully before spending any money on questions. Spend your question money wisely!

Active listening

Insist on active listening – sitting up straight, looking at the speaker, making eye contact, repeating and paraphrasing.

They show a willingness to forgive.

Exercise control

Give your pupils control over their reactions by talking them through how they are feeling and why. Teach them that they alone are responsible for how they act and feel; no-one else can MAKE them feel a certain way, if they have control.

Multiple perspectives

Multiple perspectives are similar to Edward De Bono' *Six Thinking Hats,* but use characters (either fictional or real) to address a problem. It can help children understand different perspectives and why individuals may choose to argue from a selfless or selfish point of view. If we are examining a hot debating point such as 'should all bullies be permanently excluded from school?' it may be insightful to have to argue the case from the point of view of characters who could be fictional or real, contemporary or historical. For example:

- fictional – Spiderman, Homer Simpson, Buzz Lightyear, Shrek, Luke Skywalker, the Tin Man
- real – the prime minister, Simon Cowell, Sir Alan Sugar, Jeremy Clarkson, Oprah Winfrey
- historical – Henry VIII, Martin Luther King, Oliver Cromwell, Jesus, Helen Keller, Queen Elizabeth I

Self-knowledge – If it's to be it's up to me

They minimize unhelpful comparisons with others.

Invidious comparisons

As a teacher, don't make comparisons between pupils. Banish comments similar to those below from your vocabulary:

'Look, it's not rocket science, even Set 3 got it. Why can't you?'

'Fred, can't you be quiet and get on with it like Jane over there?'

'Year 8s! You are the noisiest class I have ever taught.'

Instead try:

'It seems that I haven't explained this concept very well. Can anyone think of a better way we could learn this?'

'Fred, you've got a lot of energy for this task today. Shall we just take a second to think about it quietly?'

'Year 8, I just love the energy and enthusiasm you bring to everything. Right now, we need to show some really good listening skills, so to prepare let's all sit up straight, look at me, take three really deep breaths – in through the nose and out through the mouth. That's great, now keep looking at me while I explain what we have to do ...'

They know their strengths and weaknesses.

Malleable intelligence

On p. 47, we talked of a researcher called Carole Dweck who found that there are two views of intelligence – fixed and malleable. Children who see intelligence as something fixed are unlikely to take on a challenge in case they fail and look stupid. To avoid this, and to encourage the view that we can improve our intelligence by rising to a challenge and by trying hard, she suggests the following:

- **Don't** praise for ridiculously easy tasks. Doing so indicates to pupils that they aren't capable of doing something more challenging.
- **Do** make sure all tasks involve an element of challenge for all children.
- **Don't** tell children that they are clever. This will make them value looking clever (or not looking stupid) rather than value learning.
- **Do** praise the effort and the way in which a child has got to the end of a task.
- **Don't** lie to children and tell them they are clever so that they don't feel bad about themselves.
- **Do** tell them where they are at now and what they have to do to improve.
- **Don't** value a perfect outcome easily reached.
- **Do** apologize to the child for giving them something that didn't challenge them enough and promise to find something more challenging next time.

Learning wall

Have a learning wall in each lesson. Children can stick post-it notes on it to show what they know and what they need to find out. At the end of the lesson, they can add what they have learnt and talk about where they can find out more.

They know the difference between wants and needs.

Wants and needs activity

For older students organize the class so that they each have the checklist given below. Instruct them to interview one other person and to ring the items that the person says are needs and tick the items that the person says are wants. They should leave any others blank.

> 20 Malboro Lights, a Bacardi Breezer, a bed, books, a car, clean water, clothes, a Ferrari, a flat-screen television, food, good exam results, a Gucci handbag, a gun, good health, a house, an iPod, a job, a kidney, a knife, some lipstick, a loving partner, a mirror, a mobile phone, money, a pair of Oakley sunglasses, a packet of condoms, shampoo, shoes, a skateboard, soap, a swimming pool, transport, trusting friends, vaccinations, a washing machine, wireless broadband, a Wii console.

For younger students you can amend the list. A variation is to put some students in role and others have to guess who is in which role. The roles could be:

- a kidney failure victim
- a child in Darfur
- a spoilt teenager

- an online gaming addict
- a catwalk model
- a shipwreck survivor
- a university student

The activity stimulates lots and lots of discussion!

Integrity – To yourself be true

They tell the truth even when it is difficult to do so.

Consistency's the key

Make sure that everything you do and say is consistent with your values as a person and as a teacher. Remember why you are in the profession and what you want to do for all the children you teach. Make a list that starts with, 'I believe that …' and keep it where you can refer to it. At the end of the day, consider all that you have done and said and see if this ties in with your beliefs. If not, what can you do to change your behaviour? Or do you need to adjust your beliefs?

What makes us happy?

Alistair has devised a range of well-being activities and resources for L2, his Learning to Learn approach. One activity is called 'What makes us happy?'

He has a series of illustrated swap cards which are A5 size. Each card has a statement about something that could make an individual happy. There is an illustration and a coloured border. The border is colour coded and represents a category of experience. Students are given five cards and they have five swaps to get the selection of experiences which would make them most happy. Later, and as a group, they share their cards to find any similarities and differences. They also discuss what the categories might be. Here is what is pictorially represented on the cards. (The headings are not on the cards.)

Yourself (yellow)

- being on my own
- reading
- walking
- thinking quietly
- daydreaming

Others (orange)

- being with friends
- doing something with my family
- seeing a relative
- hanging out with my mates
- going on holiday

Growth (green)

- making someone smile
- giving someone a present
- being in church
- making someone else happy
- helping out at home

Needs (purple)

- being warm in bed
- eating ice-cream
- hearing the rain outside
- laughing at a joke
- being given a cuddle

Possessions (blue)

- dressing up
- playing on my computer
- playing with a pet
- being on my bike
- texting

Activity (red)

- going on a ride
- doing a sport
- learning something new

- doing a hobby
- watching a film on television

Students are captivated by this activity. What it teaches them is not so much about happiness but about 'otherness'.

Give a little bit

Give something of yourself. Start sentences with things like: 'You'll never guess what happened to me in the car park when I got to school this morning ...' or 'When my wife and I were walking to town at the weekend ...'

Have an 'all about me' board that has photos of yourself, your hobbies, your likes and dislikes, etc.

They have an emerging set of values.

The friends test

Put these simple criteria onto a card and then ask your students to quietly and in confidence list five people who they may call friends, ideally not people in the class. Now for each 'friend' apply the test by giving a mark out of five for each of the questions below (with five being the top score and one the bottom score).

1 **Shared background**

   Do you have a lot in common?

2 **Duration**

   Have you known each other a long time?

3 **Disclosure**

   Are you able to confidently share secrets?

4 **Adversity**

   Have you faced and overcome a difficulty together?

5 **Trust**

   Could you trust this person to look after a valued personal possession?

6 **Others**

   In your absence, would this person speak positively about you to others?

7 **Forgoing**

   Would this person give up something of true worth to them on your behalf?

The outcomes are treated with confidence but the criteria can be discussed openly. It helps students understand that relationships are secured by more than vested interest.

They know the difference between right and wrong.

Problem page

Working in groups, students are given 'problem page' scenarios based on an appreciation of typical everyday challenges. The teacher loads the problems so that there is an element of right and wrong to each without it being a simple 'yes' or 'no'. They can be genuine moral dilemmas.

The students have to generate solutions to each problem and then, in turn, present those solutions back to the other groups.

Safe to succeed

HEALTH in the classroom is about making sure that everyone is at their peak for learning, both physically and emotionally. Negative emotions make us defensive, critical and unlikely to take risks. Positive emotions make us think more creatively. They also make us more productive and inclined to learn faster.

Security

In a classroom, feeling secure is about knowing exactly what is required of you and being comfortable to ask if you are unsure. It is about not having to second-guess what you should be doing and being humiliated if you inadvertently do something wrong. Pupils will have this security when any explanations are clearly expressed and when they are followed up by, for example, asking them to clarify within their home groups how they will go about a task. Security also comes from having clear rules and boundaries for behaviour and can be added to by giving pupils control over what they are doing and ensuring that they have a say in how they are learning and what they are doing.

Well-being

As a teacher, look after yourself and you will spread your well-being to those you teach. Positivity and enthusiasm for learning are spread initially from the teacher and then around every member of the class. They are contagious! A class in which the well-being of the pupils is held in high regard will be full of children who have fun when they are learning and who regularly achieve FLOW (which may not necessarily be quiet, in fact it will often be noisy!).

Cooperation

When the whole class is working together towards the same goal the individuals within that class will learn more than if they are left to their own devices. Explaining what you have learnt to others impacts positively upon your own learning. In a class of pupils who are able to cooperate, no-one shies away from a challenge. To sail through a lesson without challenge will not bring FLOW, nor will it improve self-esteem. Make sure that the members of your class are regularly brought to the edge of their comfort zones, while giving them opportunity to speak up if they are unsure or need help.

Happier classrooms questionnaire: Health section

Below is the third and final section of the classroom questionnaire. Complete this and score as with the previous section:

1 = This statement **never** applies to the members of my class.
2 = This statement **rarely** applies to the members of my class.
3 = This statement **sometimes** applies to the members of my class.
4 = This statement **often** applies to the members of my class.
5 = This statement **always** applies to the members of my class.

Write your totals in the appropriate boxes, turn to the Winning the H Factor classrooms wheel on p. 143 and shade in the Health section.

As you did in the previous two sections, identify the areas in which you would like to make improvements and start to think about how you can go about this. There are suggestions below should you need some more ideas.

Security – The wind beneath my wings

They feel a strong sense of belonging.

	1	2	3	4	5	Total
Security – the wind beneath my wings						
They feel a strong sense of belonging						
They feel secure						
They have a say in what they do						
Well-being – I'm OK, you're OK						
They are encouraged to have a wide variety of interests						
They understand the importance of a healthy lifestyle						
They have fun						
Cooperation – together everyone achieves more						
They learn to appreciate and say 'thank you'						
They enjoy a challenge						
They look after someone or something						

Feeling opinionated

Seek the opinions of your class members on how your class operates and on how they will learn. You can do this during lessons and you could also have a suggestions box by the door so that they can make comments privately as well.

Give them a choice in how they will present their findings – will they write a report, do a role play, make a PowerPoint presentation or pretend to be television presenters, for example?

They feel secure.

Positive spin

When visiting a school recently, we were surprised to see the posters in some classrooms. There was obviously an attempt being made to be positive in a fairly challenging environment. One poster read: 'We are kind to each other … no spitting at other people.' A second said: 'We respect other people's opinions … do not tell other people to "shut up".' All these posters serve to do is to draw attention to the undesirable behaviour, instead of towards the behaviour that we do want. They are possibly an invitation to some children who perhaps hadn't thought of spitting or telling someone to shut up to do just that. What they don't do is show children how to be kind to others and how to listen to others' opinions.

Think about the way you talk. Do you use positive language? Avoid negative statements. Try 'walk', instead of 'don't run', for example. Point out the things children are doing well and the effort they are putting into their work. Talk of challenges and solutions not problems. Concentrate on 'can' not 'can't'. Use 'when', not 'if'. For example, 'When you have succeeded in this task, you will ...'. Insist that your pupils do the same.

No put-down zone

Never, ever put a child down. Never humiliate them or make them feel small. Value everything about them. At the entrance to your classroom have a sign that says 'You are entering a no put-down zone' at your learners' eye-level. Deal with put-downs quickly and with no fuss by simply saying, 'No put-downs, thank you'. Everyone understands the rule and everyone is expected to follow it.

Understood?

Give children an opportunity to check their understanding. Explain that if they haven't all understood it is because you have not explained it clearly (i.e. it is your problem, not theirs). If you say, 'Hands up if you don't understand' chances are several pupils will think this means 'Hands up if you are stupid' and will never admit to not understanding. Instead, allow pupils two minutes to explain a task to their neighbour before starting it so that they are sure they have understood it. Alternatively, you could have three pieces of coloured card on each desk – green means 'Go on, I understand', yellow is 'I think I'm OK, but I'd like some clarification' and red means 'Stop, I need help here'. If your pupils use whiteboards, you can ask them just to mark a scale of one to five for how confident they feel to carry on and get them to hold it up, or to place it on the side of their desks for you to check as you move around the room.

Worry box

Have a worry box by the door. Ask children to write it down if they have any worries and put them into the box, where they will leave them for the rest of the lesson or day. That way, they can forget about their worries and concentrate on learning.

Out and about

When you are not teaching, maintain a high profile. Greet your pupils when you meet them in the corridors, in the lunch queue or in the playground. Talking to them outside a classroom setting will help you get to know them. Show that you care about them as well as their education. Remember things they have told you that are important to them – ask after their rabbit that was sick, or how their swimming test went, for example.

They have a say in what they do.

If you don't ask …

If you don't ask their opinion, then your pupils can never have a say in what they do and how they do it. Discuss with them what went well with a lesson, what they liked, what they would like to do more or less of and how they like to learn best.

Let them lead

Go with spontaneous child initiated learning opportunities when they come up – this shows that you respect their input. It may take imagination to fit it into the curriculum but it can be done.

Well-being – I'm OK, you're OK

They are encouraged to have a variety of interests.

Go clubbing

Make sure that every child in your class or tutor group does at least one after school club. Talk to them about their hobbies and interests. Get them to talk to each other about what they are interested in, what they like about it and about what they would like to do in the future.

Things to do

Look into local activities and suggest them to members of your class. Imagine the impression it would make on someone's self-esteem to be told: 'Mark, you ask really good questions, and your writing style is so clear. I've heard of this great youth magazine. You should see if you could get involved.'

Interesting you

Have a wide variety of interests yourself. Talk about books you have read, music you have heard and films you have seen, bring in anything you collect (or collected as a child) or tell them about the tennis or football match you played. Add to your 'All about me' board (see p. 166) regularly.

They understand the importance of a healthy lifestyle.

Apple for the teacher

Look after yourself and your own health and well-being. You will teach best when you look after yourself well. Work through Chapter 3 of this book if you haven't done so already. Set a good example. Include things about your healthy lifestyle on your 'All about me' board (see p. 166).

Teach to relax

Use simple meditation techniques to help children be calm and form the right mindset for learning. Whilst some people believe meditation has religious connotations, it does not and is about relaxation and improving memory.[169] It has also been found to improve self-esteem and behaviour.[170]

Wake and shake

Have a 'wake and shake' time to music if your class has been sitting down for a while or if your pupils come to you feeling lethargic. This can be equally effective for older children as it is for primary children. Get the blood pumping around their bodies and get them ready to be creative and responsive.

Fluid intake

Encourage members of your class to always have water to hand and to drink some regularly.

They have fun.

Make it worth their while

Start every lesson with something that will bring the children running in from the playground. Grab their attention from the outset. (Hint – this will not be achieved by asking them to sit silently to copy the learning objectives from the board. You can go over these later.)

Make a connection

Have a selection of connecting activities that will bring children racing to your lessons. Think about how you can adapt childhood games or quiz programmes to your subject. For example, What's the time Mr Wolf?, Chinese whispers, zip and bong, Blockbusters, Mastermind, etc. Go to websites like www.funny–videos.co.uk and type in key words to find something relevant to your subject or the learning outcomes and show a short video clip to grab attention. Wrap up an artefact or something relevant to your lesson and get pupils to guess what it is and why you have it. Start them thinking about what they are going to be learning in the opening moments of your lesson.

Go green

Get outside! Use different learning environments. One school we work with asked their pupils where they feel that they learn most – the classroom came way down the list. Studies in Scandinavia have found that playing in nature improves children's social play and concentration.[171] One American study has found that children with ADHD can function better than usual when taking part in activities in green settings. The study also found that the positive effect lasted for activities that took place after the children had been in the green setting.[172]

Learning versus engagement

Use a learning versus engagement matrix to analyse the activities you do regularly with your class. Are there any activities (such as worksheets) that would be better off in the cylindrical filing cabinet?

You're having a laugh!

Restore your sense of humour.

Cooperation – Together everyone achieves more

They learn to appreciate and say 'thank you'.

A simple thank you

Say 'thank you' and 'well done' more often. Expect your pupils to do the same to you and each other – point out to them times when they could thank someone. When a child offers you thanks, recognize it and say: 'I'm so glad that you enjoyed yourself/ that helped you. Thanks for letting me know. I shall do more of that from now on.'

Happy list

Have a list in your classroom of the things that have happened today that have made you or someone else happy. Encourage pupils to add to it if appropriate. Pick some out at the end of the day and share them with pupils.

They enjoy a challenge.

'We want him to feel that he can achieve anything.' (Parent of a Year 7 pupil)

Comfort zones

Every lesson should contain a challenge for every pupil. Bring them to the edge of their comfort zones. If they are not used to this, explain to them that it is what you are going to be doing from this point on. To get them to understand the concept of the comfort zone, put them into pairs (ideally with someone they don't know too well) and ask them to stand on either side of the classroom facing each other. Get one person to gradually walk towards the other, until one or other of them doesn't feel comfortable about being any nearer. That is the edge of their comfort zone, and that is where you will be bringing them when they are learning.

Teach about intelligence

Whatever a child's IQ, one day he or she will come across something that will challenge thinking. The child that copes with this challenge will be one who views their intelligence as malleable and as something that can be improved with effort, not one who has never been challenged before. Discourage children from having a fixed view of their intelligence (see pp. 47 and 162 for further information and tips).

Challenging behaviour!

Talk about challenges with enthusiasm: 'Today, I've got a challenge for you guys! We're really going to get those brain cogs whirring. It won't be easy, but you're going to love it! Now, are you ready?'

Solve those problems

Encourage your pupils to think of solutions to problems themselves before they come to you for help. Talk about how to problem solve, who to ask for ideas and where to look for help. Tell them: 'When you come to me with a problem, I want you to be able to talk me through one possible solution you have thought of yourself or with your partner/home group.' To start with, you may need to come up with some solutions with them (but not *for* them).

They look after something or someone.

Adopt someone

Look after someone. For example, as a class adopt an elderly person locally. Come up with a plan and rota for helping with their shopping, gardening, dog walking, etc. Alternatively, adopt a school or class in the third world. Organize a means of communicating with them – through letters, visits and (maybe after a while) through the internet. Fundraise for the school, talk to them about their learning and way of life.

Furry life

Look after something as a class. Have a class pet of some kind and give children responsibility for its care. Giving some aspect of care to the animal could be used as a reward for showing caring behaviour. Having a class pet will also encourage the children to behave in ways that are good for the animal (for example, to talk quietly, be calm, handle it gently, etc.) and will teach them about hygiene. Obviously, you will need to take into account the requirements of the animal, the age of your pupils and your own circumstances so that the animal is properly cared for.

Build, broaden and balance activity

- Complete the questionnaire and fill in the wheel.
- Review the wheel for any obvious gaps and imbalances.
- Create an action plan to build, broaden and balance.
- Use your action plan.
- Look at the BBB strategies and note those which you have used or could use.
- Reflect on what works and set a date to repeat the questionnaire.

5

Happier schools

In this section we focus on the following topics:

> **Leadership and happier schools**
>
> **Identifying the benefits of thinking in terms of happier schools**
>
> **Ways of influencing school culture and shaping core purpose**
>
> **Methods for building even more positive relationships**
>
> **Working to an agreed set of values**
>
> **Supporting each other through strong affiliation networks**

And answer the following questions:

> *What does leadership of a happy school look and feel like?*
>
> *Are there bottom line benefits associated with happy schools?*
>
> *Is it possible to shift a school's culture by focusing on core purpose?*
>
> *How is it possible to be brutally honest and build positive relationships at the same time?*
>
> *Is it ever possible to agree a set of values and work to them?*
>
> *What are the do's and don'ts regarding staff groups?*

- Leading the happy school
- The benefits of a happy school
- Culture and purpose
- Thriving together
- Making the worthwhile difference
- Looking out for each other

Leading the happy school

Park Lane High School has a school brochure which says it loud and says it proud. Written across the front of the school prospectus is the school mission, which is: 'Creating success through happiness'. This is accompanied by the phrase, 'A happy student is a Park Lane student'. The school is on the up. It is one of the top 20 most improved schools in the country.

As part of a thinly veiled attempt to smoke out similar schools that considered themselves to be positive and happy places, Alistair, through his company Alite, ran a national competition to find the country's happiest school. The entries were not large in number, which said something about the perception of the worth of promoting oneself as 'happy', and those who did respond were usually coy and wrote in the third person. One could argue that the response was a perfect barometer of our willingness to be positive about our achievements. In an irony for Alistair there were no entries from Scotland!

The winning school, a secondary in Stevenage, was remarkable in the consistency of the messages given when Alistair went to interview a cross-section of pupils, staff and support workers. The school was not chosen because of its published reports, academic successes or a presence on the conference circuit. It is not held up as an exemplar. It was chosen because there was a clear sense of community. Students were tenacious in their defence of the school and indeed in their championing of any minority or disadvantaged groups. They knew right and wrong and were proud to be part of their school community. It was clear that the school – which had recently absorbed 50 per cent of its students from another school following an amalgamation – was on a journey. Not everything it needed for that journey was in place but there were some early indicators of why people were so positive. These were:

- visible leadership
- open communication
- focus on children
- community cohesion – sustained by active involvement of parents and helpers
- attention to 'hygiene' factors such as good accommodation, good food and safe spaces in which to work and learn
- lots of charitable giving
- informal social activities for staff

You can watch the video of the school at http://www.alite.co.uk/events/winningthehfactor.html.

In a study of state schools in Chicago[173] it was found that schools that perform best academically also have a high score for what the authors of the study called 'relational trust'. By relational trust, they mean the relationships and dynamics between all stakeholders in the school (teachers, non-teaching staff, the leadership team, pupils, parents, governors and the community). These relationships are built, say the study's authors, through the daily exchanges within a school's community and they help everyone to work together to make improvements. If relationships are good and levels of trust are high, then people are more likely to work together, to be creative and to take risks in the name of improving learning outcomes.

Trust and good relationships alone will not, however, improve learning outcomes – it is essential that these are combined with high standards of teaching.

So, as a school leader, how do you build this trust and ensure that relationships are good? Well, you have already begun by asking the opinions of others. You have shown respect for everyone's opinion and have given everyone a voice. Through these conversations, you have also made your high expectations clear and you and your leadership team model the behaviour you want to see. By having the difficult conversations, you are ensuring that incompetence or lack of motivation are not allowed to persist – should you allow them to, trust within your school will decrease.

To build relationships, make communication with your staff direct. Emails can be so readily misinterpreted. Talk to faces instead. Cut out the middle man and don't pass information through a third party. On 23 September 1999, the Mars Climate Orbiter was heading towards its goal. It had cost NASA $125 million, and some of the world's best minds had been working on it. Two teams had been involved in the project and they were excitedly watching the progress of the probe as it was heading closer to Mars. It had been travelling for about 9 months when it began to look like something was terribly wrong. It had got too close to the red planet's atmosphere. Eventually, contact was lost and the assumption was made that it had burnt up in Mars' atmosphere. What had gone wrong? The mission failed because of lack of communication – all those amazing brains, but no-one had communicated about measurements. Consequently, one team had used pounds, inches and feet and the other had used metric measurements! No wonder the probe missed its target.

Some further tips for improving and maintaining relationships and communication in your school are outlined below:

- Foster relationships with parents – some of them may have had negative school experiences themselves. Be aware of their fears. Make any visits they need to make to the school as pleasant as possible – offer drinks and snacks if appropriate. Make sure that any paperwork sent home is easy to read and not in teacher-speak. If it helps, have a parent who is prepared to read through it in advance of it being sent.

- Think very carefully before investing in any virtual learning environment for your school. Ask key questions such as how will it enhance learning? Is its operation consistent with what we say about learning and about feedback? What is its primary purpose? How will it make access to data easier for all, including students and parents?

- Run a 'learning for parents' programme, or have a parents' forum that meets once each half term. Alistair has authored an online parent learning programme called PAL (Parents as Learners) which contains ten essential communications – for example, help your child be safe, help your child with reading, help your child with maths – in the 11 most widely used languages in UK schools. See www.alite.co.uk/pal for more information.

- Time can be a barrier to communication. Make more time by cutting out excess paperwork and only doing the things that are in line with your core purpose. Don't ask people to do things that won't improve learning. Free up time for your staff by asking them what stops them from doing their jobs properly and acting accordingly.

- Information helps us improve relationships. Consider how broad your knowledge is of your colleagues – do you see them as individuals or as part of a crowd? In order to get to know them you will need to listen properly when you talk to them and to ask the right type of question to draw out information.

- Align your aims so that everyone is working towards the same goals.

- Resolve conflicts early. Trying to avoid confrontation will only allow feelings to fester and resentment to build.

- Give feedback that refers to a task or job, rather than to someone's personality.

Author, Brian Tracy, suggests that you imagine that once a day you had to swallow a plump, greeny-brown frog. There is no getting out of it; you have to do it. When would you do it? The chances are that you would do it first thing in the morning and get it over and done with. Then you could get on with the rest of the day without having to think about it again. Do the same with difficult conversations. Swallow the frog, and have them.

Managing the happy school is all about managing relationships. Speak to any difficult staff. Deal with them. Do not allow them to poison the culture you and others are working so hard for. Just as parents so often tell their children on the first morning of the school holidays, 'Do your project now, then you can enjoy the rest of the break without it playing on your mind', do the thing that makes you feel uncomfortable now and don't put it off.

Once you have spoken to those that are finding it hard to come into line you will need to find something to motivate them. Find them a role to bring them on board, give them a project or some extra responsibility, or ask them to bring you their solutions to a particular challenge that the school is facing. If this fails to work and the core purpose of your school is to give children the best possible education, then it is essential that a head teacher is prepared to go down the line of competency proceedings if a member of staff is not prepared to come on board.

On one occasion, Sir John had to have a difficult conversation with a maths teacher who was two years from retirement. The teacher had been moaning about the school management, the pupils, the workload and anything else that came to mind. He was dragging down other members of staff and letting down his pupils. After Sir John had encouraged him to speak for a while about his concerns, he asked him to imagine his final day at school and the moment when his head of department would give his leaving speech. Sir John left him with two simple questions to mull over: 'What is your head of department going to say?' and 'What do you want her to say?'

When faced with considering the sort of footprint he would leave behind, the maths teacher began to reshape his thinking. None of us want to be thought of badly by others. We would all prefer that people have something positive to say about us. Sir John followed up the conversation by giving the teacher responsibility for a group of Year 10 boys who were at risk of not achieving their full potential. By the time the boys left at the end of Year 11, the maths teacher had a new lease of life for his job and was even referring to them as 'my boys'.

The Shackleton model of leadership

Ernest Shackleton was a pre-First World War polar explorer famous for surviving the loss of his ship in the Antarctic. After months of camping on an ice cap, he was forced to abandon some of his crew and to row with five others for 16 days in an open boat and across some of the worst seas in the world. On landing, they spent three days walking mountainous terrain to reach a whaling station, from where Shackleton organized the rescue of his men.

Despite terrible odds, every member of his crew survived, and Shackleton's name has become synonymous with good leadership. How did he manage to secure the safety of his men and to find this place in history, despite the fact that his initial mission failed?

- Shackleton was able to reassess his goals – when getting to the Antarctic looked impossible, he focused on survival. He showed flexibility when he needed it and was capable of double loop thinking.
- Even in the hardest times, Shackleton maintained his optimism and belief that they would survive.
- He treated everyone as equal, whatever their role. Officers received the same treatment as all of the men. In the final days of the journey, Shackleton gave his mittens to the photographer who had lost his on the boat and suffered frostbite himself as a result.
- At all times, he led by example and modelled the behaviour he expected to see from his men. When they abandoned ship, leaving all non-essential items behind, he tore two pages out of his bible to keep and threw the remainder into snow.
- Shackleton had values and beliefs that he stuck to. He was a man of integrity. When things began to go wrong, he could have pushed on towards the pole and his men would, most probably, have died. However, he put saving them first.
- Prior to the expedition, Shackleton selected a team that he felt would be most able to cope with the challenges ahead. He did not make his selection solely on the basis of technical ability, but he also made sure that the members of his team were optimistic individuals.
- He made it his business to know his team well. He noticed, for example, that one more pessimistic member responded to flattery and to being included in team meetings. When he responded to this it stopped the spread of negativity.
- When they were stuck on the ice, Shackleton gave his men other interests – at particularly negative times, he got them to play cards or started a game of football.

The benefits of a happy school

In 2006 at the beginning of April, the *Times Educational Supplement* reported on a school in Surrey that had introduced well-being targets for staff as part of its appraisal system. The head teacher explained that she had very high expectations for the performance of staff and that she wanted to make their lives easier so that they could deliver outstanding lessons all day, every day. Members of staff were asked what got in the way of them preparing, delivering and evaluating high-quality learning experiences for students. Many of their responses were related to the challenges of time management and of achieving a work-life balance. Teachers said that the thing that

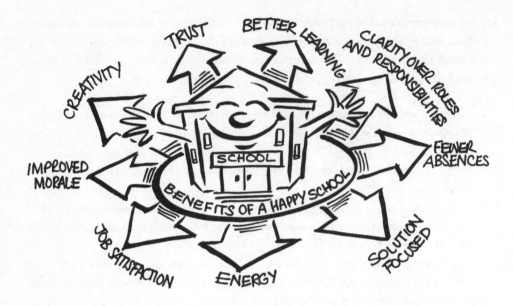

most got in the way was life itself! For many this meant time taken up by ironing, washing and feeding, taxiing, counselling and motivating others; family life is full on!

After some careful deliberation, and taking the view that schools such as theirs had purchasing power and so could be positioned to help ease some of the staff's burdens, they began to introduce some more radical solutions than tea and sympathy.

They introduced an ironing service, a dry-cleaning service, on-site car servicing and MOT, delivery of organic vegetables, shiatsu massage, corporate health club membership, free staffroom drinks and free social events each term. In addition, they held an early morning staff choir practice and banished unnecessary paperwork and meetings. The newspaper article prompted an immediate response from more than 30 teachers from across the country claiming to have read the article and spotted the 'deliberate April Fools' Day joke'!

However, this was no joke – the school did, and still does, offer staff all kinds of services to make their lives easier and more enjoyable. Combined with this are exceedingly high expectations of staff and their teaching. Because of the services, teachers have the time to prepare outstanding lessons and because of the emphasis on their well-being and work-life balance, they maintain the positive state of mind needed to deliver these outstanding lessons.

Practically, having the H Factor in your school will help you do the following:

Reduce absence

88 per cent of parents see full and stable staffing levels as essential for their ideal school. A further 10 per cent view this as desirable.[174]

If your school is happy and productive, then staff and pupils alike will want to be there. If lessons are interesting and suitably challenging, pupils will enjoy attending them and their behaviour will be good. Because of your culture of high expectations, teachers will be teaching and learners will be learning.

Just like happiness, absence is catching! A study[175] has found that a worker takes an extra day of absence for sickness if their average co-worker takes 12 more days (in primary schools) or eight more days (in secondary schools) off per quarter than them. If people see a co-worker take time off, they will be inclined to follow suit.

In England in 2007 there were, on average, 5.4 days sickness absence per teacher that worked in the maintained sector.[176] That was a small increase on the previous year and amounted to around 2.5 million days of lost teaching in English schools. In 2000, the *Times Educational Supplement* reported that, were every absent teacher replaced by a supply teacher (rather than covering their lessons internally), then the cost to schools would be £300 million.

Of course, the cost of teacher absence is not just monetary. Pupils have to cope with a lesson that will either be taught by a supply teacher or by a cover teacher. With the best will in the world, the learning outcomes are unlikely to be as good as with their own teacher who knows the syllabus and the children. And covering the lessons puts additional pressure on other members of staff who could otherwise be concentrating on preparing their own fantastic lessons or on giving productive feedback to pupils.

Short but regular absence has been found to be more problematic than long-term sick leave for school managers to deal with[177] as they often come unannounced and are difficult to plan for. If we seriously look after the well-being of staff, then they are less likely to feel the need to take an odd day off for 'recuperation' in times of stress. Studies[178] have found that, to prevent absence, school managers should worry about the health and well-being of their staff. However, this culture of caring for welfare is best combined with a directive leadership approach that is not tolerant of people who create more work for their colleagues by taking time off work.[179] If a school management team expects a lot from its staff in terms of commitment to learning and teaching, then it also owes it to them to also be concerned about their well-being, general health and work-life balance.

> I always want to go to school because if I don't I'll miss something exciting. (Dwayne, Year 8)

Increase participation

> We want Thomas to be happy at school. If he is happy, everything else will fall into place. (A parent's aspirations for her son in Reception)

How do we learn if we are not engaged? In a happy school, everyone will be keen to participate both within and beyond their own roles. Children will participate in lessons, will take responsibility for their own learning and will know that their voices count, so they are more likely to want to participate in the larger decisions about the school community itself. Staff will participate by always planning stimulating lessons in which learning is the focus, they will participate in staff meetings and in staff training and they will help make the difficult decisions. With everyone involved and working towards the same core purpose, the only way is up!

Improve performance

With everyone present and with everyone participating, then the performance of individuals and of the school as a whole can only improve.

Happy people work harder and learn more effectively. When levels of well-being improve the more easily measurable things such as exam results, attendance, behaviour and value added will also improve.

Schools that are both performing to a high standard and that look after their staff and pupils are likely to have fewer problems with recruitment. The H Factor can help you recruit and retain good, committed staff. And that brings us back around in the loop – these members of staff will be less likely to take time off, will participate fully and will be committed to further improvements. This will lead to an oversubscribed school with improved inspection results.

In summary, the H Factor can bring you and your school:

- a better working environment
- a distinct, and positive, ethos
- improved academic results
- less absence
- enhanced recruitment and retention of the staff
- higher levels of participation leading to better learning outcomes
- improved job satisfaction for staff
- a positive impact on inspection outcomes.

Culture and purpose

> A school's culture has far more influence on life and learning in the schoolhouse than the president of the country, the state department of education, the super-intendent, the school board, or even the principal, teachers, and parents can ever have.[180] (Barth 2002)

Defining a school's culture is more difficult than identifying its signifiers. A school's culture emerges from the relationships within that school, the language used, the values, the physical environment, the teaching and learning practices. Culture is defined by all sorts of traditions, words, actions and symbols; by a school's displays, the experiences that learners have, by how someone answers the phone, by the responsibility people take for their environment. It includes how we deal with problems, how we celebrate success and how we support one another.

For the web 2.0 generation, tagging has been a shortcut to visually representing the preoccupations of a website. Words and terms which are most frequently searched for and used gain greater prominence. They appear in larger and more distinct fonts. If it were possible to eavesdrop and record the most frequently used words and phrases in an electronic format, tagging would be a great way to get a visual summary of a school's culture!

To us, school culture is best understood by listening to the prevalence of topics within everyday 'corridor conversations' and tuning the ear to pick out the frequency of the words and phrases used. The underpinning belief systems will drive the frequency of these words and phrases. By listening carefully you can quickly isolate the drivers. The term 'word cloud' is associated with the frequency with which a word or phrase is used on any website; the larger the word, the more frequent its appearance. It is an instant visual summary of the prevalence of a topic. Here are two sample clouds from two 'imaginary' schools based on 'corridor conversations'.

School corridor 1:

Behaviour, Assistance, Incident, Exam, Break, Problems Issues, Reports, Detention, Shout, Care, Challenges, Control, Order, Listen, Visit, Disturb, *Inspection*, Argument, Too Little Too Late, Holiday, Support, Scream, Isolate, Tantrum, Typical, Heat, Discuss, Sort It Out, Teach, Test, Disorder, Head Teacher, Queue, Initiative, Breather, Wait, Yet Another

And, school corridor 2:

Learning, Support, Feedback, Exam, Study, Groupings Help, Reports, Rewards, Discuss, Develop, *Challenge*, Transition, Stretch, Motivate, Push, **Encourage**, Inspection, Promote, Plan Ahead, Agree, *Detail*, Mentor, Invite, Calm, Discuss, Progress, Manage, Teach, Lead, Measure, Database, Networks, Learning Platform, Developments, Creativity, Improve, Thinking

Culture for some is all about the things that those who are part of the school agree are true. For example: 'With the right support, everyone can reach their full potential', 'Everyone should be treated with respect' or 'Teachers will perform best when they have a good work-life balance'. Culture is also about the things that we agree are right and the things that we agree are wrong.

For some, culture is 'the way we do things around here'.

> Beneath the conscious awareness of everyday life in schools, there is a stream of thought and activity. This underground flow of feelings and folkways wends its way within schools, dragging people, programs, and ideas towards often-unstated purposes ... Students deserve the best schools we can give them — schools full of heart, soul, and ample opportunities to learn and grow. Too often, students are being short-changed. They are stifled by sterile, toxic places that turn them against learning rather than turn them on to it[181]. (Deal and Peterson 1999)

The culture of a school is probably the single thing that has the most profound effect on everyone who is part of that school. As long ago as the 1980s, it was found that a 'safe, orderly climate...'[182] conducive to learning (Edmonds 1982) leads to higher pupil achievement.

A healthy, positive, happy culture will motivate staff and pupils alike, improve cooperation between all stakeholders and help you to make the difficult decisions that are sometimes necessary in a large organization. Researchers have consistently found that a positive and supportive school culture improves learning outcomes, staff productivity and pupil achievement.[183]

In contrast, a negative culture will prevent change for the better, will de-motivate staff (which, in turn, will have a negative effect on the pupils' attitudes and achievements) and will lead to a downhill spiral towards low attendance, poor performance and poor behaviour.

Of course, there is a balance to be struck between a culture that focuses solely on behaviour management and rigid discipline and one that is warm and nurturing but forgets to have high expectations. Take the Surrey school mentioned above – the well-being 'perks' are combined with high expectations of teaching standards and the head teacher is fully prepared to hold members of staff accountable – they are expected to meet the standards or they are encouraged to leave. Simply introducing well-being targets and health club membership alone is not sufficient to maximize learning outcomes. As we have said before, the H Factor is not something discreet that you can just bolt on to your school.

In order to help children reach their full potential, schools must have a positive atmosphere combined with a culture of strong 'academic press' (Lee and Smith

1999).[184] ('Academic press' being high expectations for learning for all pupils and high expectations of teachers to deliver this learning.)

> There are too many schools that have succeeded in building warm and caring and nurturing places for children but have failed to translate that into a culture of high expectations.[185] (Eressy 2005)

Our belief is that learning must lie at the heart of everything you do in your school, but that this learning need not, indeed should not, be drudgery for all concerned. What is the point in dragging reluctant children kicking and screaming through exams so that they get results that put your school high up the league tables if the same children leave school thoroughly de-motivated and put off learning for life? Why should we not be able to combine warmth and humour with pushing the boundaries of achievement and a pleasant working environment with helping people learn? When you achieve this, you will have children that get the exam results to put you at the top of the league tables and who then leave school with positive thoughts about learning and education. Then your school will have the H Factor.

This brings us to how you create the right culture within your school. To finding your core purpose. Having a core purpose that is agreed upon and constantly striven for by all stakeholders is a certain route to obtaining the culture you wish for in your school. To achieve this core purpose it is not enough to banish the negatives, but you must also establish an agreed set of principles and ideals that underpin every single thing that takes place in the school.

> A truly positive school climate is not characterized simply by the absence of gangs, violence, or discipline problems, but also by the presence of a set of norms and values that focus everyone's attention on what is most important and motivate them to work hard toward a common purpose.[186] (Jerald 2006)

Few would dispute that schools are centres of learning. Introducing the H Factor is not a call for schools to stop caring about teaching and learning. Not for a minute should we lower our ambitions for pupils' academic achievement. However, newspaper headlines like, 'Classrooms are for work, not fun'[187] (*Telegraph* 2006), and articles[188] quoting the then chief inspector of schools saying, 'School is a place of work preparing youngsters for the world of work ... not a house of fun ...' (Smith, M. 2006), are, quite frankly, depressing! The implication of this statement is that both learning and work should be drudgery. Why can't learning be fun? For that matter, why can't work be enjoyable? Why shouldn't schools strive to be happy and secure places that prepare young people to live contented and fulfilled lives of which work is only a part? If we go about teaching and learning in the po-faced manner suggested by some journalists, it is no wonder that young people are put off work before they ever even start.

> that subject [happiness] wasn't on the curriculum when I was a lad, and yet somehow we managed to pull through. 'Moth' Reeve, the Latin teacher, may have given Jones W a thorough coating for failing to master the ablative absolute ('That's right, Jones, it's about time you had a jolly good blub!') but the rest of us tittered behind our textbooks …'[189] (Henderson 2007)

So, that's OK then – only Jones W was thoroughly miserable and the rest of the class had a good laugh at his expense! Or did perhaps some of the tittering come from the fact that they were relieved that 'Moth' hadn't chosen them to explain the ablative absolute? That it wasn't them being humiliated? And they 'pulled through'; but don't we want more for children today than pulling through? What happened to flourishing and to reaching their full potential? This attitude of 'in my day I was given the odd good slap with the slipper and it didn't do me any harm' is damaging in that it prevents movement forward to something better, more creative and more suitable for young people and society today. It may not have done any long-term harm (though that is debatable), but it doesn't make it right.

In Denmark, there is one word to translate something that in English can only be done in three: love of learning; 'lærelyst'. Perhaps this is because Danish schools focus on 'teaching children to think and be independent-minded, democratic citizens'[190] rather than on pushing them through examinations. And, of course, the Danes repeatedly come at or near the top of international well-being tables.

So, how do we get our ladder back to the right wall? To do this, we have to establish our core purpose. Once we have defined our reason for being here, we can look to a vision of what we want for our school and for the people who are part of it and who make it what it is. From this vision arise our ideals and our school culture.

Take time to consider the following questions with regard to your school:

- What are we here for?
- Who are we here for?
- What do we want for each and every pupil in our school? What do we want for the staff?
- Is learning at the centre of everything we do?
- Are our lessons worth behaving for?
- What do we celebrate with most enthusiasm?
- Who are our staff role models?
- Which is more important, the welfare of the staff or the welfare of the students?
- Who determines our standards – the school or the individual?

By answering these sorts of questions, you should come some way to discovering your school's core purpose.

As you walk the corridors of your school, observe the learning that is taking place or sit in meetings try to attune yourself to the core purpose. What do you overhear, see and experience that gives you an idea of where your school is and where it is headed? For instance, where the core purpose is around best serving learners and learning, you don't hear management talk endlessly about preparing for Ofsted, about SEF and about behaviour. But where the core purpose is about coping, that is all you hear about.

As a member of the leadership team, start by considering what you are getting right. Then look at where things may be going awry. Walk around the school, listen in to what is being said, take note of feelings that are being expressed and look at your mission statement – does it tie in with your core purpose?

Here's a short word about mission statements; consider yours carefully. Firstly, think about whether it is in line with your school's core purpose. If it is not, change it (involve everybody in the school in deciding what would be more appropriate). If it is in line with your core purpose, do you live up to its expectations? It is of no use, for example, having a mission statement such as: 'Where everybody is of equal value' when members of staff always shoot to the front of the dinner queue or moan about being 'stuck with' a low-ability class. And who could take seriously a mission statement such as: 'We believe that every child should have an equal opportunity to succeed (unless, of course, they behave really badly, in which case they will be put into sets lower than their actual ability).'

At one of the schools where Sir John was head teacher (Ruffwood School in Merseyside) the children were involved in writing the mission statement. Here's what they came up with:

> To go further than I thought
> To run faster than I hoped
> To reach higher than I dreamed
> To become the person I need to be

So, you have paced the corridors, popped into classrooms and listened in on conversations. Now that you know where your school stands and what you think you should be aiming for, you will need to involve everybody in achieving it. Agree with everybody – and that includes staff, pupils, parents, governors and the community – on your values and beliefs and what your core purpose is. You could start by identifying four 'movers and shakers' to have firmly on your side, then begin to involve everyone else in the process. Once you have agreed upon your core purpose, display it in prominent positions, refer to it regularly and keep it in the top of everybody's minds.

From the core purpose, you can begin to establish the sort of culture you want for your school. What are the key words that would cover your desired culture? A few to start you off may be learning, respect, relationships, high expectations, high standards of behaviour, kindness, happiness, well-being. Now consider every aspect of your school – your displays, staff meetings, assemblies, lessons, traditions, awards, rewards, sanctions, the language used, study leave, end of term arrangements, term dates, etc. – do these tie in with the culture you want? If they do, keep them and develop them. If not, bin them and start afresh.

Make sure that any behaviour you expect to see is modelled by yourself and the rest of the leadership team – governors are also included in this. Governors should show – and be shown – appreciation, should be expected to participate in training, to work hard for the school and to contribute to the school culture.

Involve your staff and pupils in the decision making and in making any changes. At one school that was experiencing problems with poor attendance and behaviour, Sir John asked the staff and pupils to name the three things that they would most like changed. The top three were:

1) The toilets – these were redesigned to have no doors to the toilet block itself. They were updated and painted and mirrors were put up. They were stocked with soap dispensers and soft toilet tissue. A member of staff visited then regularly during the school day to make sure that behaviour was appropriate.

2) The buses – the queuing system for the buses at the end of the day was reorganized, pupils were reminded of the rules for behaviour on the buses and older pupils were given responsibility for reporting incidents of poor behaviour. The buses were provided with television screens and DVD players.

3) The dining area – this was made more open plan and modernized. After consultation with parents, staff and pupils, the menu was designed to be healthy and appealing to everyone. A row of benches was put in the queuing area so that pupils could 'shuffle up' while they waited for their turn – this minimized queue jumping and made the waiting more pleasant.

Of course, everyone then wanted to nominate another three things for change, but that was OK; with each change people saw that their views were respected. The behaviour of pupils began to improve and this was not just because of the changes themselves but because of their involvement in the process of change – pupils and staff had been given control.

What gets measured gets done

As a school leader it is easy to feel overburdened by the volume of initiatives, demands on your time and things that need measuring! Later, we are bold enough to suggest that if something lands on your desk that does not meet your core purpose you should throw it in the bin. A good manager may follow all initiatives, dotting the i's and crossing the t's. But a good leader will decide which initiatives benefit their school's core purpose and will put their energy into these.

> Management is doing things right; leadership is doing the right things.[191] (Drucker 2001)

In the UK, schools are measured for just about anything. In, a study of more than 4,000 teachers in 134 schools,[192] teachers from all schools (both high and low performing) put 'measuring and monitoring results' at the top of a list of the things that their schools concentrate on most. Is this what schools are for? Is this what you came into teaching and/or school management to do? Is it part of your core purpose as a teacher and as a school?

Measurements are made for attendance figures, attainment, exclusions, value added and carbon emissions to name but a few. Because these measurements are then made public, parents are encouraged to use them to help decide about where to send their children to school. And, of course, funding follows the children. As our primary school case study showed, the media and government attention given to these measurements has overlooked the fact that parents actually want other things for their children!

In an Ipsos MORI[193] poll of more than 1,000 adults, parents said that good discipline, manners, regular communication, a balance of ethnicity and frequent friendly chats with teachers about progress were all more important to them than good academic results. The immense pressure upon schools to perform well in national tests and to come as high as possible in league tables can make us lose sight of what we are really here for – of our core purpose.

Targets can lead to the temptation to find the shortest available route to meet them. Consider the things you may do in your school in order to meet targets – perhaps you nominate a group of children in key years who look like they may fall short of a particular academic target (Level 3 SATs, 5 A–C grades, for example). That's great – for your figures and for that small group of children. But what about those who don't fall into that particular category? A more inclusive solution would be to target all children who are in danger of not meeting their full potential at the earliest possible opportunity – rather than waiting for key exam years. Some schools focus on children whose attendance falls below a certain point – again, this is beneficial for those children. But surely a better, long-term solution is to make school a positive place in which learning comes high up the agenda and in which lessons are so stimulating that all children want to be there?

I would like him to do well academically, but feel his happiness is more important.
(Parent of an infant school pupil)

Worrying only about short-term targets – for example, how to get the current Year 6/Year 11 pupils through their exams – leads to short-term strategies (carrying out scores of practice papers or giving them a piece of paper with loads of facts and telling them to 'just go and learn it', for example). If, however, we get our core purpose right at the very start and we know what we are aiming to do for all of our pupils, then those Year 6 and Year 11 pupils will have been given all the coaching and all the help and support they need throughout their careers at school. This, along with inspiring lessons, will mean that there will be no need for short-term measures at key times of their school careers.

Even more dangerously, there is the temptation to 'game' the system. It is not unheard of for schools to set standards lower so that the targets are easy to reach, or to refuse to enter a child for an exam if that child may not achieve the grade required to meet the target.

The moment you introduce targets, people will find the most economical strategies to achieve them.[194] (Shayer 2008)

An overemphasis on meeting targets based on examination results naturally leads to a tendency to teach to the test. Then, once the tests are over, everyone takes a huge sigh of relief and relaxes. This comes at the expense of the overall education of children and encourages teachers to feel that they must impart as much information as possible and drag children kicking and screaming through their exams. Professor Shayer, who has been testing young people's thinking skills since 1976, claims that children can no longer think for themselves in the way they used to and their problem-solving skills are poorer. He maintains that children today have poor thinking skills in comparison to 30 years ago. They are less able to think deeply and to formulate and test hypothesis.[195]

> Although it's [the A–C benchmark] the stupidest measure … For one reason because it's raw data, and the other reason is of course because it's incredibly dependent on a small number of children at the … threshold of performance. So it's the silliest measure anybody ever came up with, but it's totally engrained on the public psyche, isn't it?[196] (A head teacher)

When asked, two-thirds of head teachers say that the parents' view of how their school is doing is the most important issue to them.[197] That being the case, perhaps we are rather too hung up on the league tables. A poll[198] taken in 2006 showed that parents feel that schools are doing well in the academic areas (preparing children for further education and for exams), but less well in the social areas.

> In a climate in which testing is king in the drive to push up standards, pastoral provision takes lower priority – but it may be the key to unlocking potential in some young people.[199] (Sodha 2008)

In a climate where only factors that can be measured are of any importance, and in which 'successful' schools are identified by their rates of progress, improved attainment and 'value added' scores it is little wonder that, as those responsible for marketing their schools, leadership teams concentrate on the areas that are measured.

So, if we humans have a tendency to value the things that we can measure, and if happiness and well-being are difficult to measure, how do we measure the things we value? Firstly we define them. On the following pages, we define the H Factor by looking at its three components; heart, head and health and by further breaking down these three components. The H Factor wheel and questionnaires have been designed to enable you to measure well-being in your school. You will then be encouraged to identify areas of improvement and to plan to make those improvements.

School

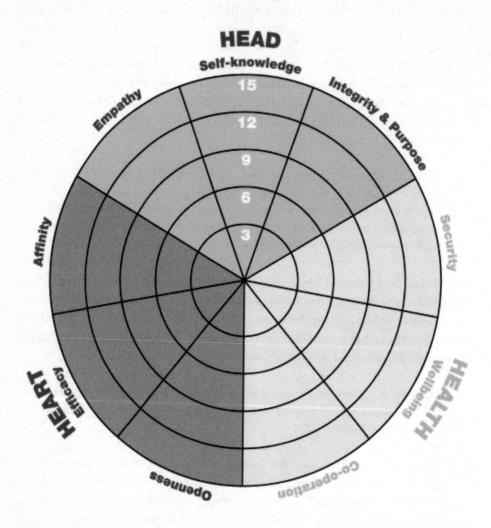

Thriving together

HEART is about making sure that everyone thrives; that nobody is just getting by. This involves all stakeholders – staff, students, governors, parents and the local community. Heart is about relationships – there is a mutual respect, people share ideas and planning time and people feel free to express opinions. Heart is about making sure that everyone is working towards a shared goal. Everybody knows what the school's core purpose is and everything that is done in the school is judged by its value to that core purpose. The difficult questions such as, 'Are our lessons worth behaving for?' are asked and answered.

Read the three explanations below, and use them to help you to complete the first section of our questionnaire. Score as follows: five points = always like my school, four points = often like my school, three points = sometimes like my school, two points = rarely like my school, one point = never like my school.

Openness

Your school should have an appropriate forum for feelings to emerge. You may feel that everyone has an opportunity to express their opinions, but have you really taken into account that some people may have something important to say but are not of the personality type to express their opinions in a public setting?

People enjoy being part of an open school because it is a positive place with high expectations of behaviour and achievement. Consider what the last thing you celebrated as a whole school was – hopefully it wasn't the end of term. In one secondary school we visited, we noticed a large sign outside the staffroom. It said: '23 days to go' in bold red letters. This was not a reminder to staff and pupils of an important coursework deadline, but a reminder of the number of days before Year 11 pupils went on study leave. They were counting down until the day that they got rid of one year group! Consider what that said to the pupils about the importance of lessons and learning and about the staff's feelings for them.

In an open school people feel confident to have the difficult conversations. They do not worry about confrontation, because they know that their opinions are respected. Consequently, concerns do not fester and become something bigger than they actually are.

Efficacy

Do you as a school cope with setbacks optimistically, or does everyone mope around and focus on the problem rather than the solution? Consider the last setback you suffered as a school – worse than hoped-for results, a disappointing inspection or negative behaviour from a group of pupils, for example. How did you cope with it? Did everyone moan about the lack of effort on behalf of the pupils, about the fairness of the system or that particular group of children? Did you make excuses for your disappointment (what would you expect from that year group/ in this area/from those children?). Or did you put your heads together and work as a team to learn from mistakes, to move forward and to find solutions so that the setback didn't reoccur? How you cope as a whole school with setbacks and disappointments will greatly affect future outcomes.

Consider whether everyone has the same goals – are you all working together towards a shared vision, or do some people have other plans? Is there collaboration or competition between departments and year groups?

In a school with high levels of efficacy, people believe that they can achieve what they have set out to achieve. Think about your policies. Firstly, do they fit in with your core purpose? And secondly, do you always turn what those policies say into practice?

Affinity: No man is an island

Consider the relationships in your school. Take into account all relationships (staff, pupils, governors, the local community) and think about the levels of relational trust as mentioned above. To what extent do each of the stakeholders in the school trust each other to carry their roles effectively? To what extent do your members of staff work together in the name of learning and making improvements?

If your members of staff feel affinity for each other, then internal collaboration will come as a matter of course. High levels of affinity and empathy will lead to people feeling confident to express concerns about their own teaching without fearing that this may indicate a weakness. Do your members of staff share ideas and good practice? Do they help each other at difficult times? Do you encourage people to work together and do you welcome creative ideas? Do you collaborate with each other in order to reach your common goals?

Collaboration needs to go beyond the members of the school. Consider how you collaborate with external bodies. For example, how well do you work with your local primary/secondary schools? And what about other schools that are similar to your own but further away? Do you share good practice with others, or do you keep your good ideas to yourselves? Consider also your links with other external services – the police, social services, local teacher training colleges and anyone else that could help you improve learning and well-being in your school.

Happier schools questionnaire: Heart section

Once you have added up your score, turn to the wheel on p. 194 and shade in the results. As you do so, we would like you to consider the areas in which your school's scores are the lowest. Then come up with an action plan for making the necessary improvements in these areas. It may be that something specific comes to mind immediately, in which case note it down. Alternatively, you may wish to consider some of the suggestions on the following pages:

	1	2	3	4	5	Total
Openness – what you see is what you get						
We have an appropriate forum for feelings to emerge						
We enjoy being here						
We are able to hold difficult conversations						
Efficacy – whether you think you can or whether you think you can't you're probably right						
We cope optimistically with setbacks						
We are committed to a shared vision						
We always turn policy into practice						
Affinity – no man is an island						
We nurture close working relationships						
We find real energy for internal collaboration						
We find real energy for external collaboration						

Openness – What you see is what you get

We have an appropriate forum for feelings to emerge.

Collegiality

Studies have a found a statistical correlation between a positive school climate – focused on collegiality and professionalism – and student achievement.[200] Fullan and Hargreaves (1996)[201] characterized collegiality as including:

- open sharing of mistakes and failures
- demonstrating respect for each other
- constructively analysing and criticising practices and procedures

However, many people do not feel confident enough to express their views in front of a large group of people. During staff meetings, give people an opportunity to work in 'mini-groups'. This will help break up the meeting and will also give everyone an opportunity to express feelings and opinions that may otherwise have been left unsaid. Putting staff with different roles, skills and length of service in groups together could generate new and creative ideas.

Post-it solutions

At staff meetings, give every member of staff a post-it note and ask them to write on it three things that would make their lives easier. You will find that some really simple things come up – 'I need a key to my room', 'The heating doesn't work in my office', etc. Act on what they say.

Raise the bar

If you set high standards for yourself and the rest of the leadership team, then it is easier to expect high standards from everyone else. Be open and ask people how you are doing. Not only will it motivate them because they feel that they have a say, but you will also find out a lot about yourself. Ask members of staff to write down three things that the senior leadership team (SLT) does well and three things they could do better.

We enjoy being here.

Seattle sound

If you've ever been to the Pike Place fish market in Seattle, you'll see people who really enjoy their job. When someone orders a salmon, a shout goes up: 'One salmon!' This is followed by, 'One salmon!', which is shouted by every person in the place – salespeople, customers and onlookers alike. Then the chances are that a salmon will be thrown through the air and caught by a salesperson, who will wrap it up and throw it back for the customer. The atmosphere is lively, full of fun and enjoyment and it pulls in the crowds. But not only that, it sells fish!

If people enjoy work, they will put their heart, soul and energy into it. If they do this, then they will be more productive. If you bring the atmosphere of the Seattle fish market into your school, the sense of fun and enjoyment will increase productivity and improve learning.

You may not be able to throw fish around the staffroom, but there are plenty of ways to make it a more enjoyable place to be:

- Have a weekly award for the person who has cheered everyone up.
- Each month, take nominations for members of staff who have gone beyond the call of duty (these can come from parents, staff and pupils). At the end of the month, put all of the names in a hat and draw out a winner. Let all of the people who have been nominated know that their names came up as well.
- Have a morning briefing that is only for positive messages – towards the end of the week when people are getting tired is good. Call it 'Positive Thursday' and ask staff to only give positive messages about pupils. Show photos if possible and then make sure that those pupils are congratulated during the day by as many people as possible.
- Make sure that tea and coffee are free.
- Provide biscuits, cake or fruit at low or busy times.

- Make your staffroom relaxing. Have a table so that staff can sit together to eat.
- Have a relaxing area with comfortable chairs, plants and pictures.
- Have a separate work area where people know that they will not be disturbed.
- Offer Salsa lessons, yoga, pilates or singing lessons for staff one lunchtime a fortnight.
- Use the skills of your own staff members – what can they offer to teach each other?
- Have a staff band, choir or orchestra. Make sure they perform at school events.

Celebrate

Periodically celebrate what *everyone* has achieved. Create a yearbook for all of your year groups. Include the pupils' strengths, dreams and hopes. Have a page for teachers' comments (only positive ones, of course). With online companies offering all sorts of services, they are not hard work and your pupils can be heavily involved in the design.

Theme days

On a charity day organized at the primary school where Joanna is a governor, she noticed an increased buzz among parents, staff and pupils. On a Friday towards the end of term, when everyone was often tired, coming to school in pyjamas seemed to bring back a sense of fun. To know that this fun was also raising money for the children's charity chosen by the pupils themselves added to the feel-good factor. Notably, the school still concentrated on learning – it was not an excuse for a day off, but it did renew everyone's enthusiasm.

Engagement versus learning

Make sure that lessons are fun. Use the engagement versus learning matrix on p. 258 to decide which activities to use. Ensure that lessons have a high level of engagement and induce FLOW in the pupils. However, be sure to avoid high-engagement, low-learning activities like worksheets and colouring

We are able to hold difficult conversations.

It may be that you need to arm yourself with a few well-chosen phrases such as, 'Personally, I don't want to have this conversation, but professionally I must'. Make sure that you prepare yourself by knowing what outcome you want from the conversation – if you believe that some good will come from it, it is more likely that it actually will! During this conversation, allow them to talk to you. When you counter their arguments, make sure that you refer back to what they have said, 'You said … I have seen, however, that …'.

Model problem solving

In staff forums, briefings and as part of the staff meeting structure encourage and model the use of simple problem-solving protocols which are solution focused, easy to use and replicate. Practise the use of decision trees, priority matrices, SWOT analysis, driving versus resisting, simple tools which will become part of the repertoire of shared decision making.

Outcomes first

Agree before any formal meeting what outcomes you seek to achieve. For example, 'By six o'clock we will have considered and prioritized a range of solutions to the issue of unruly behaviour at the school gates'. Write up the desired outcome, which will be different to the solution ('Pupils will enter and leave the school in an orderly and polite fashion'), and refer to it throughout your meeting. Ask, 'Are we still striving to reach our desired outcome?'

Teach fierce conversations

Provide training for all staff – including all support staff – on conflict management, priority and time management and holding fierce conversations. Teach children the same topics and notice how it has a positive consequence.

Efficacy – Whether you think you can or think you can't you are probably right

We cope optimistically with setbacks.

Solution focus protocol

Move away from dwelling on problems and towards thinking about solutions.

A key method of doing this is to use Seligman's ABCDE method whenever you hit a setback. Seligman developed this plan to help people get out of a negative mindset.

> **A = Adversity:** You have a problem, challenge or difficult situation. (For example, two Year 10 boys have had a fight.) To start with, you need to identify it. Know what the problem is and, if it helps, write it down.

> **B = Belief:** You have a belief about this challenge or situation. (The boys involved come from a rough estate. All children from there are difficult – their parents were

just as bad.) Be aware of your beliefs and what you think about the situation. Ask yourself whether you are feeling optimistic or pessimistic. Do you think you will be able to overcome the challenge? Long-held beliefs that are based on semi-truths and have never been questioned can become 'thought viruses'[202] that can limit your thinking and your actions. Remind yourself that what you feel and how you react come about from your beliefs, NOT from the event or situation.

C = Consequence: This is what you do as a result of your above belief. (You temporarily exclude them both.) Before you act, think about the consequences of having your beliefs.

Pessimists often stop here.

But not in your school. Once you have explained the ABCDE method to all staff and used it to practise overcoming some of your school's key challenges you can make it clear that people mustn't bring you a problem until they have visited D and E. Have as sign on your door saying, 'Before you come in, have you done D and E?'

D = Dispute: Before you act, examine if there is any evidence for your belief. Is there any evidence against it? (Maybe last year, several children from that estate did well in your school, for example.) If you have pessimistic thoughts, argue against them. Your thoughts and beliefs are just that – they are not necessarily facts. Write down what they are and then write down arguments against them. Is there any benefit to you or your school from having that belief? (No, quite the opposite. If we continue to have this belief things will never change for the children from the estate.) If you believed something else, would it help? (Absolutely. If you believe that these children can overcome their social circumstances you will do whatever is necessary to help them. That can only be good for the children and the school.)

E = Energize: Now you have changed your beliefs you should feel full of the energy you need to overcome the challenge. (You can help these children; how can you do it?) Now you can come up with some ways of solving the problem long term. Make a list of what you can do, ask advice and find out what others have done in the same situation.

When a challenge arises, act quickly. Set up a task group, focus on outcomes you want and follow the ABCDE method until you come up with a solution.

Feed the optimist in you

An optimistic outlook makes us more likely to step up to a challenge and to overcome it. Feed optimism among your staff and pupils. If someone comes to you with an idea, let them run with it. There is nothing worse for motivation than being told: 'Hmm, we tried that three years ago and it didn't work'. Next time that person has an idea, they will be likely to keep it to themselves. If you have reservations about the value of someone's idea, ask for a full plan of how they will go about implementing it, the challenges they will need to overcome and the benefits it will have to learning and teaching.

Words alone

Understand the power of language and use it with care. Here are some positive alternatives for you:

- 'yes' and not 'yes, but'
- challenges not problems
- learning not behaviour
- setbacks not crises.

Ban phrases that begin with negatives, such as: 'At my last school no-one …', 'We will never …' or 'It's not possible to …'.

Contingency planning

Plan for contingencies. Alistair works with professional athletes on contingency planning. This involves them mentally rehearsing 'winning' solutions to potential pitfalls. For example, turning up at an athletics event with the wrong set of running spikes or feeling sick the evening before or having a late lane change. By anticipating the problem well in advance and focusing on, and re-visiting, the solutions if the need arises the remedy is already in place. The athlete is less likely to be stressed and so can perform better. In schools this contingency planning falls short because there is insufficient focus on positive solutions. Often we get stuck on the problem, fixate on it, breathe life into it and then beat ourselves up over it! The important stage is to look at potential and alternative solutions which are in themselves positive.

We are committed to a shared vision.

Define core purpose

Work together to define your core purpose. Involve governors, staff and children in this. What is it you are there for? What do you want children to leave with? What is the minimum you would accept for every pupil in your school? Judge everything the school does by its contribution to core purpose. Do all of your celebrations, traditions, assemblies and lessons support the core purpose? Is the language used in your school positive and in line with your core purpose? Do the displays show what you are trying to achieve? Do any learning days off site meet the core purpose? If something does not help you achieve your core purpose, scrap it.

Work the dissonance

Dissonance is the tension which arises when people are asked, incentivized or forced to behave in ways that contradict their own attitudes and beliefs. The experience of dissonance can work to advantage as a short- to medium-term motivator or it can disable if experienced for prolonged periods.

When an individual, group or community is forced to behave in ways which are inconsistent to what is held to be of value and to be true – such as in defiance of core purpose – then a disabling dissonance can arise. Being especially clear about accountability, roles and responsibilities and core purpose will help overcome debilitating feelings of guilt. Ensuring that everyone has a say in establishing the core purpose will also help avoid dissonance.

You could, however, use dissonance to your advantage if you create a tension between 'where we are' and 'where we could be'. Once you know where you are going, you will need to agree the milestones along the way. Have a visual timeline to show what you are aiming for. Talk to your staff about it: 'When we have done all of this, where will we be, what will it feel like, what will the community say of us?'

Sell the dream

Think about how you display your vision – which is a simple expression of core purpose. Make it clear to everybody within and outside school what you are aiming for. Have branding carrying your school's message. Have a set of cards with the school mission statement and an explanation on the rear. Give them to parents, staff and pupils. Have the mission statement printed on school bags, clothing and student and staff planners. Have it in visible places outside the school and in the reception areas. Talk about it in assemblies. Make sure that everyone knows where you are going.

We always turn policy into practice.

Urgent versus important

Use tools such as the urgent versus important matrix on p. 258 with your staff and governors and get from this a list of the major challenges faced by your school.

Make sure that any policy you have will be followed. Don't write a policy just to jump through a hoop.

Zero tolerance on the signifiers

Make sure that you have zero tolerance on the things that may seem small but have symbolic value. For example, if the rule is 'baseball hats are not worn', then do not allow them at all, ever! Set your standards high, and follow your policy through if they are not met. For example, if a child is late for school on a Monday, ensure that he or she receives a phone call between 7 a.m. and 8 a.m. on the Tuesday. Don't just let it go this once, otherwise once becomes twice and soon becomes a habit.

Affinity – No man is an island

We nurture close working relationships.

Modelling

The key to getting the culture you want in your school is by modelling the behaviour you want to see in staff and pupils alike. This can be done by sharing decision-making protocols, exhibiting high standards especially on the signifiers such as dress, personal conduct and reward systems.

Visibility

Make sure that your senior leadership team is highly visible, that it makes contact with people on a regular basis and that it is available. If it helps, have a list of the names of all members of staff (both teaching and non-teaching) and tick off who you have spoken to each day. Make sure that you speak to everyone on a regular basis.

Go walkies

Ensure that the senior leadership team is seen by pupils. Go for walkabouts, visit classrooms every day, wait for the buses and talk to the pupils about what they are going to learn today, go to the gate at the end of the day and chat about what the children have experienced during the day. Make learning a focus of these conversations.

Champion the cause

Have a network of champions. Make sure that you have people who sign up 100 per cent to what you want to achieve. Use them to spread good practice. Ensure that they use positive language and talk about *when* you reach your goals.

Strong with weak

You may wish to consider linking strong teachers with weaker ones and calling them 'learning mentors', having stress buddies to offload onto during difficult times or training staff without leadership responsibilities to become coaches.

Keep your enemies close

Remember the Shackleton model and keep the negative personalities in your boat. Keep your friends close and your antagonists closer! Do this by finding out what makes the negative personalities tick. What do they respond to? Flattery, praise, having their opinion requested, being involved in decision making? Once you know what makes them tick, use this to keep them on side.

We find real energy for internal collaboration.

Put learning first

Ask yourself – and everyone else – the question, 'Do we talk enough about learning?' Make sure that learning is at the top of everyone's agenda. It should be the focus of all meetings, briefings and training.

Use problems to build teams

Problem-solving team building (PSTB) is when a group of people come together to help solve someone else's problem in a given time frame. They do this using a protocol. For example, offer the problem, define it, generate solutions without comment, test each solution, organize then order each solution. Because of the structure, a loose group that may not have worked together before comes together and helps out someone else. The person who had the initial problem then goes away with their thinking freshened. Examples of problems which could be addressed over 45 minutes at the end of a day include:

- I run out of time in lessons.
- I can't manage my workload.
- I can't persuade my son to get up in the morning.

- I can't control this girl in Year 10.
- I'm not sure where to take my field trip.
- I need to be better at helping support staff.
- I don't know how to improve my assessments.
- I cannot get parents to come to consultation evenings.

The idea is not only to become solution focused and problem solvers but to improve relationships.

360 degree feedback

Using 360 degree feedback gives an individual the chance to see how they are doing from several different perspectives. Make sure that people from all areas of the organization give feedback on individuals. So, a head of department or year group would get feedback from children they teach, from members of their department and from their line manager as well as completing a self-assessment. They would use this to plan their future development and any training needs. The most accurate feedback has been found to come from people who have known the individual for between one and three years.[203]

Build teams

Make sure that the teams within your school are clearly defined, but also that membership to them is understood and, if necessary, open. So, if someone has an interest in a particular area, but is not already part of that team, they can become a member. That way you will benefit from the fact that they are keen to participate and will be able to use any additional expertise they may have.

Job swap

Give people a chance to take over someone else's role for a while. You could ask heads of faculties to chair someone else's meeting or ask someone different to take a staff meeting – try encouraging someone with less experience to do this. Alternatively, ask an newly qualified teacher to teach staff something that they learnt in their PGCE year. You may find that other people have some good ideas to share!

We find real energy for external collaboration.

Do lunch

Once a month, have a lunch with the head teachers of your local primary or senior schools. Get some of the pupils who went to or will be going to these schools to act as waiters and waitresses for these meals.

In the news

Talk up collaboration in your newsletters. Use as many names of other local schools, businesses and members of the community as possible. Always make sure that you thank individuals, schools or businesses that have helped your school in any way

Mutual benefit

Organize and participate in projects that have benefits both for your school and for others. These may include combined staff development training, a teacher exchange or a curriculum for a particular year group that can only be offered by combining expertise or sharing teachers. If another school locally finds it difficult to recruit offer them use of some of your teachers (state in your adverts for new staff that there will be an expectation for the successful candidate to teach a certain number of lessons at the other school).

Care for your area

Recent research has, perhaps unsurprisingly, shown that children who travel through rundown areas on their way to school are less likely to behave well and learn effectively.[204] Work with the necessary outside agencies (police, councillors, local residents) to improve your area. Perhaps you can get your pupils involved in making the area look better. Taking responsibility for removing litter may be a small step, but it will show the school's commitment to improving the area. Campaign for the facilities you need (local parks, play areas, green areas, a café, etc.) and be prepared to be involved in setting them up.

Learn from others

Make regular visits to other schools. No school is perfect and you can learn from other schools as they can from you. Offer all members of staff one day per year to visit a school of their choice to look at how to improve learning in their field.

Employ an ICT student from your local university to spend their professional year with you. They will be good value for money, full of ideas and can develop e-learning resources and your website for you.

Making the worthwhile difference

HEAD is about ensuring that everyone has an agreed set of values, that they respect each other and that they take pride in everyone's achievements. In other words, Head is about ensuring that all stakeholders have agreed upon the core purpose of the school and are working relentlessly towards achieving that core purpose. Once they are doing this, they will be making a truly worthwhile difference to the lives of everyone within the establishment.

For schools where a culture change is needed, this section is about reaching the tipping point. That is, the point at which you suddenly notice that more good things than bad things are happening; the point at which you can see that the culture is beginning to shift and the small things are beginning to make a difference (for example, you may notice that the fire alarm hasn't gone off for week or two!). In order to achieve this, it is essential for the senior leadership team to model the behaviour that it wants to see.

Read the three explanations below, and use them to help you to complete the questionnaire. Score as you did in the previous section of this chapter:

    1 = This statement **never** applies to my school.
    2 = This statement **rarely** applies to my school.
    3 = This statement **sometimes** applies to my school.
    4 = This statement **often** applies to my school.
    5 = This statement **always** applies to my school.

Empathy

Having empathy is not about tolerating weakness and making allowances. It is, however, about trying to see the perspective of other people and of making sure that everybody (staff, students, governors and the local community) has a voice; that is, the chance to express their opinions and to have these opinions listened to and seriously considered. Consider how you deal with people who come to you with problems and solutions or with ideas – do you really listen to them with an open mind, or are you so set on your own path that you pass over what they say?

Consider what percentage of your staff members have a say in where your school is headed. Is everyone given a voice? Do you ask the opinion of everybody, or does the school's leadership team simply dictate to others how things will be? And what about the pupils? Is your school council actually listened to, or is it just there so that you can say that you have one?

In a school with high levels of empathy, it is noticed when people do something well – both staff and pupils. Think about how often you focus on the good things that are happening in your school – do you always point out the positive, or do you constantly find yourself giving out negative messages in meetings and assemblies? If levels of empathy are high, the focus will be on the positive.

Self-knowledge

Self-knowledge is not about believing that your school is the 'sink school' or about ending conversations with, 'Well, what else would you expect from our children?' or the like. Consider how you use comparison data in your school. Is it used for productive comparison, or do you use it to beat yourself and others up with statistics? Comparing your school to other schools just for the sake of it does not improve learning outcomes. However, knowing the strengths and weaknesses of your establishment will help you to put plans in place to make the necessary improvements.

Knowing the difference between urgent and important will help you to focus relentlessly on your core purpose. It may take a certain amount of bravery, but when a new initiative arrives on your desk, consider it with regard to your core purpose. If it doesn't help you achieve your core purpose, it is neither urgent nor important, so throw it in the bin. To make people work hard to jump through a hoop that neither serves your school's core purpose nor improves learning outcomes is de-motivating for staff and pointless for pupils.

Integrity

In a school with integrity, people are not afraid of confronting the brutal facts. Consider whether at your school people are prepared to ask the difficult questions such as, 'Are our lessons worth behaving for?' and 'Are we doing this for the benefit of our students' learning?'

In a school with integrity, everything that takes place is in line with the core purpose. Think about every decision, every conversation, every action, every assembly, display, lesson and meeting that takes place in your school. How far does each of the above go to meeting your core purpose? If something does not meet your core purpose, it is of no value and no longer has a place in your school.

Integrity is about doing the right thing even if no-one is looking, so all stakeholders in a school with integrity share values and judge everything they do and say by those values.

Happier schools questionnaire: Head section

	1	2	3	4	5	Total
Empathy – put yourself in others' shoes						
We work hard at understanding each others' perspective						
We give everyone a voice						
We catch people doing well						
Self-knowledge – if it's to be, it's up to me						
We minimize unhelpful comparisons with others						
We know our strengths and weaknesses						
We know the difference between urgent and important						
Integrity – to yourself be true						
We confront the brutal facts						
We focus relentlessly on our core purpose						
We behave in ways that are consistent with our values						

Once you have added up your score, turn to the wheel on p. 194 and shade in the results. As you do so, we would like you to consider the areas in which you are weakest. You will then come up with an action plan for making the necessary improvements in these areas. It may be that something specific comes to mind immediately, in which case note it down. Alternatively, you may wish to consider some of the suggestions below.

Empathy – Put yourself in others' shoes

We work hard at understanding each others' perspective.

Culture survey

Carry out the Hay Group survey on school culture. You can purchase and download it from www.transforminglearning.co.uk. Include every adult member of the school community – governors, teaching staff and non-teaching staff. Have the leadership team complete it in a group of its own so that everyone feels safe to be candid. You may be surprised by the results. Most importantly, act upon them. Decide together where you are getting it right, where you can improve and how you can do this.

Community matters

Invite members of the local community to school events. By this, we mean local residents, not just high-profile people. Allow them to see what you do and what your school is about. Let them get to know you and your students, and allow your students to see them as real people with opinions and feelings. Use students to show them around the school and to tell them about what they are learning.

Chatham House

Chatham House is the origin of the confidentiality rule known as the Chatham House rule, which provides that members attending a seminar may discuss the results of the seminar in the outside world, but may not discuss who attended or identify what a specific individual said. The Chatham House rule evolved to facilitate frank and honest discussion on controversial or unpopular issues by speakers who may not have otherwise had the appropriate forum to speak freely. In staff or departmental meetings this convention may encourage more respectful listening.

We give everyone a voice.

Solutions wall

Have a solutions wall in the staffroom. At your Monday morning briefing, pose a problem that needs solving and ask staff to write their ideas for solving it on this wall. Nominate a member of your support staff to be responsible for collating the suggestions onto a maximum of one side of A4 paper for further discussion at a staff meeting, for example. Always follow this up. Include, 'How can we make the school happier?' on this solutions wall.

Opinions matter

Ask for the opinions of stakeholders at every possible opportunity. For example, parents at parents' evenings, members of the community when they visit or rent facilities, students through student councils, governors at meetings and school visits. Insist that student councils focus on teaching and learning as well as other issues. Take time to find out what helps your staff to do their jobs and what hinders them. Ask them the following: 'Did anything frustrate you today? Did anything take longer than it should have done? What aspect of your job is too complicated/could be made simpler?'

Student voice

Give students a voice by inviting them to attend governors meetings. Provide them with an email address to report maintenance issues. Every half term get the members of your school council to hold surgeries in which they sit somewhere busy (outside the dining hall, for example) and listen to other students' suggestions and ideas. Give your student council a budget. Talk to students as they leave school each day. Ask them what they learnt, what they enjoyed, what didn't go so well and why.

Lead learners

Develop lead learning teams of pupils who are skilled at specific aspects of learning. Encourage these individuals to share their skills in and around learning. For example, students who are good at running de-briefing sessions such as plenaries can take a lead in their own lessons and also be deployed in other lessons. When in other lessons, they may have no subject knowledge but they do have process knowledge, so they will develop questioning skills and will have to draw the knowledge from other pupils. That way the other pupils have to share their learning and improve their skills in the process. Use the terms 'learning detectives' and 'process investigators' to define the roles of students who are encouraged to draw attention to specific learning behaviours, such as great group work, clever use of questions, active listening and independent thinking, and then report back on what they have spotted to the whole group.

You said ... we did ...

Make sure that, once you have given everyone an opportunity to voice their opinions, you let them know that they have been taken on board. Have a section in your newsletter that is dedicated to reporting on how you have responded to parent/pupil/community suggestions. Have a 'You said ... We did ...' board in a prominent position to show how you have reacted to suggestions and comments.

Reflect awhile

Uses staff meetings and conversations as opportunities to do more than discuss action. Many schools benefit from staff retreats or a focus that is more about being well than about being busy!

We catch people doing well.

Scrolling screens

Have television screens or a scrolling PowerPoint in the canteen and in other key areas of the school with news and praise for students who have done things well. This may include good test results, good or improved attendance, smart uniform or rewarding someone for doing the ordinary extraordinarily well. Include pictures of 'cool' children looking smart in their uniforms with the reasons why they wear the correct uniform scrolling underneath.

Public praise, private criticism

Praise in public and criticise in private. Only ever give out positive messages in assembly. What child is going to go to lessons keen to learn if they have just been lectured about poor behaviour on the buses when they personally walk to school? Equally, in morning staff briefings, stick to the positive. Save the negative for the individuals who need to hear it, not for the general masses.

Be proud and say it loud

Make a public display of how proud you are of your pupils and your school. Display huge photographs of children looking happy and engaged. Make sure that these include the students who have street cred! Play music written by your pupils in reception, or put it on the answer phone.

Make sure that your website is full of examples of the things your school and pupils excel at. Ensure that your reception area shows examples of pupils being busy. Move away from displaying products – artwork, ceramics, exam portfolios – in favour of showing them learning. Learning for many is a mysterious process which is done to us at school. Your reception and public areas provide an opportunity to show students and staff busy unravelling some of its mysteries!

Have 'I am proud of my school because ...' quotes written by all stakeholders in the school displayed in prominent positions – where visitors, staff and pupils can see them.

The power of thank you

Learn the power of a genuine thank you. A Moritz research project found that 28 per cent of people who had recently moved jobs did so partly because they did not feel valued or appreciated. Just saying 'thank you' can be enough – be specific and make sure you say why you are grateful or how someone has helped you. Buy some unusual post-it notes to write thank you notes and put them somewhere they will be found (on computer screens, desks, whiteboards, etc.). Alternatively, leave a personal note in a pigeon hole, possibly with a chocolate bar. Let staff know the difference they are making to you and to your pupils – be specific when you can.

Happiness is … 'Having people come up to me on the street and say, "Great job, Mayor!" (And not just my relatives.)'[205] (Bloomberg 2008)

Flower power

Send flowers/chocolates/a card home to the 'other halves' of members of staff who have been working particularly hard.

Staff Baftas

Have staff awards for anything you feel is appropriate – attendance, fantastic learning outcomes, effort, going beyond the call of duty.

Hero of the week

Consider who are the heroes and heroines of your staff. Display a picture of the staff 'hero of the week' in the staffroom, along with the reason why. Get your colleagues to make suggestions.

Praise a pupil

Send letters or postcards home to parents when a child has done something well. Alternatively, make a phone call or send a text or email. Find reasons to praise children who may often be overlooked. Have a set of pre-printed labels stating 'Excellent attendance/Homework well done/Fantastic behaviour', etc. to stick in pupils' homework diaries when appropriate. Have a celebration breakfast served by the SLT for pupils who are nominated by staff. Develop an award system for pupils that is easy to use and that ensures that all pupils are recognized. Show photographs of pupils to target for praise in your morning briefings, nominate star of the week pupils, have a role of honour board for each department or year group on which you display pupils' photos half-termly. Have a list of pupils' names in the staffroom for teachers to tick when they have sent a letter or made a phone call home and spot who is being left out – once spotted, find a reason to praise them.

Pupil praise

It is also important that your pupils learn the benefits of saying 'thank you'. Get members of your student council to give an award to the teacher who has made a difference every half term. Let them think of other appropriate awards for teachers.

Newsworthy

Find something positive to report in the local paper every week. Make sure that you publicise *everything* good that happens in your school (and the things that your pupils have achieved outside school – making sure, of course that your school's name appears too!). Drip feed to the local public what a good job you are doing and how much the children are learning and achieving.

Self-knowledge – If it's to be, it's up to me

We minimize unhelpful comparisons with others.

Invidious comparisons

Minimize unhelpful comparisons with other schools or other systems. Do this by protecting members of staff from data that is not useful to them. If specific data won't help them make improvements to learning and teaching, then only give it to them if they request it, or have it available online for them to access if they wish. Giving them the grades that each student should get is enough. Avoid de-motivating less successful people and departments through making comparisons and cramming statistics down their throats. Simply concentrate on how the stronger ones can help them. Link your strong departments, year groups or teachers with your weaker ones

Data protection

Similarly, protect children and parents from unnecessary data. An expected grade or level for each subject is sufficient. Then make sure that they know what they have to do to reach that grade or level. Give them clear guidance as to what is involved and how they can make the necessary improvements.

Famous encouragement

Use positive comparisons. Write to famous people and ask them to wish your exam group luck or to send a message of encouragement to your pupils. It has been known for schools to get a response from the prime minister!

We know our strengths and weaknesses.

Problem projects

Make a problem person your project. If you are aware of a particularly negative person among the staff, think of how you can get them to come on board. Speak to them, talk about what they are in the job for, motivate them and find them something to do that gives them their energy for their job back. If a particular pupil or group of pupils is making life less happy and secure for others, make them your project. Consider how you can get them back on board – try whatever it takes.

Do the right things

Start senior leadership team meetings by asking the question: 'What have we done since we last met to improve learning?' If the answer is 'nothing', then you have been doing the wrong things. Consider what you should have been doing and put it into practice.

Shovel negative upwards

In one school that we have worked with, there was a deputy head who referred to the school as 'this place'. Obviously, this negative attitude spread and affected the overall culture of the school. How could other members of staff possibly remain upbeat, when they heard this in the staffroom from a member of the school's management? And imagine how hard it was for the pupils to feel proud of their school and their achievements if they knew it was being spoken of in that way. While you may be aware of weaknesses in your school, have a rule that your senior leadership team can shovel negative upwards, but never downwards. When dealing with other members of staff, parents, pupils and members of the community, the SLT should remain positive and upbeat.

Touch through targets

Make sure that every member of staff has a realistic but challenging target for every child. They could write this target on their seating plans so that they are constantly reminded of it and can see immediately if a child is in danger of not reaching it. Target underperforming children as early as possible. Don't wait until they are in key years. Put their photographs up in a highly visible part of the staffroom so that everyone knows who they are. Refer to these photographs at staff meetings and encourage comment on what works and what doesn't work regarding motivating these children.

We know the difference between urgent and important.

Urgent versus important

Use the urgent versus important matrix on p. 258 to establish what you need to do as a school each week/half term/year. Enlarge it and have it in an obvious place in the staffroom. Encourage departments/year groups/individuals to have one in their own areas.

Attendance matters

Make sure that your students and their parents know what is important. Take every opportunity to talk about learning – in assemblies, as students are coming to and leaving school, at parents' evenings, at celebrations. Provide parents with the facts. If they ask to take their child on holiday in term time, let them know that missing school has a negative impact on a child's achievement generally and in SAT results, and on his or her friendships and social skills.[206] In fact, if attendance improves by 1 per cent, then attainment improves by 5–6 per cent.[207]

Set your own agenda

Work a to-do list that is based on the priorities you set yourself (as opposed to government initiatives). If it improves learning and teaching, do it. If not, bin it.

Integrity – To yourself be true

We confront the brutal facts.

Swallow the frog

Deal with people who don't sign up to the agreed values and beliefs. Do it now! If you had to eat a frog every day, you would do it first thing in the morning.[208] Eat the frog and have the difficult conversations. Prepare yourself with phrases that will help, such as: 'I don't want to have this conversation personally, but I must have it professionally.' Get these people to imagine how it will feel to be working as a member of the team and helping everyone work to the core purpose. Ask them to visualize their leaving party in however many years' time when they can talk about what they have done and achieved for the children in their care. Then give them a role that will help them to come onboard. For example, put them in charge of a group of children who are in danger of falling by the wayside.

Competence procedure

If you need it, use it. Do all you can to help individuals become competent and sign up to the core purpose. If they can't or won't, then you owe it to the children in your school to use the competence procedure.

We focus relentlessly on core purpose.

Core purpose test

Make sure that the entire school community regularly revisits core purpose and puts what is done through tradition, precedent or laziness to the 'core purpose' test.

Ban passive activities that have no impact on learning. Be bold in doing so. For example, copying down notes, study leave, Christmas 'wind-down' activities, word searches and watching DVDs don't have any learning outcome. Ditch them, however longstanding they may be. Replace them with something more suitable like deep learning days, Year 11 results improvement lessons and student-led learning activities.

What's stopping us?

Presuming that your core purpose has something to do with providing quality learning experiences for all learners (and we would strongly suggest that it is), you will need to involve everybody in looking at what may be preventing this and at what can be done to improve the chances of doing this? Try having a 'What's stopping us?' questionnaire and act on the results.

Remove obstacles

When a school in Surrey asked everybody what it was that prevented them from always planning fantastic lessons the results were perhaps unsurprising – they had other demands on their time, they didn't all know how and they didn't have the access they would have liked to the leadership team. The school responded by providing an ironing service, organizing for a garage to collect cars from the school when they needed servicing or MOTs, taking the doors off the leadership team's offices and by producing a shared model of learning across the school with staff working in teams to prepare outstanding lessons.

Some other ideas you may choose to implement are: have prescriptions delivered/fetched, provide membership to a local health club, provide breakfast in the morning for staff who get to school early, ban payments for tea/coffee, have someone to serve coffee and pack the dishwasher, provide members of staff with a laptop each, provide staff with dictaphones to record anecdotal evidence/reports and a member of support staff to type up notes.

Meeting motivation

Ensure that all meetings focus on learning and teaching, not on administration. Scrap any meetings that do not have an impact on pupils' learning. Make sure that your meetings follow a good learning model. Encourage department and/or year group meetings to have an agenda item called 'sharing of good practice' at every meeting. Every member must bring something of which they are proud because of its excellent learning outcomes. Shift the focus from 'What can I get them to do?' or 'What shall I teach?' to 'What will the pupils learn?' and 'How will they learn best?'

Register your use of time

Reconsider registration time. Some schools spend as much as 75 hours (plus) per year in registration. Is this a good use of time? Does it improve teaching and learning? Does it meet your core purpose? How could the time be better spent? (For example, could you offer revision classes to Year 11 students?)

Maintenance versus development

Divide all of your school's development plans into two: maintenance and development. Maintenance issues are what keep things ticking along nicely and development issues are the things that make your school an even better place. Maintenance tasks should be coloured in red, because they are dangerous and can prevent you from looking for improvement. Development tasks are those involving creativity and are the tasks that are probably most worth concentrating on.

Put learning at the top

Have a member of the SLT who is responsible solely for learning and teaching. Ensure that this is what your school focuses on – throw unnecessary paperwork in the bin. Be brave – all governments introduce new strategies and hoops to jump through. If they won't help you improve learning, put them to one side. No child will thank you for your school's wonderful policies. They will, however, thank you for opening up a whole new world of learning for them. Get rid of any unnecessary paperwork that keeps your staff from delivering excellent lessons.

We behave in ways that are consistent with our values.

What's the message?

Ensure that the school telephone is answered promptly, professionally and politely. Call up and test it on occasions. Make sure that the first option on your answer phone message isn't for staff calling in to report that they will be absent. This does not set a good tone! Ideally, have a completely different telephone number for staff absences.

Double loop thinking

Question long-held beliefs that may have become 'thought viruses'.[209] Consider the beliefs that are held in your school which may have been accepted as general truths, but are maybe only partially true. For example:

- 'No-one in the bottom sets can cope with learning languages.'
- 'Good discipline is the most important thing for a teacher to have.'
- 'Teaching the children as much content as possible to get them through exams is the best thing we can do for them.'

Talk these through with your staff, hold discussions on them and get them to start thinking about the validity of such beliefs. Highlight one such belief each week and display it with room for people to write their arguments for and against, have a discussion forum on your staff intranet or talk the beliefs through at meetings.

Morale hoovers

Some people invest heavily in gloom. They are your morale hoovers and their undue pessimism can go unchecked. Check that your staff values are aligned with your school's values. If they are not, address the member(s) of staff concerned. Don't let the morale hoovers shape the staffroom culture. Make it clear that they will need to change or go.

Smart recruitment

Advertise for and employ people who sign up to your core values. Make it very clear in your adverts what you are looking for and make sure that the questions you ask during interviews reflect your school's core purpose and values.

Ingredients of a great lesson

Involve all staff and pupils in deciding what makes a great learning experience. Agree and then define the characteristics of a great learning experience and make sure it is understood, regularly tested and communicated at all levels. An understanding of learning should shape the architecture of schemes of work, the way lessons are constructed and delivered and be a key component of staff development.

Grasp the nettle

If something isn't right, don't leave it. You must act. Deal with it! It may be painful, but you must always act with the interests of your pupils in mind. For example, if it means you have to speak to a difficult member of staff, or have to swap classes and teachers during the year, just bite the bullet and go for it.

Looking out for each other

HEALTH is about our mutual wellbeing. It is about looking after each other and about being looked after. It concerns both physical and mental well-being. Happy people are healthier – they are less likely to take time off work and they are more productive. Happier people receive better evaluations from their co-workers and managers and also more pay awards than their unhappier peers.

Security

When you are completing this section of the questionnaire, consider whether people really feel that they belong in your school, or whether they just turn up to carry out their work and then go home? Think about how much members of staff all do together (all members of staff that is, not just teaching staff). Are cleaning staff and non-teaching staff invited to social occasions; do they have their own uniforms? Are their contributions appreciated? And what about the pupils – do they feel that they belong to the school, that they are respected and trusted?

Consider both the physical safety of your staff and pupils and the environment in which they teach and learn – do they have control over their teaching and learning?

Feeling secure is essential if you want people to be creative and to come up with new ideas and make improvements. If they are in fear of being shot down, then they will keep their ideas to themselves. Do you encourage others to have a say in the future of your school? Do you listen to ideas and suggestions?

Well-being

A 2004 study[210] found that 29 per cent of people who left their job did so because they wanted a better work-life balance. Are your members of staff actively encouraged to have interests outside school, or are they just left to get on with it and work until they drop? What is done, if anything, to make the lives of your members of staff easier?

Consider the health of everyone in your school community. What is done to promote a healthy lifestyle for children and adults alike?

Well-being is also about the professional development of staff. How carefully do you consider individuals' developmental needs and what sort of training do you offer? Think about what sort of in-house training you offer – are your INSET days well planned, well delivered and relevant to your goals and core purpose? Perhaps you make use of the expertise of individuals to offer additional training above and beyond the required INSET?

Cooperation

Pulling together makes success far more likely. And pulling together involves making a sincere effort to appreciate the things other people do. Think about the things that are noticed in your school – are people given suitable recognition when they go above and beyond the call of duty, or is it simply expected of them without thanks? A thank you is cheap and takes little time, but the effect it can have on the recipient is immense.

A cooperative team will share a challenge, rather than watch on from a dry bank while others may be sinking. Do you talk to your staff and pupils about the challenges you face as a school? Do you invite their opinions and suggestions for possible solutions? Or do you closely guard them in an attempt to prevent others from finding out about them?

When a team is cooperating, its members will willingly help each other out. Consider your team – how much do people do for each other? Are they keen to offer advice and to give their time to others, or do they keep away from the staffroom in order to avoid being asked for help?

1 = This statement **never** applies to my school.
2 = This statement **rarely** applies to my school.
3 = This statement **sometimes** applies to my school.
4 = This statement **often** applies to my school.
5 = This statement **always** applies to my school.

Happier schools questionnaire: Health section

Security – The wind beneath my wings

We feel a strong sense of belonging.

	1	2	3	4	5	Total
Security – the wind beneath my wings						
We feel a strong sense of belonging						
We feel secure						
We have a say in the future of the organization						
Well-being – I'm OK, you're OK						
We encourage interests outside of our organization						
We promote a healthy lifestyle						
We prioritize the development of individuals						
Cooperation – together everyone achieves more						
We actively appreciate what people do						
We share every challenge						
We all give willingly and freely to help others						

Small is beautiful

Why not have more little schools within your big school? It is easier to retain the BASICS – belonging, aspiration, safety, identity, challenge and success – when you exist in a smaller unit. This is not an argument for more schools but for greater consideration of human scale when it comes to how we organize and lead our existing schools.

Well-being policies

Review all school policies which 'flow' into well-being and so contribute to happiness. For example bullying, reward systems, behaviour and personal safety policies.

Restorative justice

Restorative justice is a relationship management strategy where the focus is on repairing harm done to relationships rather than pointing the finger of blame or giving out punishments. It works through 'shuttle dialogue' and 'restorative conferencing' involving both the victim and perpetrator of any wrong doing.

Vertical tutoring groups

Vertical tutoring groups can contribute to the sense of belonging and being part of an integrated network which is such an important component of individual happiness.

Sing up at the back ...

Build a strong sense of belonging through a varied programme of social events. Ask your staff what they would participate in and when, then make sure that it happens. If it helps, have some of your key members of staff (those that can make everyone laugh at a drop of a hat and are able to get everyone up and moving) to work as a staff social committee and to organize a series of social events and cajole people who may be reluctant into attending.

Staff R Us

Your ancillary staff members are as much part of the team as anyone else. Provide them with branded uniforms. Make sure that these are both practical and stylish – they will be counter productive if people don't feel good wearing them! Invite midday supervisors, premises managers, cleaners and all support staff to Christmas meals, parties, Ofsted celebrations, staff meetings, INSET, etc. Make sure that they know that they are as included and as valuable as anyone else in your team.

Delete if ...

In order to manage the relationships in your school make communication direct; cut out emails as these can so easily be misinterpreted. Instead talk to faces. Try to cut out the middle man by avoiding passing information through a third party. If there is a need to send emails, start the title with 'DELETE IF' (for example, 'DELETE IF you don't teach Year 4'); that way people don't waste time opening irrelevant messages.

Build relationships

Know your staff. Acknowledge individuals. Being aloof or stand-offish makes them feel that they are not worth talking to or knowing. If remembering names and details doesn't come easily to you, write them down (include all of your non-teaching and cleaning staff). Talk to people and make it your business to remember details about them – ask them about their hobbies and family, etc. and refer back to things they have told you about in the past.

Staff roles

Rather than sticking to a simple display of staff photographs with names, have a display that includes what individuals do to contribute to learning. For example: 'I am the caretaker (or premises manager) and I contribute to learning by ensuring that the school is a clean, safe place in which to learn.' Or: 'I am a midday supervisor. I contribute to learning by ensuring that students and staff have a good lunch so that they are at their peak to learn and teach in the afternoon.'

Here I am ...

Have a list of all staff with photos, interests outside school, likes and dislikes and anything they feel comfortable about showing about themselves on the school intranet. You could get pupils to interview staff on their favourite books, television programmes, etc. and to put it onto the intranet for you.

We feel secure.

Work alongside agencies

Work with any agencies that support your core purpose. Have youth workers on your staff. Include the school in the police beat and ask them to help take an active part in some of the learning activities.

Safe journeys

When members of staff are working late at night, find out about their home journeys and make sure that they are safe and/or accompanied.

Car park corners

Ensure that your car park is well lit and clean and that there are no dark corners.

Site maintenance

The state of your building and its surroundings make a significant impression upon how secure people feel within them. Remove any graffiti immediately that appears where it shouldn't. Remove chewing gum from the carpet immediately; redecorate wherever is needed when it is needed. Take stock by walking around all of the school and its grounds. Imagine that you are a visitor coming to the site for the first time. Are there any fences that are looking tatty? Do the lines in the car park need painting? Are there balls stuck in the ceiling of the sports hall? Is there a lack of shrubbery and trees? If so, get them sorted out. If possible, get someone who hasn't been there for a while (or at all) to come and look with you – fresh eyes are likely to spot things that you have become used to seeing.

Washroom wiles

School toilets are well known as the places where pupils can feel least safe. Make sure they are clean, bright and hygienic and are visited regularly by staff members. Some schools we know of have part-time cloakroom attendants who will also look after personal belongings in a hotel-like cloakroom system.

Action group

Create an action group of pupils and young people who are committed to tackling whole community issues such as bullying, anti-social behaviour, personal safety, etc. Help them to work with the police, health agencies, the local council and other outside agencies so that their voices can be heard.

Peer mentoring

Have a peer mentoring system within your school in which older children support younger children. It is essential that the older children receive thorough training in order to be able to take on this role effectively.

We have a say in the future of the organization.

Flourishing ratios

A feedback ratio of 3:1 seems to be the best for balancing positive feedback to negative. Work done by Losada[211] found that flourishing teams engage in positive to negative speech acts on a ratio of 3:1 and are characterized by higher levels of enquiry-based questioning rather than advocacy and advice giving; more discussion about the organization rather refer the competition, and more outcomes related to those involved in the discussion as opposed to those who were not present. Losada also found that low performing teams got stuck in self-absorbed advocacy modes very early and stayed there.

Gottman's[212] longitudinal studies of 79 couples married on average for five years, looked at the balance of positive speech acts and positive observations made by partners. He found that marriages which flourished had a mean positivity ratio of 4.9:1. Marriages which were languishing had a ratio of 0.8:1.

Remarkable coherence exists[213] around these positivity ratios – whether it is for individuals, partnerships or organizations.

Some schools apply flourishing ratios to tools like WWW (What Went Well?) and EBI (Even Better If?) to solicit feedback on shared experiences such as INSET events.

Impact versus do-ability

Have a meeting in which you start by brainstorming ideas for improving your school. At this stage, anything goes. Once you have made a list, ask everyone to tick their top three. Then take the most popular ideas and put them onto an impact versus do-ability matrix to decide which ideas you will take forward.

Well-being – I'm OK, you're OK

We encourage interests outside of our organization.

No certificates, we're active

A study has found that employees who receive healthy, activity-based rewards get strong positive feelings from these and that the memories of the experience can last indefinitely. Moreover the study found that these feelings were even stronger and longer lasting when the employees got to share the reward with family, friends or colleagues.[214]

A taste of well-being

Have well-being events for all staff and provide incentives for those who go beyond the call of duty. Offer things like Indian head massage, pilates, yoga or fitness classes at lunchtime or after school. Reward staff with vouchers for a local health club. Organize exciting outdoor adventure days that staff may otherwise not experience (canoeing, climbing, archery lessons, mountain biking, etc.). Use well-being experiences to enhance problem solving. For example, over the course of a morning you might:

- Meet in groups to pose problems to do with the school.
- Choose to do one of the following therapeutic activities: line dancing, spin cycling, choral singing, head massage, swimming, pilates, yoga.
- Revisit groups to provide initial solutions to the problems posed.
- Choose and carry out a second therapeutic activity.
- Revisit groups to provide final and best solutions to the initial problems posed.
- Meet as a whole school to pool the thinking.

Pixar

Employees at Pixar (makers of *Toy Story* and *Wall-e* and one of the most innovative and creative companies of the current time) are encouraged to take courses that are outside of their own comfort zone and field of interests. The company understands that to get the very best out of their employees, they should have a good work-life balance and a variety of interests. Encourage your members of staff to have interests outside school. In a non-obtrusive and supportive way, make one of their performance management targets something that is completely unrelated to teaching and entirely to do with their physical, emotional or spiritual well-being.

Chief happiness officer

The technology giant Hewlett Packard employs a chief happiness officer. He is a Dane called Alexander Kjerulf. The Danes have a word for happiness on the job – it is *arbejdsglaede* – and worker productivity in Denmark is among the highest in the world. Of Fortune magazine's 100 best companies in America, those whose employees consistently cited them as good places to work outperformed others by providing a 14 per cent annual return as opposed to 6 per cent, between 1998 and 2005. According to Alex Edmans, a finance professor at Wharton Business School, this means that companies are having to revisit traditional practices. Have a chief happiness officer or a head of well-being in your school.

Pupil well-being days

Have well-being days or weeks for students around ECM topics. For example, you may have a Health Week, during which all subjects include something about having a healthy lifestyle – discuss foods and activities in foreign language lessons, teach repeating patterns by making fruit kebabs, have a healthy lunchbox competition, complete surveys on activities in numeracy, compare the food Victorians ate with the food we eat now, etc. You may be asking your staff to think a little differently and to come up with creative ideas for teaching their curriculum, but you will probably find that, given the time to be creative, they will rise to the challenge and will find it interesting and stimulating.

Shared strengths

Make the most of the strengths of your team of staff. Because you have made an effort to get to know them as we suggested in the previous section, you will know what these are! Encourage members of staff to use their own interests to help with homework clubs, after-school activities and activity weeks. Think how you can build these skills into the curriculum and maximize people's strengths. If, for example, you have a member of staff who can do circus tricks, get them to pass these skills on (to adults as well as children!).

We promote a healthy lifestyle.

Balancing acts

Do more than talk about work-life balance. Treat it seriously. Sample the working hours of a cross-section of your staff from the point of view of balance. You may find that some are spending an unhealthy amount of time in preparation and marking.

Radical marking

Get staff to mark less and pupils to self- and peer assess more. Have a marking policy which does not mention the word marking! Talk up peer evaluation and teach the skills of doing so. Talk up feedback forums where teachers talk through and reflect upon success criteria. Use Success Mats such as those Alistair recommends to help pupils with smart marking and smart coaching. Provide feedback guidelines and share a feedback vocabulary with pupils. (A Success Mat is a laminated A2 sheet which outlines a learning process. The card sits on a table or desk and is used to guide a group of students through a process. A Smart Marking Success Mat would give a step by step method of giving formative feedback. The mat would also contain key words and useful phrases to use.)

Head of well-being

Appoint a head of well-being who has responsibility for both staff and student well-being.

Five a day

Put a fruit bowl in the staffroom and fill it up a couple of times a week.

Cool it

Have water coolers in the staffroom and in department offices around the school.

Occupational health unit

Join with other schools to share the costs of having an occupational health unit.

Stress support

Make your staff aware of where they can get help in times of stress. As well as support systems you may offer within your school, teachers can access advice from websites such as those recommended at the back of the book.

We prioritize the development of individuals.

Have a go

It is natural for people to want to be a part of their organization and to understand how it works. When Pixar set up their on-site university, they found that it was not just illustrators and animators who attended the courses. Very often, an accountant would attend a course about animation. Involve all staff in key staff development activities and invite all staff to meetings and training, even if it is not in their personal field.

Effective CPD

Find and provide the right training. Plan and deliver an effective continuing professional development (CPD) programme. Encourage all members of staff to have a portfolio which includes certificates of attendance at training sessions. At the same time consider how you will cover for members of staff who are absent whilst attending training. They may be learning something to help improve teaching and learning (T&L), but what about the learning of the children they are not teaching? Make sure that any training during school time will be sufficiently beneficial to warrant losing the teacher for a day.

Run weekly CPD sessions, over and above the legal requirement, run by members of staff. Advertise them at the beginning of each term and ask staff to sign up. These are advantageous both for those attending and those running the training.

Cooperation – Together everyone achieves more

We actively appreciate what people do.

Kounaikenshuu

In Japan, teachers receive at least 20 days in-service training in their first year in the job.[215] The training takes the form of lesson study where groups of teachers meet regularly over long periods of time to work on the design of a few research lessons which are then revisited and improved. This intensely focused method is highly valued by Japanese teachers.

Appreciation night

If people do not feel appreciated for the work that they do, they are likely to leave. In contrast, those who are listened to and who are openly appreciated are more likely to stay in their jobs longer, work harder while they are there and have better relationships with their colleagues and pupils. Have your own Teacher's Oscars with slightly off-beat awards. For example: teacher with the biggest grin/person who has cheered everyone up the most/person who has gone beyond the call of duty.

Retention

Create an advanced skills teacher post in order to keep your best teachers who might otherwise move on.

Catch them doing something right

The moment you see someone (staff or pupils) do something right point it out and thank them. This can be anything from picking up a piece of litter, an excellent classroom display, some brilliant learning or teaching, a creative idea, to organizing and running successful residential trip or getting fantastic GCSE grades.

We share every challenge.

Solution focus INSET

Have a school solution focus INSET. Prior to the INSET, ask individuals and departments or teams to write down any challenges that they are facing. Put these in a hat and during the INSET pull some out. Set small focus teams to work on generating as many solutions as possible. Allow time for conclusions to be drawn and a plan of action to be drawn up.

We all give willingly and freely to help others.

Shared planning

Organize time for your teachers to plan together. Pair up people with different skills, for example creative people with practical people. It may be that people from very different departments, subject areas or year groups can still help each other prepare fantastic lessons. A fresh viewpoint could really help put a new spin on teaching!

Induction for all

Ensure that all new members of staff, whatever their level of experience, have the best possible induction training – partner them up with your very best teachers and make sure that they are made very aware of the culture of your school. Provide induction for non-teaching members of staff and for governors too.

Intranet storage

Have a place on the school intranet for staff to store and access short videos to use as connection activities (for more information, see p. 172). They could also post teaching ideas, share good practice and discuss any challenges they may be facing.

Build, broaden and balance activity

- Complete the questionnaire and fill in the wheel.
- Review the wheel for any obvious gaps and imbalances.
- Create an action plan to build, broaden and balance.
- Use your action plan.
- Look at the BBB strategies and note those which you have used or could use.
- Reflect on what you have done.
- Set a date to come back and revisit the questionnaire.

And finally ...

Gold Cup Festival week in Cheltenham is an exciting time. A sudden influx of thousands of people who drink 214,000 pints of Guinness over four days brings the relatively small town to life.

Residents love the buzz of being part of such an enormous event, but they know not to venture out in their cars until all of the race-goers are firmly ensconced at the racecourse! Here's what happened to one of Joanna's friends during the 2009 Festival:

> I'd got my timing just right. I came out of the house just after the start of the first race and was going to do a dash round the supermarket, meet some clients and head home after the racing was over for the day. If you get it wrong, you can sit for 90 minutes in traffic and move only half a mile! I was just climbing into the car when a heard two men berating a third for failing to order a taxi.
>
> 'For Gore's sake, Sean, would you not furget yer head if it werenut screwed on yer neck?'

They were stranded, five miles from the racecourse and no taxi.

> I told them I was going past the racecourse and to jump in. They didn't need asking twice. I got them to the course in time for the second race and, when they offered

to pay me the taxi rate, I refused. I'd enjoyed having them in the car, and I hadn't gone out of my way at all. (Though it was a good job I didn't have the kids with me, or they'd have picked up some colourful language to say the least!) As a parting shot, Sean, who had quickly been forgiven, promised to put a bet on for me.

I thought no more of it, although I did enjoy telling my clients some of what I'd heard in the car. When I got home, however, there was an envelope on the doormat, with a scrawled note; 'Cheers for the lift! Had a good day. Your horse came in too. If we got the wrong house, this'll make your neighbours' day!' There was £150 stuffed into the envelope. I still don't know which horse or which race, but it was quite some thank you for a lift!

Happiness is not so much the destination; it's more the experience along the way. Its fullest expression comes through the accumulation of internal moments and not the acquisition of external things. The £150 will soon evaporate but the feelings it engendered will linger on. Be brave – go for the H Factor.

6　Happier ever after

- Recommended books
- Recommended websites
- Glossary of terms used

Recommended books

Argyle, M. (1987), *The Psychology of Happiness*. London: Methuen.

Boniwell, I. (2007), *Positive Psychology in a Nutshell*. London: PWBC.

Brown, Stephanie, L. Nesse, M. Randolph, A. D. Vinokur, D. M. Smith and M. Dylan (2003), 'Providing social support may be more beneficial than receiving it: Results from a prospective study of mortality'. *Psychological Science*, 14(4), 320–7.

Carr, A. (2004), *Positive Psychology*. London: Brunner Routledge.

Carr, J. and L. Greeves (2006), *The Naked Jape: Uncovering the Hidden World of Jokes*. London: Michael Joseph.

Cohen, S., W. J. Doyle, D. P. Skoner, B. S.Rabin and J. M. Gwaltney, Jr (1997), 'Social ties and susceptibility to the common cold'. *Journal of the American Medical Association*, 277, 1940–4.

Csikszentmihaly, M. (1990), *Flow: The Psychology of Optimal Experience*. New York: Harper and Row.

Csikszentmihaly, M. (1997), *Living Well: The Psychology of Everyday Life*. New York: Basic Books.

Danner, D., D. Snowdon and W. Friesen (2001), 'Positive emotions in early life and longevity: Findings from the Nun Study'. *Journal of Personality and Social Psychology*, 80(5), 814–15.

Davidson R. J., J. Kabat-Zinn J, J. Schumacher, M. Rosenkrantz, D. Muller, S. F. Santorelli et al. (2003), 'Alterations in brain and immune function produced by mindfulness meditation'. *Psychosomatic Medicine*, 65, 564–70.

Diener, E. (1984), 'Subjective well-being'. *Psycological Bulletin*, 95, 542–75.

Diener, E. and M. E. P. Seligman (2004), 'Beyond money: Toward an economy of well-being'. *Psychological Science in the Public Interest*, 5, 1–31.

Fontana, David and Ingrid Slack (2007), Teaching Meditation to Children. UK: Watkins Publishing.

Fredrickson, B. L. (2001), 'The role of positive emotions in positive psychology: The broaden and build theory of positive emotions'. *American Psychologist*, 56, 218–26.

Gilbert, Daniel (2006), Stumbling on Happiness. London: HarperCollins.

Goldstein, Josef and Sharon Salzburg (2002), *Insight Meditation Kit. A Step-by-Step Course on How to Meditate* (audio book). Louisville: Sounds True.

Goldstein, Martin and Robert Cialdini (2007), *Yes! 50 Secrets from The Science Of Persuasion*. London: Profile.

Helliwell, J. and R. D. Putnam (2005), 'The social context of well-being', in F. A. Huppert, B. Keverne and N. Baylis (eds), *The Science of Well-being*. Oxford: Oxford University Press, pp. 435–460.

Hoddings, Nell (2003), *Happiness and Education*. Cambridge: Cambridge University Press.

Huppert, F. A. et al. (2005), *The Science of Well-being*. Oxford: Oxford University Press.

Huppert, F. A. (2005), 'Positive mental health: Individual and population flourishing', in F. A. Huppert, B. Keverne and N. Baylis (eds), *The Science of Well-being*. Oxford: Oxford University Press, pp. 307–40.

Kabat-Zinn, J. (2005), *Guided Mindfulness Meditation* (with CD). Louisville: Sounds True.

Kahneman, D., E. Diener and N. Schwarz (eds) (1999), *Well-being: The Foundations of Hedonic Psychology*. New York: Russell Sage Foundation.

Langer, E. J. (1989), *Mindfulness*. Reading, MA: Addison Wesley.

Layard, R. (2005), *Happiness: Lessons from a New Science*. New York: Penguin

Marar, Z. (2003), *The Happiness Paradox*. London: Reaktion Books.

Martin, Paul (2005), *Making Happy People: The Nature of Happiness and Its Origins in Childhood*. London: Fourth Estate.

Meaney, M. J. (2001), 'Maternal care, gene expression, and the transmission of individual differences in stress reactivity across generations'. *Annual Reviews of Neuroscience*, 21, 1161–92.

Nettle, D. (2005), *Happiness: The Science behind Your Smile*. Oxford: Oxford University Press.

Ornish, Dean M. D. and Stephan Bodian (2006), *Meditation for Dummies*. New Jersey: Wiley Publishing.

Persaud, R. (2001), *Staying Sane: How to Make Your Mind Work for You*. London: Bantam Books.

Peterson, C. and M. E. P. Seligman (2004), *Character Strengths and Virtues: A Handbook and Classification*. New York: American Psychological Association and Oxford University Press.

Provine, R. (2000), *Laughter: A Scientific Investigation*. London: Faber and Faber.

Puttnam, R. (2000), *Bowling Alone. The Collapse and Revival Of American Community*. New York: Simon and Schuster.

Ryan, R. M. and E. L. Deci (2001), 'On happiness and human potentials: A review of research on hedonic and eudaimonic well-being'. *Annual Reviews of Psychology*, 52, 141–66.

Seligman, M. E. P. (2002), *Authentic Happiness*. New York: The Free Press.

Seligman, M. E. P. (1990), *Learned Optimism*. New York: Simon and Schuster.

Smith, Alistair (2002), *The Brains behind It: New Knowledge about the Brain and Learning*. London: Network Continuum.

Weare, K. and G. Grey (2003), What Works in Promoting Children's Emotional and Social Competence and Well-being. London: DFES.

Recommended website

www.alite.co.uk
The Alite website gives details of our courses and programmes for educators, developers and parents. There are also links to the video resources for some of the lessons outlined in this book.

www.positivepsychology.org
The Positive Psychology Centre, Penn University of Pennsylvania has resources for teachers, questionnaires for personal use and for use with students, more information about positive psychology plus the opportunity to take part in Seligman's research online.

www.authentichappiness.org
This is the official Martin Seligman site containing online questionnaires and profiles.

http://www.psych.uiuc.edu/~ediener/
Ed Diener's website has answers to FAQs, a short questionnaire to judge your satisfaction with life plus research articles and PowerPoint presentations.

http://www.faculty.ucr.edu/~sonja/
The homepage of Sonja Lyubomirski.

http://www.unc.edu/peplab/barb_fredrickson_page.html
The homepage of Barbara Fredrickson.

http://www-psych.stanford.edu/~dweck/
Carol Dweck's personal page on the Stanford University website.

http://www.indiana.edu/~intell/index.shtml
This is a human intelligence website with biographical profiles of key researchers, such as Carol Dweck.

www.enpp.org
The European Network for Positive Psychology includes teaching notes to deliver positive psychology courses – these can be copied and used for educational but not commercial purposes. This website also has details of conferences and meetings.

http://www.cambridgewellbeing.org/
This website includes details of work that Cambridge University's psychology department is undergoing with its education department to develop school-based well-being programmes.

www.6seconds.org/index.php
This is a commercial organization promoting emotional intelligence.

www.antidote.org.uk
Antidote promotes well-being among young people in the UK.

www.centreforconfidence.co.uk
This is a Glasgow-based charity with a national brief to support individual, organizational and cultural change mainly through the dissemination of learning from positive psychology. Find further information on happiness, optimism and mindset, plus much more.

www.cappeu.org
This is a commercial organization promoting positive psychology.

www.eiworld.org
EI world is a commercial organization offering practical strategies to improve emotional intelligence.

www.gallupippi.com
The Gallup Institute for Global Well-Being

www.happiness.co.uk
The happiness website of author Robert Holden offers a daily 'coaching success' tip plus information on commercial courses for the individual's happiness.

www1.eur.nl/fsw/happiness/
The World Database of Happiness brings together scientific research on 'the subjective enjoyment of life'.

www.neweconomics.org
The New Economics Foundation is a 'think and do tank'. It is the organization behind GDH or Gross Domestic Happiness and its centre for well-being aims to 'enhance individual and collective well-being in ways that are environmentally sustainable and socially just'.

www.happyplanetindex.org
The HPI looks at the environmental impact of delivering well-being from country to country. Complete an online questionnaire to discover your life expectancy, your well-being levels, your carbon footprint and tips on how to improve these.

http://www.mhf.org.uk/publications/?EntryId5=43106
This training pack is a free to download resource for teachers to develop debate and activities on mental health promotion across their school. It can be used flexibly and at a pace that suits the school. The pack features a variety of activities, including the use of peer support and circle time, discussions about teachers' mental well-being and a range of handouts.

http://www.mhf.org.uk/welcome/
The Mental Health Foundation is a UK charity. The website has a section on children and young people and details research, information on mental health issues, real-life stories and podcasts to help with daily stress, etc.

http://www.right–here.org.uk/
This website details a current five-year project to promote well-being and improve mental health services for young people (aged 16–25).

http://www.thecalmzone.net
The 'Campaign against Living Miserably' raises awareness of depression among young men across Manchester, Merseyside, Cumbria and Bedfordshire.

http://www.roots.group.cam.ac.uk
The Roots Project looked into why some teenagers cope with problems and others don't. The website has simple information for teenagers and adults on the brain, diet, hormones, puberty and genes.

http://www.learningmeditation.com/
A website with suggested reading, tips on how to relax and links to further websites for people who want to know more about meditation and relaxation.

http://www.forgivenessproject.com/
A website that does what it says on the tin.

http://www.stressinstitute.com/
A website with suggestions for coping with stress.
The weak can never forgive. Forgiveness is the attribute of the strong. (Gandhi)
http://www.quotationspage.com/quote/2188.html 13.10.09

http://quotationsbook.com/quote/40990/ date accessed 13.10.09.
Money never made a man happy yet, nor will it … The more a man has, the more he wants. Instead of filling a vacuum, it makes one. (Benjamin Franklin)

http://thinkexist.com/quotation/i-do-not-try-to-dance-better-than-anyone-else-i/361529.html date accessed 13.10.09
A house may be large or small; as long as the neighbouring houses are likewise small, it satisfies all social requirement for a residence. But let there arise next to the little house a palace, and the little house shrinks to a hut … the occupant of the relatively little house will always find himself more uncomfortable, more dissatisfied, more cramped within his four walls.[76]

http://thinkexist.com/quotation/some_cause_happiness_wherever_they_go-others/ 157620.html date accessed 13.10.09
Some cause happiness wherever they go; others whenever they go. (Oscar Wilde)

http://thinkexist.com/quotation/life_would_be_infinitely_happier_if_we_could_only/181597.html date accessed 13.10.09
Life would be infinitely happier if we could only be born at the age of eighty and gradually approach eighteen. (Mark Twain)

http://www.quoteb.com/quotes/1973 date accessed 13.10.09
People are about as happy as they make their minds up to be. (Abraham Lincoln)

http://www.paradise-engineering.com/quotation/index.html accessed 14.10.09
It is better to be happy for a moment and be burned up with beauty than to live a long time and be bored all the while. (D. Marquis)

http://quote.robertgenn.com/getquotes.php?catid=133 13.10.09
It is not in doing what you like, but in liking what you do is the secret of happiness. (J. Barrie)

http://www.quotationspage.com/quote/2188.html 13.10.09
The weak can never forgive. Forgiveness is the attribute of the strong. (Gandhi)

http://quotationsbook.com/quote/6227/ date accessed 15.10.09
The best way to cheer oneself up is to try to cheer someone else up. (Twain)

Glossary of terms used

- Affinity – our capacity to form and sustain relationships with others.
- Attribution theory – how we as individuals explain the causes of any given success or failure.
- Build, balance and broaden – our recommended method for developing the signature characteristics of individual, departmental and school happiness.
- Construal theory – some say 'there are no facts, only events' and we constantly process or construe those events in order to make sense of them.
- Cooperation – living and working together in harmony.
- Core purpose – the essence of an individual or organization.
- Cortisol – chemical secreted by the adrenal gland as a consequence of stress.
- Desire-satisfaction theory – the theory states that, if all of our desires are met (regardless of whether they bring us pleasure or not), then our well-being will increase.
- Dissonance – an uncomfortable feeling caused by holding two contradictory ideas simultane-

ously. The 'ideas' or 'cognitions' in question may include attitudes and beliefs, and also the awareness of one's behaviour.

- Efficacy – the capacity to exercise control over one's circumstances.
- Empathy – the ability to see things from others' perspectives.
- Eudomania – Greek term meaning to reach your full potential.
- Explanatory style – indicates how people explain to themselves why they experience a particular event, either positive or negative. Psychologists have identified three components in explanatory style: personal – 'to what extent am I responsible?', permanence – 'is this likely to recur?', pervasiveness – 'does it happen to everyone?'.
- Fierce conversations – the ability to hold really difficult conversations touching upon sensitive issues but doing so with dignity and calm.
- Fixed and growth mindsets – based on a model by psychologist Carol Dweck which suggests we can 'lock in' to a way of thinking which is either 'fixed' (we perceive ourselves as having a given or limited ability) or 'growth' (we believe we can better ourselves through effort).
- Flourishing ratios – coherence of 3:1 around positive to negative feedback.
- Hedonism – the pursuit of happiness through the acquisition of happy moments or material possessions.
- Home and away groups – a simple method of organizing groups of learners by friendship or non-friendship.
- Humour – laughter which arises from a shared experience.
- Immune system – our physical ability to detect and resist disease.
- Integrity – 'doing the right thing, especially when no-one is looking'.
- Longitudinal study – following the participants over a course of years.
- Malleable intelligence – the belief that intelligence is not fixed but adaptable and capable of developing over time.
- Modelling – exhibiting the behaviours you wish to see in others by adopting them yourself.
- Obesity – a condition in which excess body fat has accumulated to an extent that health may be negatively affected. Obesity is commonly defined as a body mass index (BMI) of 30 kg/m^2 or higher.
- Objective list theory – the objective list theory takes things such as friendship, beauty, knowledge, health, creativity and virtue. The theory states that our lives will go best if we can fill our lives with as many items from the list as possible
- Openness – readiness to disclose feelings.
- Optimism – tendency to take a favourable view and see opportunity.
- Pessimism – negative tendency to perceive difficulties and find problems.
- Pester power – situations engineered by advertisers to encourage children to pester their parents for consumer products.

- Problem-solving team building – opportunity to solve local problems with help of colleagues using a problem-solving protocol.

- Security – feeling of personal safety.

- Self-theory – psychological basis of how we construct views about ourselves.

- Self-knowledge – degree to which we either understand or fail to understand our own motivations, behaviours and desires.

- Set point – the 'fixed' or set quality of personality determined by genetic inheritance.

- Signifiers – small gestures, incidents or interventions which suggest something of greater and different significance.

- Single and double loop thinking – single loop thinking is characterized by an inability to question the status or premise of the original approach, hence C follows B which follows A. Double loop thinking may question the validity of the sequence and its constituents.

- Social capital – the value which arises from well-formed relationship and kinship structures in any society. Social capital emerges from the prevalence of groups such as football leagues, badminton clubs, women's groups and reading clubs.

- Solutions wall – a problem-solving tool where solutions are posted then organized.

- Student voice – an opportunity for students to be more actively involved in their learning.

- Subjective well-being – how we as individuals define our own lives and levels of happiness.

- TAPIN – Take stock, Accept responsibility, Plan improvements, Imagine success, Negotiate a new path.

- The 5 Rs – Resilience, Resourcefulness, Responsibility, Reasoning and Reflection.

- Visible leadership – being seen to be active in the leadership role.

- Well-being – maintaining a healthy lifestyle in mind and body.

Endnotes

1 Thatcher, M. (1987), 'Aids, education and the year 2000!', *Woman's Own Magazine*, pp. 8–10.

2 Hicks, D. and Stone, R. (2007), '"Unlucky for some": The social impact of bingo club closures', *HCHLV*, 6, 47.

3 Putnam, R. (2000), *Bowling Alone: The Collapse and Revival of American Community*. New York: Simon and Schuster.

4 Gladwell, M. (2008), *Outliers: The Story of Success*. New York: Little, Brown and Company.

5 Speaking about research in, Steptoe, A., O'Donnell, K., Badrick, E., Kumari, M., and Marmot, M. (2008), 'Neuroendocrine and inflammatory factors associated with positive affect in healthy men and women'. *American Journal of Epidemiology*, 167(1), 96–102.

6 Fowler, J. and N. Christakis (2009), 'Dynamic spread of happiness in a large social network – longitudinal analysis of the Framlington heart study social network'. *British Medical Journal*, 338, 23.

7 Self, A. (2008), 'Social trends 38', *UK Office of National Statistics*, xxvii.

8 Childwise, (2009), 'Monitor report – mobile phones', *CHILDWISE*. p. 62.

9 Self, A. (2008), 'Social trends 38', *UK Office of National Statistics*, 174.

10 Earlier figures are total deaths – childhood deaths statistics not available.

11 Layard, R. (2005), 'Mental health, Britain's biggest social problem?', http://cep.lse.ac.uk/textonly/research/mentalhealth/RL414d.pdf. Date accessed 23 July 2009.

12 Hickman, M. (2007), 'For the first time, Britons' personal debt exceeds Britain's GDP', *Independent*, http://www.independent.co.uk/money/loans–credit/for–the–first–time–britons–personal–debt–exceeds–britains–gdp–462825.html. Date accessed 5 June 2009.

13 Hitchens, P. (2005), 'The Reward for Our Greed, a Generation of Young Savages', *Mail on Sunday*, http://www.dailymail.co.uk/debate/columnists/article–345243/The–reward–greed–generation–young–savages.html. Date accessed 5 June 2009.

14 Hughes, E., L. Pople, R. Medforth, G. Rees and C. Rutherford (2006), 'The good childhood? A question for our times'. A paper from The Children's Society.

15 Gibson, W. (2007), 'A review of *Toxic Childhood* (Sue Palmer)', http://www.childrenwebmag.com/books/books-reviews-child-care/toxic-childhood-by-sue-palmer. Date accessed 6 July 2009.

16 Rand, N. (2008), 'The "peace and plenty" generation: Understanding teenagers' lives'. *Young Consumers: Insight and Ideas for Responsible Marketers*, 5(1), 45–52.

17 UNICEF (2007), 'Child poverty in perspective: An overview of child well-being in rich countries', The United Nations' Childrens' Fund Innocenti Report Card 7, *UNICEF Innocenti Research Centre Florence*, p. 7.

18 Bullen, R. (2006), 'Kids seeking reality TV fame instead of exam passes'. *Learning and Skills Council*, p. 336.

19 NHS information Centre (2008) The National Child Measurement programme, summary of key facts, http://www.ic.nhs.uk/statistics–and–data–collections/ supporting–information/health–and–lifestyles–supporting–information/ obesity/the–national–child–measurement–programme/national–child– measurement–programme–2006/07/ncmp–2006–07–report. Date accessed 9 July 2009.

20 Gerberding, J. (2003), Centre for Disease Control and Prevention, in speech at University of Georgia's Atlanta Alumni centre.

21 Kirby, T. (2006), 'Massive increase in obesity means one-third of children are overweight', *Independent*, http://www.independent.co.uk/life–style/ health–and–families/health–news/massive–increase–in–obesity–means–onethird– of–children–are–overweight–475136.html. Date accessed 8 July 2009.

22 Street Porter, J. (2008), 'The growth industry that is now obesity', *Independent*, http://www.independent.co.uk/opinion/commentators/janet–street–porter/ janet–streetporter–the–growth–industry–that–is–now–obesity–954487.html. Date accessed 9 July 2009.

23 Dr Foster and Abbott Laboratories Ltd (2005), 'Obesity Management in the UK', http://www.drfosterintelligence.co.uk/newsPublications/publications/ reports/obesityBackground.asp. Date accessed 15 July 2009.

24 Ryan, S. and N. Beta (2009), 'Childhood obesity epidemic a myth, says research', the *Australian*, http://www.theaustralian.news.com.au/ story/0,25197,24889986–601,00.html. Date accessed 15 July 2009.

25 About Cozzolini, J. (2008), Motorola survey, Motorola, http://www.motorola. com. Date accessed 9 July 2009.

26 Future Foundation (2006), Experian from Easier.com motoring, (2006), 'Kids now have a bigger say in the car buying decision', http://www.autoindustry. co.uk/press_releases/11–08–06. Date accessed 13 July 2009.

27 Hughes, E., L. Pople, R. Medforth, G. Rees and C. Rutherford (2006), 'The good childhood? A question for our times'. A paper from The Children's Society.

28 New Girlguiding UK and Mental Health Foundation (2008), 'A generation under stress', http://www.mentalhealth.org.uk/media/news–releases/news– releases–2008/14–july–2008/. 12 July 2009.

29 Zurbriggen, E., R. Collins, S. Lamb, T. Roberts, D. Tolman, L. Ward and J. Blake (2007), 'Report of the APA Task Force on the Sexualization of Girls', American Psychological Association, http://www.apa.org/pi/wpo/sexulaizationsum.html. Date accessed 23 August 2009.

30 McFadyean, M. (1986), 'Youth in distress. Letters to *Just Seventeen*'. *Health Education Journal*, 45(1), 49–51.

31 The British Association of Aesthetic Plastic Surgeons, (2005), 'Plastic surgery: It's not teens, it's their grandparents!', http://www.baaps.org.uk/content/view/131/62/. Date accessed 15 July 2009.

32 Ipsos MORI (2004), 'Media image of young people', *Young People Now Magazine*, http://www.ipsos–mori.com/researchpublications/researcharchive/poll.aspx?oItemId=761. Date accessed 15 July 2009.

33 Dorfman, L. and V. Schiraldi (2001), 'OFF BALANCE: Youth, Race & Crime in the News', http://www.buildingblocksforyouth.org/media/media.html. Date accessed 15 July 2009.

34 Bawdon, F. (2009), 'Hoodies or altar boys? What is media stereotyping doing to our boys?', *Women in Journalism*, http://www.womeninjournalism.co.uk/node/325. Date accessed 13 July 2009.

35 Ipsos MORI youth survey (2008), 'Young people in education', http://www.yjb.gov.uk/Publications/Resources/Downloads/MORI_08_fullreport_EDU.pdf. Date accessed 13 July 2009.

36 Russell, B. (2009), 'One third of children admit to carrying a gun or knife', *Independent*, http://www.independent.co.uk/news/uk/crime/one–third–of–children–admit–to–carrying–a–gun–or–knife–1638512.html. Date accessed 14 July 2009.

37 Ipsos MORI youth survey (2008), 'Young people in education', http://www.yjb.gov.uk/Publications/Resources/Downloads/MORI_08_fullreport_EDU.pdf. Date accessed 13 July 2009.

38 Telegraph.co.uk, (2009), 'One crime committed every two minutes by British youths', http://www.telegraph.co.uk/news/newstopics/politics/lawandorder/4946255/One–crime–committed–every–two–minutes–by–British–youths.html. Date accessed 15 July 2009.

39 UNICEF, (2007) 'Child poverty in perspective: An overview of child well-being in rich countries', The United Nations' Childrens' Fund Innocenti Report Card 7, *UNICEF Innocenti Research Centre Florence*, p. 7.

40 Morris, D. (2008), to news conference. BBC News, http://news.bbc.co.uk/1/hi/wales/7253788.stm. Date accessed 15 July 2009.

41 Bailey, S. (2007), Child mental health ills 'rife'. BBC News, http://news.bbc.co.uk/1/hi/health/6221240.stm. Date accessed 23 July 2009.

42 McCulloch, A. (2008), Mental Health Foundation, http://www.mentalhealth. org.uk/media/news–releases/news–releases–2008/21–october–2008/. Date accessed 15 July 2009.

43 Bellamy, C. (2001), 'Unicef Young Voices Poll of 2000–2001', http://www. unicef.org/polls/. Date accessed 14 July 2009.

44 Mental Health Foundation, (2008), 'Children and young people, good mental health', http://www.mentalhealth.org.uk/information/mental–health–a–z/ children–and–young–people/. Date accessed 15 July 2009.

45 Steptoe, A. (2008), commenting to press on Steptoe, A., K. O'Donnell, E. Badrick, M. Kumari and M. Marmot (2008), 'Neuroendocrine and inflammatory factors associated with positive affect in healthy men and women. The Whitehall II Study'. *American Journal of Epidemiology*, 167(1), 96–102.

46 Harman, N. (2009), 'Andy Murray made to work hard for semi-final place by Ivan Ljubicic', *Times Online*, http://www.timesonline.co.uk/tol/sport/tennis/ article5941750.ece. Date accessed 13 July 2009.

47 Hodgkinson, M. (2009), 'Britain's Andy Murray made to sweat by Ivan Ljubicic', *Telegraph.co.uk*, http://www.telegraph.co.uk/sport/tennis/ andymurray/5019361/Britains–Andy–Murray–made–to–sweat–by–Ivan– Ljubicic.html. Date accessed 13 July 2009.

48 Craig, C. (2009) to Radio 4's Today Programme.

49 The Missouri Department of Economic Development (2008), Missouri job vacancy survey, Missouri Economic Research and Information Centre, http:// ded.mo.gov/cgi–bin/dispress.pl?txtpressid=103. Date accessed 13 July 2009; Stasz, C., K. Ramsey, R. Eden, E. Melamid and T. Kaganoff (1996), 'Workplace skills in practice case studies of technical work', RAND Corporation, http:// www.rand.org/pubs/monograph_reports/MR722/index.html. Date accessed 13 September 2007.

50 Margo, J. and M. Dixon with N. Pearce and H. Reed (2006) 'Freedoms orphans: Raising youth in a changing world', *IPPR*.

51 Clake, R. (2006), 'UK employers seek school-leavers with soft skills, finds quarterly CIPD/KPMG Labour Market Outlook', http:// www.epolitix.com/stakeholder-websites/press-releases/press- release-details/newsarticle/uk-employers-seek-school-leavers-with- soft-skills-finds-quarterly-cipdkpmg-labour-market-outlook///sites/ chartered-institute-of-personnel-and-development/. Date accessed 23 July 2009.

52 Lyubomisky, S., E. Diener and L. King (2005), 'The benefits of frequent positive affect: Does happiness lead to success?'. *Psychological Bulletin*, 131(6), 803–55.

53 Conti, G., A. Galeotti, G. Mueller and S. Pudney (2009), 'Popularity', Institute for Social and Economic Research, http://www.iser.essex.ac.uk/publications/working–papers/iser/2009–03.pdf. Date accessed 12 July 2009.

54 Ipsos MORI (2008), Young people omnibus survey – 2008, Sutton Trust, pp. 1–3.

55 Marks, N. H. Shah and A. Westall (2004), 'The power and potential of well-being indicators: Measuring young people's well-being in Nottingham', New Economics Foundation (NEF) and Nottingham City Council.

56 Pring, R. (2008), 'The Nuffield Review of 14–19 education and training, England and Wales issues paper 6: Aims and values', http://www.nuffield14-19review.org.uk/files/news58-2.pdf. Date accessed 23 July 2009, pp. 1–8.

57 Cox, D. (2006), 'The health benefits of happiness', BBC News, http://news.bbc.co.uk/1/low/programmes/happiness_formula/4924180.stm. Date accessed 13 July 2009.

58 Danner, D., D. Snowdon and W. Friesen (2001), 'Positive emotions in early life and longevity: Findings from the Nun Study'. *Journal of Personality and Social Psychology*, 80(5), 804–13.

59 Cohen, S., W. Doyle, R. Turner, C. Alper and D. Skoner (2003), 'Emotional style and susceptibility to the common cold'. *Psychosomatic Medicine*, 65(4), 652–7.

60 47 Veenhoven, R. (2008), 'Healthy happiness: Effects of happiness on physical health and the consequences for preventive health care'. *Journal of Happiness Studies*, 9, 3.

61 Steptoe, A., J. Wardle and M. Marmot (2005), 'Positive affect and health-related neuroendocrine, cardiovascular, and inflammatory processes'. *Proceedings of the National Academy of Science*, http://www.pnas.org/content/102/18/6508.full?ck=nck#sec-1. Date accessed 14 July 2009.

62 Veenhoven, R. (2008), 'Healthy happiness: Effects of happiness on physical health and the consequences for preventive health care'. *Journal of Happiness Studies*, 9, 3.

63 Steptoe, A., K. O'Donnell, E. Badrick, M. Kumari and M. Marmot (2008), 'Neuroendocrine and inflammatory factors associated with positive affect in healthy men and women. The Whitehall II Study'. *American Journal of Epidemiology*, 167(1), 96–102.

64 Weissberg, B. (2005), BBC News, http://news.bbc.co.uk/1/hi/health/4449199.stm. Date accessed 12 July 2009.

65 Frederickson, B. (1998), 'What good are positive emotions?'. *Review of General Psychology*, 2, 300–19.

66 Veenhoven, R. (2007), 'Healthy happiness: Effects of happiness on physical health and the consequences for preventive health care'. *Springer Science+Business*

Media, 12–13, http://www.springerlink.com/content/0474658172222350/ fulltext.pdf. Date accessed 12 July 2009.

67 Schulz, W. (1985), 'Lebensqualität in Österreich (Quality of Life in Austria) Report', vol. 10,1 and vol. 10,2. Institute of Sociology of the Faculty of Social and Economic Sciences, University of Vienna.

68 Lederman, S., V. Rauh, L. Weiss, J. Stein, L. Hoepner, M. Becker and F. Perera (2004), 'The effects of the World Trade Center event on birth outcomes among term deliveries at three Lower Manhattan hospitals'. *Environ. Health Perspect.*, 112(17), 1772–8.

69 McCrae, R. and P. Costa (1986), 'Cross-sectional studies of personality in a national sample: Development and validation of survey measures'. *Psychology and Aging*, 1, 140–3.

70 Diener, E., E. Suh and S. Oishi (1997), 'Recent findings on subjective well-being'. *Indian Journal of Clinical Psychology*, 24(1), 25–41.

71 Giles, O. (2007), *Times Online*, http://women.timesonline.co.uk/tol/life_and_style/women/the_way_we_live/article2688285.ece. Date accessed 13 July 2009.

72 Giles, O. (2007), *Times Online*, http://women.timesonline.co.uk/tol/life_and_style/women/the_way_we_live/article2688285.ece. Date accessed 13 July 2009.

73 Brickman, P., D. Coates and R. Janoff-Bulman (1978), 'Lottery winners and accident victims: Is happiness relative?'. *Journal of Personality and Social Psychology*, 36, 917–27.

74 Diener, E., J. Horowitz and R. Emmons (1985), 'Happiness of the very wealthy', *Social Indicators Research*, 16, 263–74.

75 Brickman, P., D. Coates and R. Janoff-Bulman (1978), 'Lottery winners and accident victims: Is happiness relative?'. *Journal of Personality and Social Psychology*, 36, 917–27.

76 Marx, 1891. Marx, K. (1998), *Wage Labour and Capital*. Peking: Foreign Languages Press. http://www.marx2mao.com/M&E/WLC47.html#TP. Date accessed 25 July 2009.

77 Zheren, W. (2008), 'Relative income positions and labor migration: A panel study based on a rural household survey in China', *Discussion Papers in Economics and Business*, Osaka University, Graduate School of Economics and Osaka School of International Public Policy, 8–24.

78 HM Revenue and Customs data (2000–2003), National Statistics.

79 Wilkinson, R. and K. Pickett (2009), *The Spirit Level: Why More Equal Societies Almost Always Do Better*. London: Allen Lane.

80 Solnick, S. and D. Hemenway (1997), 'Is more always better? A survey of positional concerns'. *Journal of Economic Behaviour and Organization*, 37, 373–83.

81 Lyubomirski, S. and L. Ross (1997), 'Hedonic consequences of social comparison: A contrast of happy and unhappy people'. *Journal of Personality and Social Psychology*, 73, 1141–57.

82 Pruessner, J., M. Baldwin and S. Lupien (2005), 'Self-esteem, locus of control, hippocampal volume, and cortisol regulation in young and old adulthood'. *Neuroimage*, 28(4), 815–26.

83 Huppert, F. (2003), BBC News, 'Low self-esteem "shrinks brain"', http://news.bbc.co.uk/1/hi/health/3224674.stm. Date accessed 15 July 2009.

84 Brody, A. (2007), 'Ben Affleck's sweet revenge', FilmStew, http://www.filmstew.com/showArticle.aspx?ContentID=14786. Date accessed 15 July 2009.

85 Van Boven, L. and T. Gilovich (2003), 'To do or to have? That is the question'. *Journal of Personality and Social Psychology*, 85(6), 1193–1202.

86 Numbers only include surgeons who are members of BAAPs.

87 Krebs, D. and A. Adinolfi (1975), 'Physical attractiveness, social relations, and personality style'. *Journal of Personality and Social Psychology*, 31(2), 245–53.

88 Diener, E., B. Wolsic and F. Fujita (1995), 'Physical attractiveness and subjective well-being'. *Journal of Personality and Social Psychology*, 69(1), 120–9.

89 Försterling, F., S. Preikschas and M. Agthe (2007), 'Ability, luck, and looks: An evolutionary look at achievement ascriptions and the sexual attribution bias'. *Journal of Personality and Social Psychology*, 92(5), 775–88.

90 Försterling, F., S. Preikschas and M. Agthe (2007), 'Ability, luck, and looks: An evolutionary look at achievement ascriptions and the sexual attribution bias'. *Journal of Personality and Social Psychology*, 92(5), 775–88.

91 Eagley, A., R. Ashmore, M. Makhijani and I. Longo (1991), 'What is beautiful is good, but … A meta-analytic review of research on the physical attractiveness stereotype'. *Psychological Bulletin*. 110, 109–28.

92 Dermer, M. and D. Thiel (1975), 'When beauty may fail'. *Journal of Personality and Social Psychology*, 31(6), 1168–76.

93 Freeman, H. (1985), 'Somatic attractiveness: As in other things, moderation is best'. *Psychology of Women Quarterly*, 9(3), 311–22.

94 Taylor, S. and M. Butcher (2007), British Psychological Society's Annual Conference.

95 Farrow, M. (2008), The Star.com, http://www.thestar.com/comment/columnists/article/306547. Date accessed 23 July 2009.

96 Redelmeier, D . and S. Singh (2001), 'Appearances are deceptive. Longevity of screenwriters who win an academy award: Longitudinal study'. *BMJ*, 323, 1491–6.

97 Chesterton, G. (1910), *Heretics*, London: J. Lane.

98 Seligman, M., http://www.authentichappiness.sas.upenn.edu/Default.aspx. Date accessed 23 July 2009.

99 Wallis, C. (2005), 'The new science of happiness', *Time Magazine*, 9 January.

100 Thompson, E. (2008), 'Proust questionnaire', *Vanity Fair*, http://www.vanityfair.com/culture/features/2008/07/proust_thompson200807. Date accessed 12 July 2009.

101 Lykken, D. and A. Tellegen (1996), 'Happiness is a stochastic phenomenon'. *Psychological Science*, 7(3); Weiss, A., T. Bates and M. Luciano (2008), 'Happiness is a personal(ity) thing: The genetics of personality and well-being in a representative sample'. *Psychological Science*, 19(3), 205–10.

102 Lyubomirsky, S. (2008), *The How of Happiness: A Scientific Approach to Getting the Life you Want*. New York: Penguin.

103 Clark, A., E. Diener and R. Lucas (2008), 'Lags and leads in life satisfaction: A test of the baseline hypothesis'. *Economic Journal*, 118, F222–F443.

104 Bandura, A. (1986), *Social Foundations of Thought and Action: A Social Cognitive Theory*. New Jersey: Prentice-Hall, p. 25.

105 Bandura, A. (1977), *Social Learning Theory*. New York: General Learning Press.

106 Seligman, M. (2003) to Sample, I., *Guardian*, http://www.guardian.co.uk/society/2003/nov/19/1. Date accessed 23 July 2009.

107 McCain, J. (2008) to Republican Convention. Source: BBC News, http://news.bbc.co.uk/1/hi/world/americas/7599422.stm . Date accessed 15 July 2009.

108 Lyumomirsky, S. (2001), 'Why are some people happier than others? The role of cognitive and motivational processes in well-being'. *American Psychologist*, 56(3), 239–49.

109 Fredrickson, B. and T. Joiner (2002), 'Positive emotions trigger upward spirals toward positive well-being'. *Psychological Science*, 13(2), pp. 172–5.

110 Gilbert, D.(2006), *Stumbling on Happiness*. London: Harper Press.

111 National child development study (begun in 1958), Centre for Longitudinal Studies.

112 Golstein, N., S. Martin and R. Cialdini (2007), *Yes: The Science of Persuasion*. London, Profile.

113 Craig, C. (2007), 'The potential dangers of a systematic, explicit approach to teaching social and emotional skills (SEAL). An overview and summary of the arguments', Glasgow: Centre for Positive Psychology, p. 6.

114 Smith, A. and N. Call (2001), *The ALPS Approach Resource Book*. Stafford: Network Educational Press.

115 Heifetz, R. and M. Linksy (2002), *Leadership On The Line: Staying Alive Through The Dangers Of Leading*. Harvard: Harvard School Press.

116 de La Rochefoucauld, F., in Blech, B. (2004), *Taking Stoc:, A Spiritual Guide to Rising Above Life's Financial Ups and Downs*. New Jersey and Canada: John Wiley and Sons.

117 Fontana, D. and I. Slack (2007), *Teaching Meditation to Children, A Practical Guide to the Use and Benefits of Meditation Techniques*. UK: Watkins Publishing.

118 Stockdale, J. and S. Stockdale (1984), *In Love and War*. New York, Harper and Row, (revised 1990).

119 Stockdale, J. and S. Stockdale (1984), *In Love and War*. New York, Harper and Row, (revised 1990).

120 Mathews, M., Lemonade Stand, http://www.blogsbywomen.org/my–lemonade–stand.6285.html. Date accessed 13 December 2008.

121 Davis, B., in Gschwandtner, G. (2007), *Great Thoughts to Sell By: Quotes to Motivate You to Succeed*. Europe: McGraw-Hill Education.

122 Burrill, G., in Geary, J. (2005), *The World in a Phrase: A History of Aphorisms*. New York: Bloomsbury.

123 Curtis, J. (2009), Success, http://www.brainyquote.com/quotes/quotes/j/jamieleecu360539.html. Date accessed 23 July 2009.

124 Frankl, V. (1946), *Man's Search for Meaning*. Boston: Beacon Press.

125 Frankl, V. (1946), *Man's Search for Meaning*. Boston: Beacon Press.

126 Winslet, K. (2008), 'Isn't she deneuvely?', *Vanity Fair*, http://www.vanityfair.com/culture/features/2008/12/winslet200812?currentPage=2. Date accessed 12 July 2009.

127 Sullivan, B., M. Snyder and J. Sullivan (2008), *Co-operation: The Political Psychology of Effective Human Interaction*. Oxford: Blackwell.

128 Miller, M., C. Mangano, Y. Park, R. Goel, G. Plotnick and R. Vogel (2005), 'Laughter helps the blood vessels function', presented to Scientific Session of the American College of Cardiology.

129 Clark, A., A. Seidler and M. Miller (2001), 'Inverse association between sense of humor and coronary heart disease'. *International Journal of Cardiology*, 80(1), 87–8.

130 Miller, M., C. Mangano, Y. Park, R. Goel, G. Plotnick and R. Vogel (2005), 'Laughter helps the blood vessels function', presented to Scientific Session of the American College of Cardiology.

131 Berg, J., J. Dickhaut and K. McCabe (1995), 'Trust, reciprocity and social history', *Games and Economic Behaviour*, 10(1), 122–42; Falk, A., S. Gächter and J. Kovacs (1997), 'Intrinsic motivation and extrinsic incentives in a repeated game with incomplete contracts'. *Journal of Economic Psychology*, 20(3), 251–84; Fehr, E. and S. Gächter (2000), 'Fairness and retaliation: The economics of reciprocity'. *Journal of Economic Perspectives*, 14, 159–81.

132 Oatley, K., M. Djikic and R. Mar, (2008), 'The science of fiction'. *New Scientist*, 2662, 42–3.

133 Harbaugh, W., U. Mayr and D. Burghart (2007), 'Neural responses to taxation and voluntary giving reveal motives for charitable donations'. *Science*, 316(5831), 1622–5.

134 Enright, R. (1999), *Dimensions of Forgiveness, Psychological Research and Theological Perspectives*. Philadelphia: *Templeton Foundation Press*.

135 The free store: A concept for recessionary times, http://grosski.tumblr.com/. Date accessed 23 July 2009.

136 Lawler, K., J. Younger, R. Piferi, E. Billington, R. Jobe, K. Edmondson and W. Jones (2003), 'A change of heart: Cardiovascular correlates of forgiveness in response to interpersonal conflict'. *Journal of Behavioural Medicine*, 26(5), 373–93.

137 McCullough, M., L. Root and A. Cohen (2006), 'Writing about the benefits of an interpersonal transgression facilitates forgiveness'. *Journal of Consulting and Clinical Psychology*, 74, 887–97.

138 Simon, N. (2007), 'Proust questionnaire', *Vanity Fair*, http://www.vanityfair.com/culture/features/2007/10/proust_simon200710. Date accessed 12 July 2009.

139 McCollough, M. and R. Emmons (2004), *The Psychology of Gratitude*. New York: Oxford University Press.

140 Pollak, D., F. Monje, L. Zuckerman, C. Denny, M. Drew and E. Kandel (2008), 'An animal model of a behavioral intervention for depression'. *Neuron*, 60(1), 149–61.

141 Matzel, L., Y. Han, H. Grossman, M. Karnik, D. Patel, N. Scott, S. Specht and C. Gandhi (2003), 'Individual differences in the expression of a "general" learning ability in mice'. *Journal of Neuroscience*, 23(16), 6423–33.

142 Chandiramani, K. (2001), 'Meditation as efficient as psychotherapy for prisoners', lecture to Royal College of Psychiatrists Annual Meeting.

143 Kabat-Zinn, J., E. Wheeler, T. Light, A. Skillings, M. Scharf, T. Cropley, D. Hosmer and J. Bernhard (1998), 'On rates of skin clearing in patients with moderate to severe psoriasis undergoing phototherapy (UVB) and photochemotherapy (PUVA)'. *Psychosomatic Medicine*, 60, 625–32.

144 Mitchell, R. and F. Popham (2008), 'Effect of exposure to natural environment on health inequalities: An observational population study'. *The Lancet*, 372(9650), 1655–60.

145 Spencer, M. (2006), *Two Aspirins and a Comedy How Television Can Enhance Health and Society*. Colorado: Paradigm Publishers.

146 Taylor, S. (2002), *The Tending Instinct: How Nurturing is Essential to Who We Are and How We Live*. New York: Henry Holt.

147 DeNault, L. and D. McFarlane (1995), 'Reciprocal altruism between male vampire bats, Desmodus rotundus'. *Animal Behaviour*, 49(3), 855–6.

148 Gibson, M., http://www.quotedb.com/quotes/2718. Date accessed 15 July 2009.

149 Emmons, R. and M. McCullough (2004), *The Psychology of Gratitude*. New York: Oxford University Press; Seligman, M., T. Steen, N. Park and C. Peterson

(2005), 'Positive psychology progress: Empirical validation of interventions'. *American Psychologist*, 60(5), 410–21.

150 Larson, J. and Rusert, B. (2008), reporting on Maritz Poll, http://www.maritz. com/Maritz–Poll/2007/Maritz–Poll–Maritz–Unveils–Six–Distinct–Employee–Types–Based–on–Reward–Preferences.aspx. Date accessed 12 July 2009.

151 Toepfer, S. (2008), 'Letters of gratitude study – writing to improve wellbeing', http://www.kent.edu/magazine/Winter2008/AttitudesGratitude.cfm. Date accessed 23 July 2009.

152 Seligman, M. (2002), *Authentic Happiness: Using the New Positive Psychology to Realize Your Potential for Lasting Fulfillment*. New York: Free Press.

153 Hauter, S. and D. Hauter, 'Therapeutic health benefits of aquariums', *About. com*, (http://saltaquarium.about.com/cs/publicswfamilyfun/a/aa010600_2. htm) p. 2, reporting on Clay, R. (1997), 'Psychologists find animals to be a helpful adjunct to therapy', Monitor on Psychology.

154 Hay McBer, (2000), 'Research into teacher effectiveness – a model of teacher effectiveness', Department for Education and Employment, 31, http://www. dcsf.gov.uk/research/data/uploadfiles/RR216.pdf.

155 Hay McBer, (2000), 'Research into teacher effectiveness – a model of teacher effectiveness', *Department for Education and Employment*, 27, http://www.dcsf. gov.uk/research/data/uploadfiles/RR216.pdf.

156 Henderson, M. (2007), 'Of course happiness can't be taught', *Daily Telegraph*, http://www.telegraph.co.uk/comment/personal–view/3639837/Of–course–happiness–cant–be–taught.html. Date accessed 9 July 2009.

157 Juszczak, E., L. Applebey, R. McDonnell, T. Amos, K. Kiernan, H. Parrott, K. Hawton, L. Harris and S. Simkin (2000), 'Effect of death of Diana, Princess of Wales on suicide and deliberate self-harm', *British Journal of Psychiatry*, 177, 463–6.

158 Smith, A. and O. Shenton (1995), *Accelerated Learning in the Classroom*. Stafford: Network Educational Press; Smith, A. and N. Call (1999), *The ALPs Approach (Accelerated Learning in Primary Schools*. Stafford: Network Educational Press; Smith, A., M. Lovatt and D. Wise (2003), *Accelerated Learning: A User's Guide*. Stafford: Network Educational Press.

159 Frey, S. and A. Stutzer (2000), 'Happiness, economy and institutions'. *Economic Journal*, 110, 918–38.

160 Bethel-Fox, C. and F. O'Conor (2000), 'The primary and secondary school classroom climate questionnaires: Psychometric properties, links to teacher behaviours and student outcomes, and potential applications'. London: Hay Group, pp. 20–21.

161 Hattie, J. and H. Timperley (2007), 'The power of feedback', *Review of Educational Research*, 77(81), 88–112.

162 Roosevelt, T. (1899), Chicago.

163 Roosevelt, T. (1897), New York.

164 Khan, A. (2004), *Daily Telegraph*, http://www.telegraph.co.uk/sport/othersports/boxingandmma/2392356/Boxing–Khan–shows–no–rust–to–emerge–lord–of–the–ring.html. Date accessed 11 July 2009.

165 Walters, D., quoting Marriot, B. http://www.paidpublicspeaking.com/dottie-waltersstory.html. Date accessed 11 July 2009.

166 Seneca, L. (mid-first century AD)

167 Vidal, G. (1973), http://thinkexist.com/quotation/whenever_a_friend_succeeds_a_little_something_in/10930.html. Date accessed 23 July 2009.

168 Fowler, J. and N. Christakis (2008), 'Dynamic spread of happiness in a large social network: Longitudinal analysis of the Framingham Heart Study social network'. *BMJ*, 337:a2338 doi:10.1136/bmj.a2338.

169 So, K.- T., and D. Orme-Johnson (2001), 'Three randomized experiments on the holistic longitudinal effects of the Transcendental Meditation technique on cognition'. *Intelligence*, 29, 419–40.

170 Barnes, V. A., L. Bauza and F. Treiber (2003), 'Impact of stress reduction on negative school behavior in adolescents'. *Health and Quality of Life Outcomes*, 1(10), http://www.hqlo.com/content/1/1/10.

171 Bang, C., J. Braute and B. Kohen (1989), 'Naturleikplassen. Ein Stad for Leik og Laering', Universitetsforlaget, Oslo; Fjortoft, L. (1999), 'The natural environment as a playground for children. The impact of outdoor play activities in pre-primary school children', Proceedings of OMEP's 22nd World Congress and 50th Anniversary of the child's right to care, play and education; Grahn, P., F. Martensson, B. Lindblad, P. Nilsson and A. Ekman (1997), 'Ute pa Dagis. Stad & Land', Sveriges Landbruksuniversitet.

172 Faber Taylor, A., F. E. Kuo and W. C. Sullivan (2001), 'Coping with ADD: The surprising connection to green play settings'. *Environment and Behaviour*, 33(1), 54–77.

173 Anthony Bryk, A. and B. Schneider (2002), *Trust in Schools: A Core Resource for Improvement*. American Sociological Association's Rose Series in Sociology. New York: Russel Sage Foundation.

174 Ipsos MORI Poll, (2009), 'What do parents want?' *Prospect Magazine with Ipsos MORI*, 1.

175 Bradley, S., C. Green and G. Leeves (2005), 'Worker absence and shirking: Evidence from matched teacher-school data', http://www.lancs.ac.uk/staff/ecasb/papers/abs05_dec18.pdf.

176 National Statistics (2008), 'School workforce in England (including local authority level figures)', DCSF, http://www.dcsf.gov.uk/rsgateway/DB/SFR/s000813/index.shtml. Date 10 July 2009.

177 Bowers, T. and M. McIver (2000), 'Ill-health retirement and absenteeism amongst teachers', Department for Education and Employment, Research Brief No. 235, http://www.dcsf.gov.uk/research/data/uploadfiles/RB235.pdf. Date accessed 23 July 2009.

178 Dworkin, A., C. Haney, R. Dworkin and R. Telschow (1990), 'Stress and illness behaviour among urban public school teachers', *Educational Administration Quarterly*, 26(1), 60–72.

179 Imants, V. and A. van Zoelen (1995), 'Teachers' sickness absence in primary schools, school climate and teachers' sense of efficacy', *School Organization*, 15(1), 77–86.

180 Barth, R. (2002), 'The culture builder'. *Educational Leadership*, 59(8), 6–12.

181 Deal, T. and K. Peterson (1999), *Shaping School Culture: The Heart of Leadership*. San Fransisco, Jossey-Bass Education, p. 3.

182 Edmonds, R. (1982), 'Programs of school improvement: An overview', National Institute of Education, Washington, DC. Teaching and learning program 8, http://www.ascd.org/ASCD/pdf/journals/ed_lead/el_198212_edmonds.pdf. Date accessed 23 July 2009.

183 Gonder, P. and D. Hymes (1994), *Improving School Climate and Culture*. London: Rowman & Littlefield; Eccles, J., A. Wigfield, C. Midgley, D. Reuman, D. MacIverand and H. Feldlaufer (1993), 'Negative effects of traditional middle schools on students' motivation'. *Elementary School Journal*, 93(5), 553–74; Goodenow, C. and K. Grady, K. (1993), 'The relationship of school belonging and friends' values to academic motivation among urban adolescent students', *Journal of Experimental Education*, 62(1), 60–71;

184 Smith, J. (1999), 'Social support and achievement for young adolescents in Chicago: The role of school academic press', *American Educational Research Journal*, 36(4), 907–45.

185 Gerald, C. (2006), 'School Culture: The hidden curriculum', on Eressy's (2005) presentation given at the Alliance for Excellent Education's High School Achievement Forum, Washington, DC. The University Park Campus School in Worcester, Massachusetts.

186 Gerald, C. (2006), 'School Culture. The hidden curriculum', http://www.centerforcsri.org/files/Center_IB_Dec06_C.pdf. Date accessed 23 July 2009.

187 Lightfoot, L. (2006), 'Classrooms are for work, not fun', *Daily Telegraph*, http://www.telegraph.co.uk/news/uknews/1518883/Classrooms–are–for–work–not–fun.html. Date accessed 9 July 2009.

188 Smith, M. to Lightfoot, L. (2006), 'Classrooms are for work, not fun', *Daily Telegraph*, http://www.telegraph.co.uk/news/uknews/1518883/Classrooms–are–for–work–not–fun.html; (2006), 'Parents leaving children unfit for school, says Ofsted', *Mail Online*, http://www.dailymail.co.uk/news/article–386956/

Parents–leaving–children–unfit–school–says–Ofsted.html, date accessed 9 July 2009; (2006), 'Pupils should adopt work ethic at school, says watchdog chief', *Guardian.co.uk*, http://www.guardian.co.uk/education/2006/may/19/schools.uk1. Date accessed 9 July 2009.

189 Henderson, M. (2007), 'Of course happiness can't be taught', *Daily Telegraph*, http://www.telegraph.co.uk/comment/personal–view/3639837/Of–course–happiness–cant–be–taught.html. Date accessed 9 July 2009.

190 Kjerul, A. (2008) to Joanna Reid.

191 Drucker, P. (2001), *The Essential Drucker: Management, the Individual and Society*. Oxford: Butterworth-Heinemann.

192 Hobby, R. (2004), 'A Culture for Learning – an investigation into the values and beliefs associated with effective schools', http://transforminglearning.co.uk/homepage/Culture_for_Learning_Report.pdf. Date accessed 23 July 2009.

193 Ipsos MORI Poll (2009), 'What do parents want?' *Prospect Magazine with Ipsos MORI*.

194 Shayer, M. (2008), talking about 'Intelligence for education: As described by Piaget and measured by psychometrics'. *British Journal of Educational Psychology*, 78(1), 1–29.

195 Shayer, M. (2008), talking about 'Intelligence for education: As described by Piaget and measured by psychometrics'. *British Journal of Educational Psychology*, 78(1), 1–29.

196 Wilson, D., B. Croxson and A. Atkinson (2004), 'What gets measured gets done: Headteachers' responses to English secondary school performance measures'. CMPO Working Paper series no. 04/107,, p. 8.

197 Wilson, D., B. Croxson and A. Atkinson (2004), 'What gets measured gets done: headteachers' responses to English secondary school performance measures'. http://transforminglearning.co.uk/homepage/Culture_for_Learning_Report.pdf, p. 10.

198 Ipsos MORI (2006), Ipsos MORI, http://www.ipsos–mori.com/researchspecialisms/ipsosasi.aspx.

199 Sodha, S. (2008), 'The route to the top of the class', IPPR, http://www.ippr.org.uk/articles/index.asp?id=2994. Date accessed 8 July 2009.

200 Marzano, R. (2003), *What Works in Schools: Translating Research into Action' Association for Supervision and Curriculum Development*. Alexandria: Association for Supervision and Curriculum Development, p. 61.

201 Fullan, M. and Hargreaves, A. (1996), *What's Worth Fighting for in Your School?*. New York: Teachers' College Press.

202 Dilts, R. (1999), *Sleight of Mouth: The Magic of Conversational Belief Change*. Capitola, CA: Meta Publications, p. 117.

203 Eichinger, R. and M. Lombardo (2004), 'Patterns of rater accuracy in 360-degree feedback', *Human Resource Planning*, 27, 200.

204 Perpetuity Group, 'One more broken window: The impact of the physical environment on schools', NASUWT, www.nasuwt.org.uk/consum/groups/public/./nasuwt_002577.pdf. Date accessed 9 July 2009.

205 Bloomberg, M. (2008), 'Proust questionnaire', *Vanity Fair*, http://www.vanityfair.com/culture/features/2008/10/proust_bloomberg200810. Date accessed 12 July 2009.

206 Malcolm, H., V. Wilson, J. Davidson and S. Kirk (2003), 'Absence from school – a study of its causes and effects in seven LEAs'. Edinburgh: Queens Printers for DCFS, pp. 64, 76.

207 DCSF (2007), 'The correlation between attendance and attainment in secondary and primary schools'. Edinburgh: Queens Printers for DCFS, slides 2–12.

208 Tracy, B. (2006), *Eat That Frog*, Berret-Koehler, Williston, XV111.

209 Goodship, S. (1991), 'The history of the quintessential self and the thought viruses that prevent its realisation' http://www.thoughtviruses.com/downloads/TheHistoryofThoughtViruses.pdf. Date accessed 14 July 2009.

210 Maritz Travel Company study, USA.

211 Losada, M. (1999), 'The complex dynamics of high performance teams'. *Math. Comput. Mode*, 30, 179–92 and (2004), 'The role of positivity and connectivity in the performance of business teams'. *American Journal Of Behavioural Science*, 47, 740–65.

212 Gottman, J. (1994), *What Predicts Divorce: The Relationship Between Marital Process And Marital Outcomes*. New York: Laurence Erlbaum Associates.

213 Frederickson, B. (2004), 'The broaden and build theory of positive emotions'. *Philosophical Transactions of the Royal Society Biological Science*, 359(1449), 1367–77.

214 Maritz Travel Company study, USA.

215 Marzano, R. (2003), *What Works in Schools: Translating Research into Action*, Alexandria: Association Supervision and Curriculum Development, pp. 66–7.

Matrices

Place any activities/ideas for activities in the appropriate part of the matrix. The more an activity engages pupils, the further to the right it will appear. The better the learning outcomes, the higher up it will come. The activities you should be looking to do the most of will be those that come in the top right hand corner, as these are the ones that will induce 'flow'. You can substitute 'learning versus engagement' for any of the following and use the matrix in the same way; wants versus needs; urgent versus important; impact versus do-ability.

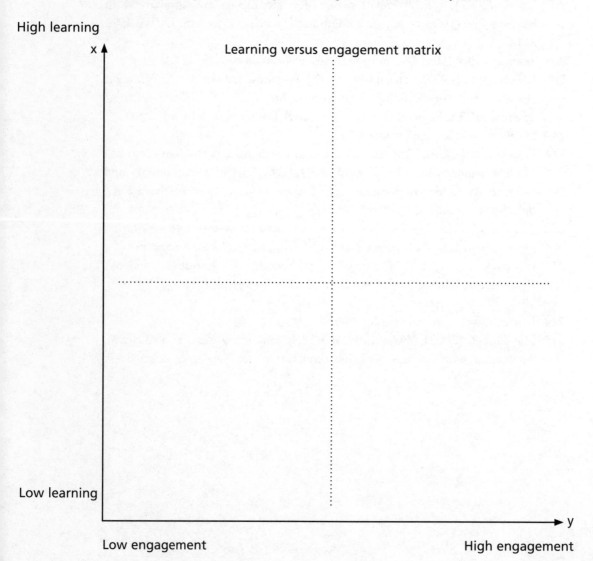

Index